A TRIP DOWN MEMORY LANE

BY

CRISTIAN POPIȘTEANU

Translated from the Romanian by Adriana Cerkez

A TRIP DOWN MEMORY LANE

BY

CRISTIAN POPIȘTEANU

Translated from the Romanian by Adriana Cerkez

EAST EUROPEAN MONOGRAPHS, BOULDER

DISTRIBUTED BY COLUMBIA UNIVERSITY PRESS, NEW YORK

2004

EAST EUROPEAN MONOGRAPHS, NO. DCXLIV

ISBN: 0-88033-542-4

Library of Congress Control Number: 2004108568

Printed in the United States of America

Dedication

To my Romanian fellow-journalists, descendants of Asachi, Barițiu, Kogălniceanu, Heliade, Mureșan, and of many other defenders of the causes of my country and of mankind, bearers of truth-fueled light.

ALSO BY CRISTIAN POPIȘTEANU:

A Small Guide to UNO and to Specialized Institutions (in Romanian), Politică Publishing House, 1965

Romania and the Balkan Entente (in Romanian), Politică Publishing House, 1968, 1971

Meetings in the World of Films, (in Romanian), Meridiane Publishing House, 1970

A Trip down Memory Lane, (in Romanian), Albatros Publishing House, 1984

Accents (in Romanian), Silex Publishing House, 1997

Greece 1936–1941 (in Romanian), vol. II, Militară Publishing House, 1980

C.C. Giurescu and the Mass-Media (in Romania between East and West, in English), Columbia University Press, New York, 1982

CO-AUTHOR TO:

Europe? Where? (in Romanian), Politică Publishing House, 1970, 1971

A Diplomatic Dictionary (in Romanian), Politică Publishing House, 1984

Romania's Foreign Policy (in Romanian) Științifică & Enciclopedică Publishing House, 1986

The Sturdzas – A Chronicle of a Family (in Romanian), *Magazin istoric* Cultural Foundation, 1995

EDITOR TO:

Martha Bibescu – A Political Journal 1939–1941 (in Romanian), Politică Publishing House, 1979

August 23, 1944 – Documents (in Romanian), Științifică & Enciclopedică Publishing House, 1984

Radu Rosetti – Pages of His Journal (in Romanian), Adevărul Publishing House, 1994

CONTENTS

THE EPHEMERAL OF THE MOMENT

Fifty years have elapsed. Are they many? Are they few? They are yours and they are less than the next to come. That's for sure. Have they been difficult? Have they been easy? Have they been full or empty? Questions you can repeat endlessly, mainly if you are in room 18. A hospital side-room. A side-room like many others, but unique at the same time. It is here that I have experienced some solitary and painful battles, perfidious pangs announcing a possible end followed by wonderful and liberating moments of good news, of victory of life.

My fifty years look different now when I am in side-room 18. Time and space seem to expand here. It is a moment against a lifetime (or against death). A moment that has got the price of life. A moment as a secret of life. How many years and how many moments? How many lives and how many moments?

It is in hospital only that one can understand time: what it means and how dear it is. I cannot tell what it is like being in prison or in war. But I know that the only chance of getting out alive from a hospital is the force you have to think of the others, to want to live for the others as well. In hospital you can discover that the moment is the sign of life. A moment can be a longer unit of time than a year and, sometimes, than a whole life. "An unreal and omnipotent secret."

As a journalist I have been guided "by the idea of duty and by the commandment that one shall live".

I started by writing foreign policy comments and I realized then what important history was. I had started to speak about a tree by describing its leaves and only leaves as if there had not been branches, a trunk, and roots – the historical roots of the events I knew so little about. I had to study history first so that I could discover those roots. There exists that "why" of historical events, concerning their causes, traditions, and motivations and the journalist must know them. The journalist – whose job is so important today that it is considered the first profession of the century – has to know everything and to understand everything. A journalist who can no longer understand the events has to quit.

When you celebrate your fiftieth anniversary in side-room 18 you are alone with the moments of your life. And then you are able to discover the beauty and the wealth of thousands and thousands of moments. The minutes and hours your fellow-journalists have given to you.

There are lots of people you have met, known, interviewed at home or abroad. You have met them once or several times, you have worked with them, laughed with them, or suffered with them. You realize that you have not given a proper place to them although they got themselves involved in the life of your country or in your own life, or in the European culture or history. They all have their right to be properly presented and spoken about. Even if both their stories and yours are ephemeral.

August 1983
"Al. Sahia" Hospital, Bucharest

INTRODUCTION

Why do I resume *A Trip down Memory Lane?*

Out of a sense of duty, I think. First of all towards me, but also towards all the people who trusted me. Out of a sense of duty towards the truth of life and out of respect for the professions of historian and journalist I have closely interwoven with passion and trust all along my life. Duty means gratitude here. In a dramatic life marked out by collapses and recoveries, I have had reasons of satisfaction and fulfillment as well – the most important one being my very job: journalism. Following 1989, when we have won liberty and also the supreme gift to speak and write with no constraint, the duty I have towards truth makes me testify for what I know only. *A Trip down Memory Lane* is a book of testimonies about what I have lived and experienced directly.

I am again in a hospital ward – this time side-room 9. Ten years have elapsed since my first attempt to grasp the ephemeral of the moment.

A Trip down Memory Lane is not meant to persuade, but to show people, attitudes, and stories. The reader will be its judge.

There are very few things I have changed in the present volume: just some sentences and paragraphs. That's all. I read the first edition and I found out that everything I wrote there was true: my thoughts, the attempts I made to pass beyond the canons and obstacles of those times (1984), the characters that had inspired my book.

I wrote *A Trip down Memory Lane* and I invoked some of the characters there – famous people whom I had met – in an attempt to defend myself from those who wanted to remove me from *Magazin istoric*. At the beginning of 1983 I was lying in hospital with a heart attack and I followed from there all the zigzags of the attempts they made to sideline me, with the permanent feeling that all was about somebody else and not about me.

I wrote then in the Preface that a person could find his/her exact measure only in war, in prison, and in hospital. I have the experience of hospitals only. For 18 years. It was in hospitals that I conceived – under terror of death and of repression – the technique meant to help me resist and keep the magazine I had identified myself with. But it was not enough. The match was not equal.

However, mention should be made that the situation, abhorrent as it seemed to be, was not in the least similar to the sufferings caused by imprisonment, conviction, and final extermination of so many hundreds of thousands of victims totalitarianism had made in Romania. What I lived in those years was a kind of Kafkian adventure populated with the phantoms of the totalitarian structures that invaded our immediate reality. And it was that immediate reality that gave me the chance to remain the editor-in-chief of *Magazin istoric* although for 80 months I had not been paid at all.

In my teens, my political ignorance had deluded me into joining communists and leftist intellectuals. However, as an adult, I learned how big the lie that had lured me was. So I started to act consequently. Of course, I was on my own account – I decided to do nothing else but what I considered that should be my own solution to my past illusion. Fortunately, along my lonely and worked out way I met many "accomplices" and opportunities that helped me not to play in the hands of the Romanian special services that I had refused since the beginning of my career.

In building my citadel, where *A Trip down Memory Lane* was an important protection wall, I was supported and encouraged, among others, by my friend, poet Florin Mugur who used all his arguments to make me write it; by Mrs. Natalia Petruț, the book editor; and by Mircea Sântimbreanu, the director of the Albatros Publishing House who used all the subterfuges he could to edit the book on his own responsibility and to avoid the Caudine Forks of censorship. When the volume came out, Mircea Sântimbreanu told me: "Cristian, this book is not about them, it is about you. You are the character here! May God help you." And last but not least, the book was written in the hospital under the careful eyes of Dr. Gheorghe Rădulescu who protected both my heart and myself against some persons with secret missions who wanted me out of hospital the soonest possible.

They all are the godfathers of *A Trip down Memory Lane* and I am happy to acknowledge here both their help and involvement.

The ten great people in the following pages, who saved many moments of my life, are lighting my way to stars now.

Bucharest – London – Paris

1994–1998

MARTHA BIBESCU,

TOMA CARAGIU,

RENÉ CASSIN,

CONSTANTIN C. GIURESCU,

MIRCEA GRIGORESCU,

GEORGE IVAȘCU,

ANDRÉ MALRAUX,

ALEXANDRU ROSETTI,

V.V. TILEA, and

ARNOLD TOYNBEE

These are the characters populating A Trip down Memory Lane – a feature report, confession, interview, essay, or document that reveals the profile of an age. Controversial or questionable, they all have left strong roots in the chronicles of their times. Two of them rest today in the French temple of eternal glory, while the other eight have known the posthumous recognition that save them from oblivion. Communism and anticommunism; rigorous research of the past and imagination of philosophy of civilizations; singularity in defending the interests of Romania and the dangers that tore it apart; antifascist complexes and Hitler's victories; espionage in the shadow of beauty and passports for the Romanian intellectuals; the distance separating genuine art and journalism from their epigones; the tragedy of the long-distance runners in search of human rights – all these and many other events hidden behind the scenes of the previous century make up Cristian Popișteanu's book.

A happy author who has found his ten characters!

ONE HUNDRED MEETINGS

Were they really one hundred?

If I think of the meetings proper I had with A.J. Toynbee, in London, it is far from that! There were only three of them.

But if I consider the innumerable meetings with his work that started when I was a little older than 20 and have continued to this very day, about a quarter of a century following his death, then there are more than one hundred.

I remember the most important ones, but let's start with the beginning. The very first meeting was with his work, of course. In my late teens I worked part time (and after that a full time editor) for *Revista elevilor* (Pupils' Magazine), for *Brigadierul* (The Brigadier), for *Tânărul muncitor* (The Young Worker), and for Radiodifuziune (The Romanian Broadcasting Corporation). At the same time I was a pupil at "Sfântul Iosif" and then "Gheorghe Lazar" high schools in Bucharest, both of them within a very short distance from the Radiodifuziune precincts. My older colleagues used to teach me contemporary history at my job, or I picked it up from the very events of the day, from the cables sent by the international press agencies, and from the comments in the Romanian and foreign newspapers. I did not study it from books, or, better to say not enough from books. At school I used to listen very carefully to the words of my teacher of French, the future diplomat Valentin Lipatti, of my teachers of Physics and Chemistry, the future professors Iosif Rișavi and Constantin Rabega, respectively, and, rather skeptical, to the stern but patriotic lessons of Remus Ilie, my teacher of history, a little too "reactionary", according to the trend of those days. A hasty judgement maybe, the same as many other hasty things in those years not exactly lacking a certain grandeur, in which the blast of a fake revolution turned everything upside down and made callow young people and adults alike often reach thoughtless conclusions. For me, the genuine history was being born across from the high school, in the offices of the newspapers or of the Radio, or on the "patriotic" work sites. In 1948, almost all the schools in Romania had a course about the 1848 revolution. Excellent subject, I think! But I did not attend it. Was I wrong? Yes, I was partly wrong, but life cannot be lived again. It would have been wonderful if I had been the best at school and at my jobs alike. It was not possible. It is rather impossible to be the best in everything you do at the same time.

Therefore, I was enthusiastic about my editorial job and later on about my job at the radio. There I broadcast live some news from the teletypewriter as I thought that my voice could thus be heard by millions of people that were, in that way, in contact with the universe. The exhilaration I felt was similar I thought with the feeling of grace experienced by poets. Of course, there was not inspiration with me, but truth. The moment I was in front of the teletypewriter and read, letter by letter, news about important events in the world, and the minutes following it, when I entered "Proust's chamber" and set down in front of the microphone to broadcast the latest news, I was confident I was a direct participant in the birth and the spreading of the Truth. (The broadcast booth was called "Proust's chamber" by my ex-desk mate at "Sfântul Iosif", the future poet Florin Mugur who used to say that the phonically isolated booth, without street windows, was similar to the room where the great novelist used to find refuge. And like the latter's work, though in a different way, it contributed to the spreading of truth.) I was enthusiastic about my job as a journalist, and, after so many years, that enthusiasm is still present. I have had the opportunity to see a lot of journalists' homes, editorial, radio or TV offices in various countries as I have always felt very close to journalists. Our politics could have been different, but that was not important. What really mattered was the fever of passion, the fever of the genuine journalism, the emblematic profession of the 20th century (as astronautics will probably be in the 21st century). And, according to the WHO statistics, one of the most dangerous too!

Let's come back to truth. The pieces of news from all over the world that we broadcast were certainly true. Nevertheless, they did not express the absolute truth, the truth that exists but nobody knows entirely. There are people who say that the absolute truth can kill. And they know what they say. They might be right. But my problem was a different one. The facts were true all right. However my aging mind could not help realizing that in the comments on those facts (comments made with a perfect good faith) the truth seemed to get a smaller "place". I could say now (I could not then) that they missed the historical foundation that could have been only attained by solid knowledge of our long history. From 1940 until 1964–1965, the Romanian public was kept away from the historical truth, but the distance got then gradually smaller as some partial truths started being told. The dictatorship of Antonescu's Iron Guard, Antonescu's dictatorship in a militarized Romania practically occupied by fascists, and then the foreign influence on Romania, had blurred the truth about the Romanian history for a long time. It was only after the removal of the foreign restrictions that the truth has gradually come to light.

Should have I realized the state of things when I was 20–22? I might have not had the right perception but I intuited something! Not even for a moment did I hesitate when I had to decide on my future career: the history of the international relationships. I was a student and a commentator on foreign policy at the Radio and, one day, in 1954–1955, at the Library of the Ministry of Foreign Affairs, I came across a collection of the famous yearbook *A Survey of International Affairs*. The Yearbook, edited by Arnold J. Toynbee (often with his future wife, Veronica Toynbee, a historian as well), was published between 1925 and 1946. You could find there very important information and brilliant, competent comments you could agree with or not, but whose force of analysis and synthesis you could not ignore. For my exams, my graduation paper, and my doctoral thesis I often referred to that extraordinary collection of studies.

So, that was the first meeting but there was no question about the work of this great scientist – "the most controversial historian of the century" – being translated and published in Romania.

I kept studying Toynbee's work till 1963 when an important event took place in the Romanian journalism: *Lumea* (The World) started being issued. The weekly was created to show the position of Romania in matters of international politics and also to inform the Romanian readers about the state of things in the world. And last but not least, the new journal was intended, among other things, to resume the thread of tradition.

A new and great chance had appeared for me. In the 15 years I had worked for the Radio, I had prepared thousands of broadcasts, but they all had vanished. I had then the opportunity to write words meant to last. Printed words. My chance was a big one indeed since I was supposed to work together with two great and influential journalists: George Ivașcu, the editor-in-chief of the journal, and Mircea Grigorescu, a genuine journalist.

After many years, our colleague, Felicia Antip, would describe our daily life at *Lumea* in one of her books (*Lumea în ziare* [The World in the Newspapers], Cartea Românească and Porto Franco, 1991) and a communist leader of that period will tell how the idea of publishing such a journal came into life in the high political circles (Paul Niculescu Mizil – *O istorie trăită* [The History I Lived], Ed. Enciclopedică, 1997).

Lumea often published excerpts from important papers issued abroad; one column was entitled "Points of View". One day, some inflammatory fragments of the idealist Toynbee were reproduced there. He was expressing his viewpoint on the United States policy and treated sarcastically their attitude in Vietnam. It was a period of energetic consumerism and Toynbee violently attacked the so-called "American lifestyle". It was also in that period that Mircea Malița published a long paper in *Contemporanul* commenting on Toynbee. I knew that Toynbee was not exactly a publicist, but his name, familiar to historians only, started to penetrate public awareness and that was a good thing indeed. In 1969, Nicolae Bagdasar published at Editura Politică *Teoreticieni ai civilizației* (Theorists of Civilization) with a study about the great historian. You can find his conclusion below: "We have revealed the drawbacks of Toynbee's conception – contradictory ideas, ambiguous terms, unfounded assertions, excessive use of metaphors, far-fetched analogies, misinterpretations, speculations, irrational and mystical theses. His conception, also known as *the theory of parallel civilizations*, ignores the unitary process of world history. Science corroborates the materialistic conception of history that defines the objective criteria of social progress and demonstrates that peoples' historical development is generated by succeeding social-economic structures, under specific conditions, following highly diversified rhythms and shapes. The idea of civilization cannot be substituted for social-economic structures, as the latter offer the key for understanding the unitary, complex and varied social-historical development of the peoples. However, his conception gets many positive sides. Let's see some of them: the British theorist has penetrated through the traditional Western circle of the *world history* (confined, in Antiquity, to Asia Minor and to the Eastern Mediterranean, and then, through the Middle Ages and the modern period, to Europe only) and recognized the existence, beyond Europe, of other civilizations, having a similar value to the Hellenistic and Western ones. He does not agree with the common opinion of the *immovable East*, of the would-be inability of the Asian peoples to evolve, to contribute again to the cultural heritage of the mankind. He is an implacable opponent of racism and savages its theoretical aberrations since he is confident that each people, irrespective of race, is able to create culture. He is also an implacable opponent of fascism and of all the totalitarian regimes that he denounces and exposes. He condemns war as a means of geographical expansionism and of solving the conflicts among countries since he is a supporter of peaceful political settlements. And last but not least, he has left aside the usual empiricism of the British historiography in an attempt to grasp the general aspect of the individual events."

So I started reading Toynbee's work. It wrote "reading" not "studying" for his 12-volume *A Study of History.* Their study would have required many long years. *Reconsideration*, the last volume, is the author's answer to the numerous criticisms, some of them extremely virulent, against his way of approaching history. I have given above the opinion of the Romanian philosopher Nicolae Bagdasar. Other opinions were fierce attacks indeed. A.J. Toynbee was contested or greatly admired, a subject of bitter controversy and high praise. He was often reproached for his literary genius, considered the very source of his scientific "incompetence". *A Study of History* had thus become, irrespective of its errors and sometimes-inconsistent points of view, a main subject of discussion among the Western philosophers and historians (similarly to Spengler's *The Decline of the West* before). After World War II, the American historian D.C. Somervell published a two-volume abridged edition, revised by Toynbee himself. Therefore, the British historian became even more popular in the West. Let's not forget that *A Study of History* included more than 30 year's work.

Today, we are happy to have a Romanian version of *A Study of History* (Somervell's synthesis, translated by Dan Amedeu Lăzărescu, was published in 1977 by Humanitas Publishing House).

And now, back again to my story.

In 1970 I was no longer so young, but I still hoped that the dream I had when I was 20 would come true: one day I would meet Toynbee. A dream, an ambition... It was more than just an ambition. In the meantime I had become a historian – I had all this time been a journalist as well – and my dream was not only to meet and talk with one of the greatest contemporary historians and philosophers, but also to persuade him to visit Romania. Alas, he was too old so I had to give up my wish very soon.

The idea of meeting him was very intimidating indeed. I had learned a lot about Toynbee. I knew for instance that he had benefited from the British system of promotion in diplomacy. After graduation, several young historians – usually former prominent students – are employed by the British Foreign Office and specialized to become experts in a certain field or another. With this aim in view they work in the British embassies abroad. After passing the practical exams as diplomats, they are free to work for the Foreign Office or not. Great many British diplomats have graduated in history. Toynbee, a specialist in the problems of East and Eastern Europe, had served as a delegate to the Paris Peace Conference (in 1919 and in 1946), he was (during World War II) the director of the research department of the Foreign Office and (for 30 years) the director of the Royal Institute of Internal Affairs. There is a memorial room Toynbee at the Institute. "It will not be an easy task to meet him" I used to think.

I cannot say if it was easy or difficult. In 1970 I was first invited to Great Britain by a relatively small institution, but with good connections in the important circles owing to the dedicated people working there: the Great Britain–East-European Center. Doreen Berry was then deputy manager. It was Miss Berry (a great friend of Romania, who then headed the Romanian section of BBC) who was so kind to help me. I had written to her that most of all I would like to meet Toynbee. Therefore, they contacted the great historian and arranged an appointment on October 30, 1970; they sent me then all the details: time of the meeting, address, the bus I was supposed to take, the stop I had to get down.

It was at 95 Oakwood Court, 3 p.m.

At 2.50 I got down the red double-decker and started looking for the house. I stopped in front of a very large yard in which a lot of children were playing despite the drizzling rain outside. I could see a multitude of alleys and several rather dull and smoked brick buildings. I started asking around: "Where does Professor Toynbee live?" The children did not know, but neither did the adults whom I asked with a growing fear that I could be late. They had never heard of Toynbee. I kept looking at my watch, I started thinking that I would never find that address when finally a young lady pointed to the building just in front of me. A rather strong building, one of the kinds built after World War I. The elevator that lifted me to the fourth floor seemed of the same age. I rang the bell and Mrs. Toynbee, Veronica Toynbee, opened the door for me. Veronica was the historian's second wife. She had been, as I have mentioned above, his assistant when he worked for the Yearbook, and also his secretary at the Royal Institute of International Affairs. An old gray-haired lady, rather short, moving briskly. She was wearing a gray dress and a sweater over it. She kindly invited me in and I entered a rather dark room, a kind of library or living room, with very comfortable armchairs, a sofa, a small table, and huge bookcases all around the walls. I would have liked to see some titles of the books, but I could hardly look a moment out of the window when Toynbee came in. I could easily see that he forced himself to go quickly, as he was a very old man indeed. I had seen some photos of his in his middle age: a tall, slender man. Well, it seemed that he had decreased. He and his wife gave one a sad, yet invigorating feeling: of strength (there was still a lot in him) and decrease at the same time. His shoulders sloped, he was wearing glasses and his clothes were gray, very elegant. So was his tie too, in perfect taste, with no trait of pose. I suddenly had a revelation… I saw a light. A great, warm light coming from the man in front of me. In the very first instant I did not realize where the light and the warmth that made me feel no longer a stranger were coming from. Then I understood: Toynbee had a hearing aid at his left ear. For more than thirty years I had interviewed hundreds of people and had asked them all to speak louder so that I could hear them. Therefore, that hearing aid seemed an unexpected, happy token of brotherhood. (I told him in that very moment about the thousands victories won in Romania by a surgeon, Dr. Doru Hociotă, in his fight with deafness). His face was the image of kindness, intelligence, and force. Suddenly I felt as we were shaking hands that I met my grandfather. The grandfather each child would like to have. *The grandfather*! He shook my right hand as he seized my left hand with the gentleness one can often meet with the English people (as if they wanted to test your moral power; they are sincere and they want to see how sincere you are as well). The English people are good at making you feel well indeed; and he was not some Englishman, he was my grandfather… I could see he knew quite a few things about myself – he had asked for full information from Miss Berry – and he did not pretend otherwise, he just asked me to confirm it. Have I really written a work on the Balkan Entente? Have I really been invited by the Great Britain–East-European Center? What am I going to do? The contact had been established from the first moment, but I had my "mission". So I took the recorder out of my briefcase and told him: "Sir, I think it is better to record you from the very beginning; I don't want to miss a word…" And I started firing questions at him for one hour and a half.

The interview was published in *Magazin istoric* (Historical Magazine), in March 1971. I still remember the huge efforts made by late Catinca Ralea to get out of the bad recording about ten minutes of clear voices for the broadcast in the English language at Radio Bucharest. I cannot help thinking now at the difference between the cozy and warm atmosphere surrounding an interview and the cold, distant printed words. All the "stage directions" are missing: the temperature of the room, the hesitating voice, a flicker of the eyes. So, I will add some brackets here and there when necessary...

"Which are, in your opinion and according to the experience of life you have, the main conclusions on history?

(As if such a question could be answered in a few words only. Well...)

"I am neither optimistic, nor pessimistic. I am a realist. I think that mankind is in a permanent state of crisis because it is in incessant change, transformation, movement. Where there is life there will always be critical moments. Today I think that we are in an unusually crucial moment."*

(What a pity I can't describe his eyes. I met him three times, I looked at him for hours, but I can't tell now if his eyes were black or blue. That lack of perceptiveness proper to men! However there were "extenuating circumstances". He was always in a dim light and I think I guess why: the hearing aid was new for him and he could not stand the idea that he was no longer able to hear well and would have to have that aid all his life. He did not want people to see him *like that*...)

"You have defended your thesis on parallel civilizations all your life. Do you think it is valid? Do you think we are facing a new civilization?"

"I think civilizations are useful units for the study of history. Anthropologists understand this phenomenon as such, but historians prefer to think in terms of development of the nations. I don't think there is any danger for the modern civilization to disappear or to be destroyed. But I think that the terrible development seizing all the world, irrespective of ideologies, will entail a huge transformation in today's civilization."

I think I hit a raw nerve there: how could he deny his lifelong beliefs? No matter whether he was right or wrong. The slight contraction of his face then makes me wonder now: was it not because of his vividly polemical spirit that this man has not been raised to nobility? Polemic against the pacemakers who were late to

---

* Translator's note: Since I could not obtain a copy of the interview transcript I had to translate Toynbee from the Romanian version into English. Unfortunately, I have done the same with many other quotations in the book as their sources are not indicated or I have not found them. I apologize for any possible misinterpretation. (A.C.)

intervene against fascists. Polemic against the American lifestyle. Polemic against so many things he did not agree with in Great Britain that he had served faithfully all his life. However that did not stop a conservative deputy accusing him in the House of Commons of "lack of patriotism and subversiveness").

"Do you think the change you are speaking about will lead us to a point where we have to build up our future history on different bases than today?"

"The external conditions will probably be different, but I think that human nature will always be the same. There exist continuity and similarity in the lives of people as biological beings. As long as human nature remains the same, the history of mankind will go on. On the other side, we are very good at technology, but the relationships among us, people, are very bad. This is one of the tragedies of mankind and it has always followed history. And I think it will still follow it."

"What is your opinion on contemporary history?"

"Today I am more alarmed than I used to be before. The increasing violence and lack of rationalism are very worrying. I want to tell you that I do not believe in a World War III. No, I do not believe."

(He was no longer speaking in a louder voice, he was simply shouting. As if he were trying to make himself sure he was right. His wife came – worried? – with a tray and two small glasses. Sherry. A sip. He did not smoke but I was almost sure he had been a hard smoker in his youth. Had I seen him smoke in a photo? I do not know. Likewise, I do not know why all the British historians I met drank the sherry. He went on.)

"Well, on the other side, I can see that the living conditions are, psychologically speaking, harder and harder. I emphasize that all this has no connection with the idea of nationality and I wonder how will mankind be able to cope with the psychical strain brought by the new development."

"Which is, in your opinion, the mission the historian has today?"

"I think the historian has to help the present generations not to repeat the mistakes of the past. Likewise, I should say that following the technological development all the people should share responsibilities and interests; I think historians could support this solidarity, helping people learn about their past, since the historical past of each compartment of mankind is very important for determining its present. Therefore, I think that historians can be extremely useful, and that their mission is extremely difficult and hard to fulfil."

(No, I do not remember his eyes. I am just looking at the photo taken three years later: he, on the left, I, on the right, my hand under his arm. I can see his white, thinning hair; the wire of the hearing aid is quite visible on the coat lapel; a tie with a large knot against the pure white of his shirt; but the eyes are just two black dashes under the high forehead. He might have tried to protect his eyes against the light. A tall old man – he is taller than I am – his face a bit sad. At the bottom of the photo I can see his left hand – a white spot. Yes, I remember his hands. I watched them all the time. They were still young and strong in spite of the dark spots caused by age; not a pianist's hands, but the hands of an intellectual worker, a man who can lift and place, on the highest shelves of a bookcase, large piles of volumes weighing sometimes more than ten kilograms... A respectful, yet funny thought is crossing my mind: the twelve volumes of the *Study of History*, together with his other 32 books, and, of course the Yearbook weigh together much more than the old man with young hands sitting in front of me...).

"What have the arms and wars races represented for the history of mankind and for each people separately?"

"Wars? I am sure that war is an extremely aggressive phenomenon and that arms race is very dangerous. I think that governments and peoples will find the best way to stop this arms race. The wealth spent for armaments could be used for so many other things, for increasing the living standard of the poor majority of mankind, for instance. Unfortunately, the great majority of people are poor, and arms are so expensive. As I've already told you, I don't think a third world war will ever come. But I think that arms race is very difficult to stop, as it has become overwhelming, indeed. Likewise, the psychological strain caused by it has a bad influence on the young generation all over the world."

"Which is, in your opinion, the role of popularizing history among the new generations?"

"I think that it is very important for the growing generations to realize that it is impossible for them to break off with the past and to have an entirely new start. The young generation is impatient and they think they can do things better than the old ones. The young do not realize, at the beginning, that there is a kind of nucleus, a certain constant importance of the past nobody can ignore. We are partly free, but not completely free. An extremely important side of the understanding between the old and the young is that the young should accept the need of continuity. And it is also very important that people should not lose patience with the young, be kind, understanding and confiding."

(Had my questions been less severe, had I met him before or wanted to challenge him – his many polemical papers and the opinions he expressed on radio or TV prove that he could be challenged quite easily –, had I wanted to reach his "sore point", I mean "popularizing history"... He would probably have told me then something about the accusations brought against him: he was too often using – even in his academic works – a light, elegant style, in the spirit of the ancient writers, in an attempt to avoid the dry, matter-of-fact exposition, exclusively professorial, of other historians. Toynbee had always been so confident in his knowledge and in his literary gift (nobody could have contested it anyway) that he took the liberty to express his extravagant opinions and to write things a less confident historian would have never dared to sign. He fancied what the life of Alexander the Great would have been if he had not died so young. Historical fiction of course, extremely attractive for the young people who want to study history. In 1972, *Magazin istoric* published *Alexander the Great's Insomnia* (the title was ours), an excerpt from *Some Problems of Greek History* (Oxford University Press, London, 1969), a large, erudite study on Ancient Greece. The Romanian editor wrote: "In the pages below, Toynbee starts from a premise that is so characteristic of his way of writing history: *what would have happened if Alexander the Great had lived longer?* The author introduces, besides authentic events, some others that never happened, but would have been possible, even probable, taking account of the circumstances of that age. It is a kind of *hypothetical history* with a hero supposed to be still alive two years following his death." Therefore, what was the reason of Alexander's insomnia? It was his mother, Olympia, an argumentative woman, who was on the point of generating important conflicts at home while Alexander was in his military expeditions far away. She used to send Alexander long letters, full of lamentations and insults. Alexander was thus forced to send her into exile in a very remote place, as the most exasperating correspondence would be more easily swallowed when the letters traveled about six months. But where and how should he exile her? How could he send Olympia somewhere far from Europe? Of course, following medical advice. And where should he send her? The answer to that question depended on the previous one. Physicians had to recommend her a mild climate, far from the heavy winters of Epirus and Macedonia. So Alexander remembered that he knew the perfect place. He had once stopped on the island of Socotra that he annexed. It was like heaven and he seemed to have forgotten to donate it to the Phoenicians. Therefore, he acted with no delay. His obliging physicians drew their conclusions the very next morning, and in the evening Olympia was already on her way to Socotra. It was hard for anybody to believe that some old people in Socotra could have had the ability to change the world for her sake. The queen was thus exiled for the rest of her life on that island. The tropical climate was not able to make her apathetic but there was no hope for her to be a regent in Epirus or Macedonia either.

I am reading again the Romanian translation of the excerpt and I cannot stop feeling sorry I did not ask Toynbee some questions that could have roused his polemical spirit against those who see in history a dry, documentary succession of facts, years, and acts. But in 1970, during our first meeting, I had more important questions to ask. And I dare say they were important not only for me).

"Do you think in the possibility of cooperation among all the powers of the world?"

"Yes, I do. Yes. And I think that even those less prone to cooperate will be forced by circumstances to do it. For instance, I think that sea and air pollution, more than war danger, will make all the regions of the world cooperate. I also think that without a genuine world cooperation, the Earth will no longer be inhabited

"You have just told me that history has reached a crucial moment. What is the role of Europe in the future history?"

"I think it would be very sad if Europe did not have a role to play. We, Europeans have got experience, and largely diversified ancient and modern cultures; yet our unity is rather strong. Therefore, Europe has to regain her place among the other continents, to be one of the main forces involved in shaping the future of mankind. The condition she has to fulfil is to be united by cooperation, and the connections between the East and the West should be resumed and developed. I am looking forward to seeing it."

"Do you think is there any compatibility between the desire of the mankind to develop interdependence and the independence and national sovereignty each country wants to preserve?

"Yes, I do. Today, no nation, irrespective of its power and wealth, is big enough to be completely separated in the international context, as all the great issues and important activities have got a world scope today. I keep saying it: that does not mean to destroy nations, but to make them cooperate more closely."

"Can you tell me the historic event that most influenced your life?"

"The outbreak of World War I. I was 25 then; it was quite an unexpected event for me. I thought that there would be eternal peace in Europe, and that we lived in a rational world, in incessant progress. My expectations were totally contradicted. The shock of the war outbreak has left an everlasting impression on me and was the starting point of my present theory on history."

(It was for the first that he mentioned his life. Three years later, when I visited him last time, he pointed to several photos over the fireplace behind his desk. Toynbee looked at those old faces and told me that they were his best friends, all killed in World War I. He could never forget them, he said. Neither could he forget the two wars although he had not been in the war zone on the continent. "The most astonishing thing was", he said, "the human nature's power of accommodation. I realized then that people could cope with unusual, sometimes extremely difficult, circumstances. When the war was over, I was extremely happy, together with all my contemporaries gathered in front of the Buckingham Palace. I thought then that I had lived a terrible experience that would be never repeated. I even thought that my best friends' deaths were of a lesser importance since war would no longer exist. At the end of the World War II I was in the same place and realized that although people were very happy that the war was over, they were much more prepared for the hard times they had to face." And I asked him then, I mean in 1973, to go on and tell me more what World War I, the most terrible event in his entire life. He looked again at the photos and added: "I was 25 in 1914. Following my studies at Oxford and in Greece, I was then at Balliol College, Oxford, absorbed by my research in the unity of the ancient times: comments on Thucydides. And then the totally unexpected outbreak of the war…"

"Which were the personalities you have met?

"I remember a lot of people. I remember heads of states, like, for instance, Jawaharlal Nehru. And there were so many historians, I can't mention them all."

"What about Winston Churchill."

"I was honored to receive, at the same time with him, a diploma at the University. Then I saw him from time to time. There were short, very interesting encounters."

"Can you tell me several names in the world history – in different periods of time – that, in your opinion, influenced their times?"

"I think of the ancient Greeks. I think that the great historians of the ancient Greece – Thucydides, Herodotus, and Polybius – influenced their contemporaries a lot.

(Some of the questions I asked then seem to be naïve now. They might be, but I render the whole interview, since his answers are extraordinary. "In your opinion", repeated several times is neither so naïve nor so inadequate as it seems. Those words have a meaning, even if some voices might say that the historian could only express his own opinion and that the repetition is rather monotonous. It might be monotonous, but do not forget that it was the very first time the historian was interviewed by a Romanian journalist-historian coming from a, then, communist country. And Toynbee had never been a communist. Quite the opposite. "In your opinion" had no trait of hostility. On the contrary, it was quite polite and it meant to indicate distance. As for the routine or too general questions, they had their purpose as well: to avoid the dangerous situation in which the great historian's opinion would have contradicted mine).

"Do you have a message for the Romanian, students, historians
and readers?"

"I have always been interested in Romania. I crossed Romania in 1929, while travelling from Pas de Calais to Istanbul. I have always been interested in the peoples speaking Romanic languages and in that unexpected historic phenomenon that made possible the preservation of the eastern wing of the Latin world. I like the interest of the Romanians in history, best illustrated by the large circulation of *Magazin istoric*. Unfortunately, I can no longer travel, but I wish my best to the Romanian people, especially to the new generations, which have to take part in solving the problems of mankind.

(Some more details. I had brought with me several copies of *Magazin istoric*; he browsed them... I had asked him if he wanted to visit Romania... He answered... But the sentence: "I crossed Romania in 1929..." has today, after I have learned more about the scientist's work and life, another meaning than it had in 1970. It was then, when he was crossing the old Thracian fields in Orient Express that he thought about his great work on the history of civilizations, the first volume of which was published in 1934. I have not got a detective mind, so I may not venture to assert that he first thought at his work while crossing Romania, but his notes clearly showed that the great idea crossed his mind during that voyage, on his way to Bulgaria and Turkey).

"If you were to start a new life and activity, would you choose the same profession?"

"There is no doubt of it. Yes I would. I would. My mother was a historian as well and she was said to have influenced me. I may say that as long as I can remember I was meant to be a historian."

(Using a joke to define his vocation, he said once: "Why am I a historian and not a physicist? For the same reasons I drink my tea and my coffee sugarless." A joke elegantly emphasizing both that Toynbee was attracted by history in the most natural way, because he liked it, and also the lack of illusions – sugar – in this science that cultivates nothing but the truth. His mother was a historian – one of the first women admitted at the University in about 1890 – and so were his wife Veronica, and his sister, Jocelyne M.C. Toynbee. Jocelyne was a professor in classical archeology at Oxford, the editor of the English edition of the famous *Trajan's Column and Dacian Wars*, by the Italian archeologist Lino Rossi. "I congratulate you", J.M.C. Toynbee wrote to me in 1974, "for the happiness of having the crucial moments of the birth of the Romanian people engraved on a monument that has defied time. I am much interested in the copy of the Column, in the Bucharest National Museum of History, and in the Roman monuments in Dobruja." Her brother told me that he had wanted to be a historian since he was four and his mother used to tell him tales with heroes of the English chronicles. "I couldn't have guessed, when I was four", he added smilingly, "that I would have such a university career.")

"As I can see, you are much interested in the young generation. How can you explain your interest?"

"Well, I have children, grandchildren, and a grand granddaughter, so I have got a personal interest in future. I have always understood the youth. I have spent the latest ten or twenty years studying and initiating the young generation. I am today very much concerned with the serious problems the young people have to face. As I have told you, I was grown up before 1914 in Western Europe, in a stable world, or that seemed to be stable. In their turn, my children and grandchildren were grown in a terribly agitated world. It is difficult, much more difficult. Here, in Europe, we are lucky to have a better cultural continuity, but the largest part of mankind faces huge difficulties and extremely special and complex prospects of development… Yes, the largest part of Asia, Latin America, and Africa… That is why I am very sympathetic to the younger generation."

"Which are, in your opinion, the main features of the British nation?"

"I think that *moderation* in politics. In the 17th century, the English people were engaged in a revolution. We had a civil war, a revolution, and then a more autocratic government than the previous one. All this created a tendency towards moderation that has continued till this very day. The English people do not think and do not make plans systematically. I think that is rather unsatisfactory. I think that the French logic is better. However, as moderation is concerned, the English people have got much more experience."

(And the monotonous "in your opinion" proves to be again useful. Toynbee suggested that for the Great Britain revolution was a matter of history. Unpleasant memories that taught the English people of the latest centuries to be moderate. Moderate above all. This psychological peculiarity of the common Britisher deserves attention and – why not? – admiration. But it is hard to believe that an empire – one of the greatest colonial empires in the world – was created and then disappeared, on moderation grounds only. It is also difficult to believe that all the revolutionary issues of the English people could be reduced to the memories concentrated in remote childhood or youthful age.... But as I did not contradict Toynbee then, when he could have answered me, it is no doubt tactless to insist too much now on his obviously wrong opinion. Geniuses have their right to be wrong sometimes...)

"How do you appreciate the role of the Romanian Countries in the Middle Ages?"

"I think that the Ottomans could not be frightened easily, but they were afraid of the attacks in Romanians' oak forests. That is why the Ottomans agreed to grant autonomy to Walachia and to Moldavia, while the rest of the countries they conquered – even Hungary – were subject to them. The Ottoman Empire was obliged to put rather acceptable conditions in Walachia and in Moldavia. In my book on Byzantium and its world, I treat on the Latin-speaking peoples living in the extreme of the Byzantine Empire. The Romanian people are among them. The Westerners think that the Byzantine civilization disappeared when the Ottomans conquered the Byzantine Empire. I think that their culture has not disappeared, that it has survived through the Middle Ages in all the countries that have stemmed their culture from that of the Byzantine Empire. For instance Romania, Serbia, Bulgaria, Ukraine, Russia. All those countries have a Byzantine culture."

"Have you met the Romanian great historian Nicolae Iorga?"

"I am sorry, I've never met him, but I read some of his works. I have a great admiration for the variety of the fields he investigated, for his activity as a writer and as a historian. I am grateful that he wrote *A History of the Ottoman Empire* – a great work indeed.

There is a German copy of it in my library. Nicolae Iorga is a great figure of historical science and he belongs to Romania, Europe, and the whole world alike. His tragic end was quite a loss indeed."

We had been talking for two hours; the room was getting dark. We both agreed that the interview was over and we breathed freely. Professor turned the light on. It was teatime. Mrs. Toynbee brought the tee and some cookies in and then she quietly left the room. We talked a lot, taking long breaks, till seven thirty. He invited me to visit his five-room flat. The rooms were tall and large enough. He kept on approaching the topics he was concerned with. First of all the youth, their situation, their problems. Besides his grand children and his grand granddaughter, he included his two sons among the young people. One of them was a literary critic, the other – a painter, and they were probably my age. He talked about the fate of the young people forced to live today in such an agitated world that would not leave them time to deep, quiet, long studies. He was also interested in journalism and he started browsing the copies of *Magazin istoric* I had brought for him. This time there was no hurry; he looked at the pictures and asked me to translate some excerpts for him. I tried my best, with the feeling that I have to pass a difficult exam. The conversation went on quietly until I told him about my book *Romania and the Balkan Entente* that had just been published in Bucharest. Suddenly, the pace changed; I could say that his interest grew, his tone was more professional... He seemed to have become somebody else. His kindness was the same, but then it was my turn to answer like a professional. He told me, in very clear wording, his opinion about the relationship between England and the Balkan Entente. He was delighted to see that a lot of our opinions were similar. Not all of them, of course. I argued all my answers and I think that what made him happy was not exactly the discussion, but my little victory, that was his as well: I proved that my knowledge of the Balkan Entente was rather good, so I could show him that he had not been wrong when he had invited me so kindly. Anyhow, his final invitation to come back one day to visit him again was rather convincing. I left a copy of my recently published book and I left.

***

In 1970 Toynbee published *Cities on the Move* (at the same time in London, New York, and Toronto); in 1979 the book was translated into Romanian and was published by Editura Politică. Before speaking about the next meeting with Toynbee, in 1971, I want to mention that the second edition of my book on Entente would have an afterword written by Toynbee. I want to mention this, because I wrote the afterword for the Romanian version of his *Cities on the Move* (his only book translated into Romanian). That was not a matter of pure coincidence. It proved, I think, Toynbee's appreciation for Romania and also his interest in the contemporary Romanian problems. The period of Balkan Entente was just an episode in the long and agitated history of Romania. He was interested in that episode as a historian and also as a man who lived and worked during those years. Likewise, he was familiar with the presence of contemporary Romania in the international life. Toynbee had made me a gift – his afterword – but he also established in this way a connection between the study of the great problems of the Romanian people and those of his own ancestors.

Volumes II, III, V, VII, and VIII of *A Study of History* mention Romanians and their ancestors. Burebista is called the "Dacian king of Transylvania"; Trajan has the same qualities as Theodoric. A worth mentioning, less known hypothesis suggests that the Goths and the Getae originated from the same tribal body and spoke an Indo-European language. His opinion on the Goths and the Getae is also very interesting. "If the European Getae in the Lower Danube region belonged to the same nomad peoples as the Tisagetae between the Volga and the Elbe, and as the Masagetae on the lower Iaxartes, then it was logical to suppose the same kinship between Davians and Dacians, the historical neighbors of the European Getae in Transylvania, and Dahians, the neighbors of the Tisagetae and Masagetae in Transcaspian. As Dacians were considered a Thracian people, it might seem, at first sight, that the tribal names of Getae or Dacians were common both to the Iranian-speaking and to the Thracian speaking branches of the Indo-European linguistic family. In the same volume II Toynbee speaks about the foundation of the Romanian Principalities, Walachia and Moldavia, both founded by Romanian, Orthodox Christian princes who had come from the Transylvanian tableland. Those princes could not have found deserted lands, but places inhabited by a numerous native population that had been living there for immemorial times; otherwise, those states could not have been founded. He also speaks about the high degree of autonomy Moldavia and Walachia kept in spite of the Ottoman domination. It must be an old belief of the author since he mentioned it during my visit to London in 1970, as well. The Romanians, Walachians and Moldavians, knew how to get from the Turks better conditions than their coreligionists did in the south of the Danube. They got the sultan's assurance that, under his suzerainty, only Christian princes would rule them. Likewise, that neither Muslim place of public worship or Turkish fiefdom, and no colonists would ever be settled on their land. That situation changed in 1683 when the principalities got a new strategic and political significance as they became border zones of the Ottoman Empire both with the Danubian monarchy of the Habsburgs and with the Russian Empire. When Peter the Great entered Moldavia in 1711, the ruling prince Dimitrie Cantemir joined him. That signal imposed a stricter control of the Ottomans, but they did not violate the letter of obligations they had assumed: the Turks appointed Orthodox princes to rule the principalities, but they were not Romanians, and had no connection with the native people. According to that rule, between 1711 and 1821, the incomes of the two states were turned into *baksheesh* (tip) of the Phanariots –

an arrangement meant to safeguard the Ottoman interests and to fill the Phanariots' pockets at the expense of the Romanian local population. Nothing about the merits (mainly cultural and modernizing) of the Phanariot rulers. Anyhow, the specification that the Phanariots were "governors of the autonomous principalities of Walachia and Moldavia" is worth mentioning. In volume VII Toynbee speaks about the Romanian principalities as possible models for the states that succeeded the Ottoman Empire. The author resumes the idea that the principalities knew how to preserve and then to strengthen their autonomy – a good example for the other peoples in that part of the world. Toynbee considered that the foundation of the national states of Greece, Serbia, Romania, and Albania was a turning point in the history of Europe (volume IX).

Therefore it is clear that Toynbee was familiar with the history of Romania. To the end of the autumn (1970) I sent to him a typewritten copy of my book (translated into English). He read and very quickly wrote a (surprising!) preface for a possible English edition. The fact that he condemned, in that preface, the position of Great Britain versus Balkan Entente was not a great surprise for those who knew Toynbee's nonconciliatory attitude. My book was not published in Great Britain, and Toynbee's preface became an afterword of the second edition published in Romania. The theses of the historical "iconoclast" have shocked too much. He demonstrates that there is no place where history *is made*, an exclusively Anglo-Saxon space, that neither Great Britain nor the United states are the only makers of history; that there is not a "center" of the world, either in Europe or in the United States, or on any other continent. There are other countries and *civilizations*, each with its specificity and power, which made their contribution to *History*.

Daniel Boorstin, ex-director of the Library of Congress, used to say that Toynbee kept trying to take History out from under the empire of Eurocentrism, provincialism, and factual descriptiveness. I met Boorstin in Bucharest in 1976, and then in Washington, in 1978. He told me then: "I am not an expert and analyst of Toynbee. I was happy enough to meet him several times and to discuss with him about his view on history. I can tell you what I admire and what I do not with Toynbee. He was a brave historian, he saw history as a hole, and did not study strictly the American, British, French history, etc. etc.; he approached it at a world level. What is important, he tried to find the truth and what is really valid in the history of mankind, with no discrimination whatsoever. He worked with much perseverance and got remarkable results, following his own ideas. But in spite of all this, no matter how hard he tried to have a general view on the world, in many aspects he had the point of view of an English Protestant, a successor of the British Empire, a supporter of the Christian virtues. I do not agree with such views. Although he tried to conciliate Islam with the other religions and with atheism within a personal view on world history, he remained loyal to the glorious period of the British Empire at the end of the 19th century, that had influenced his education. But according to Marx none of us could develop beyond the conditions of time and space, and the circumstances we live in. We, historians, have to try, as Toynbee did, and succeeded to a higher degree than other historians of his generation, to surpass in our analysis the circumstances dictating our own existence."

Cities on the Move treats on the present, past, and future role the cities have in the world and on the cities in the future. The author does not recommend anything, he simply support his hypotheses. There is no connection with war. But the obsession of racism, senseless hatred among people, lack of tolerance, cruelty, more exactly the obsession of evil that is still a part of life is present with Toynbee.

Is Toynbee's utopian "World City" a heaven or a hell? It is not an easy question to answer. As any other positivist utopian – *Cities on the Move* can be generally considered a positive utopia – Toynbee had got an optimistic view on the far future. Toynbee said about himself that he was neither optimistic, nor pessimistic, but realistic. That is true and it can be applied to Cities on the Move as well. Toynbee wrote the book at a rather old age and it goes without saying that he did not think of his future, but of the future of his descendants. That is the book of a grandfather, but not a grandfather telling fairy tales. It is a wise grandfather, rather worried than serene; he is far from an idyllic grandfather. The Western cities of today are far from making him happy. It is the book of a man who, in the latest twenty-five years, has made severe prophecies and then has repeated them, as emphasizing the dangerous injustice generated by the increasing difference between the rich, ex mother-countries, and the poor, developing ones. He approaches some other issues: the unhappy experience of colonialism, the danger of the arms race, environmental pollution, wars, violence and terrorism. Toynbee's humanism is simply shocked and frightened when faced with the contrasts existing in the large cities of the Western countries and in those in the developing countries, ex colonies, savagely exploited. Toynbee seems to keep repeating Santayana's aphorism "They who cannot remember their past are condemned to live it again".

Is Toynbee afraid of future? Nobody can give a "yes" or "no" answer. Toynbee did not seem to be afraid, either in his life, as a polemicist, or in his work that shows the same attitude of a brave man. He was not afraid of the unknown or of the distant future. He was not frightened and he did not want to spread terror. He was neither an alarmist. Even if he seems to ignore many of the essential laws of development or considers economy less important than it really is, Toynbee speaks as a lucid man, a clearly-sighted historian, an intelligent scholar who can understand and is looking for the best solutions able to remove everything is wicked, dangerous, obstructing in the Western civilization of today. A realistic grandfather? That is not so strange as it seems to be.

***

My first visit to Toynbee was an ordinary one. Ordinary and – I have explained why – wonderful for me. The second was a kind of syncope. It was in April 1971 and I was on my way to the USA. I broke my voyage in London, called to tell I was coming, got on a taxi, and stopped in front of his house. As the taxi driver was waiting for me, I entered, we shook hands, I gave him the issue of *Magazin istoric* with our interview, thanked him for having received me and for the interview, for his afterword… everything at a pace that was improper for a visit to a man in his eighties. But I remember with great pleasure that visit hasty as it was: I was no longer a stranger and Toynbee kindly allowed me to behave as if I were an old friend. Of course, I had told him I was going to call on him, but he did not expect such a short visit. When I told him I was flying to the States he wished me good luck and asked me if I read what he had written about Americans (mostly pamphlets). I replied in the affirmative and told him that it was my first voyage to the States. He told me: "Well, it's about what I have written about them. You should not take everything as if it were gospel truth. The devil is not so black as he is painted. The Americans might be naïve, they might be childish, but attention: they are very hard-working, enterprising… and rich." He added as he saw me off: "Try to study their education system. Their Universities. They are terrific – their universities are the best in the world…"

***

The third meeting was, unfortunately, the last one. I visited him at his place, in London, two years before his death. He was 84. It was December 1973. It was not a sad meeting, it was rather grave, I could say. I think Toynbee rejected sadness and any hint of lamentation. He rejected them with determination and with a kind of calmly British contempt. The crisis of energy had broken out in the world, but we could discuss quietly on that. And there was another crisis in his own life: he had been ill, was partly recovered and was going to leave London. Illness and return to his native place were serious topics but we could talk calmly about them, as well. Miss Doreen Berry arranged that meeting too. It was 10 a.m., a nice day. Toynbee had had a heart attack and pneumonia, then flu. He was extremely weak. He took again my hands into his, but his hands seemed colder as if blood had fallen deep inside, to leave place for the warmth of his gestures, his movements, his voice, and his words. He was wearing a gray slack suit (maybe the same he was wearing during my first visit), but his clothes were too large for his thin body. The light seemed to come out just from him, but it was flickering, with no force in it. There had been quite a dazzling light, but gentle at the same time. However, some solitary rays still focused his emotional vibration. No briskness, no thrill. That was my first impression that gradually faded away as we started to talk.

Before sitting down, he took my arm and we started to walk – together with Miss Berry and with Mrs. Toynbee – in the flat full of boxes. Toynbee was packing his books; he would leave for York together with his wife. His two sons and the grandchildren were to remain in London. Grandfather was preparing himself to pass away. A part of his books were going with him, the others were left to the Institute the director of which he had been for such a long time. I had come with gifts for him. He seemed delighted at the two Romanian blankets, woven by hand. He and his wife took them, went in front of the window to see them better, and put them in one of the boxes. "I will take with me these warm memories from Romania." He seemed to have enjoyed the other gift even more. It was the English version of *A History of Increase and Decrease of the Ottoman Empire*, which had just been published in Bucharest. He sat down and started browsing the book.

"This is one of the books I have always wanted to have in my library. It was quite impossible to buy a first edition copy printed in London and translated by N. Tindal in 1734–1735. I congratulate and I thank the Romanian editors and researchers who give again to Europe a work of such value for its time. My homage to Dimitrie Cantemir is paid by my belief that in a century (the 18th) that did not lack geniuses he was the proof of the creative force of the peoples in the South Eastern Europe, and mainly of the Romanian people. He was one of the greatest scholars of his time, a genuinely universal scholar. Romania can assert itself more and more prominently in the world and I wish the Romanian people the greatest success, especially to the young generations that have to take an active part in solving the problems of mankind."

(An answer revealing the two main topics of our discussion: the former about the new generations, and the latter about the solving of the problems, a matter in which Romania will play its part.)

I repeated an older question:

"Tell me, please, what does the arms race mean for the history of mankind and of each people separately?"

"Wars? I have already told you I do not think a World War III could break out although, owing to some complex factors, it is not unavoidable. We have passed beyond the epoch when the peoples could afford themselves the luxury of militarism and of praising military virtues. That time has passed when, in the Western world, war was in fashion, like hunting for instance. Wars, like a "sport of kings" in which a Richard Lion-Hearted or a knight like Bayard fought, brought much pain, and the kings making them were undoubtedly militarists. If we compare them with Charles XII of Sweden or with Frederick the Great of Prussia we can see that militarism has kept growing. Frederick the Great would have never dreamt of glorifying war as another Prussian militarist did. I mean Helmuth von Moltke who said that 'Eternal peace is just a dream; and it is not a beautiful dream. War, in exchange, is an integral part of the order of the Universe set by God'. If we think of the difference between Moltke and Hitler we can see how far militarism has gone..."

... The same opposition and huge contempt for Hitler. Some more questions and answers. A careful rereading of his answers of 1973 shows that they are almost identical with the answers he gave me three years ago. It is only natural: his concerns and worries were the same. Even his optimistic view about a third world war. I am browsing notebooks, copy books, some notes scribbled in the margins of newspapers. There is something new here. He shows that the Europeans have the chance of a great cultural continuity. He told me about it, but this example of "leap over time" is a new one: "I admire what China has succeeded to do from 1950 on. I listened with much interest what my friend, the ex- ambassador of the United States to India, John Kenneth Galbraith, told me. By the end of the millenium China will already be on the way of its original democracy."

He speaks again about the youth. His words are more or less those I recorded when I first met him, but the tone of his voice is quite different. More restrained, more grave.

"I am content," Toynbee said, and I understood he was thinking of his life. But he might have thought of his book that had just been published. He showed it to me. It was his last but one book. The last one was published after his death. Its title, *Mankind and Mother Earth*, reveals his thoughts on the old age.

"I am content" he said and added then, in a clearer voice that time: "I have done everything".

He seemed really pleased and convinced that he had done everything he was able to. Content and – something new, something unexpected for the polemist ready to defend violently his conviction, for the man a lot of people considered hard to cope with – conciliated. Conciliated (I could realize) with all the members of his large family. There may have been some conflicts too. They were quite natural with such a difficult "grandfather". Conciliated with his fate. Conciliated with what he had done and with what he was still intending to do. He was no longer concerned with himself, but with mankind, with the millions and millions of young people. Toynbee, even when he resumed the ideas he expressed in 1970 (in almost the same words), had the voice of the man that felt himself responsible for everything would happen after his death. The same as, in a strange way, he felt responsible for everything, even for what had happened before him, some 4 000 thousands years ago in China, or for Alexander the Great's fate, for the death of Decebalus or for ancient Rome and Greece, and for World War II as well. *Our fate is in our own hands*, he told me. He had written those words several times, he had told them to me, and repeated them as if apologizing for repeating such a common place truth; but he had no choice. Commonplace or not, that was, or had become, his testamentary truth. "*Our fate is in our own hands*"… When I had come, the boxes full of books had vague, slightly mysterious shapes in the foggy light of the morning. Then, the sunlight came out from behind clouds to polish book covers and spines, patches of wood, Mrs. Toynbee's thin hands, the old hands of the man who was *for sure* the greatest historian of the century, *for sure* the most controversial one among all those who, in this century have written the history of all centuries and of all civilizations. He was also a friend of Romania and – I like that thought – the idea of writing *opus magna* crossed his mind as he was crossing Romania.

When I was again in the street, after more than four hours, it was very sunny and very cold. I do not remember what I did afterwards. I think I walked a lot and when I was shivering with cold I went in somewhere to drink a cup of tea. Then I came back to my hotel. After my meeting with Toynbee – extremely grave, but invigorating at the same time – I was restless, so I went out again, in the streets of London. London is no longer the capital city of an empire and it is consequently more peaceful. Peaceful yet governed by a feeling of encouragement. The English people know that their Empire does no longer exists, they have no illusions, and try – animated by the realistic spirit Toynbee was so proud of – to rebuild their lives on new grounds. The English people do not imagine that the old days will come again, but they know that if they use the natural resources (not very rich) of their country, and their own resources of intelligence, work, economy, and character (that is very rich indeed) they will succeed to face honorably any kind of situation. Of course, this is my opinion, that is what I feel, a foreign traveler, journalist, and historian, what I can tell about the English people as I know it. Such feelings as discouragement, despair, and panic are quite strange to them.

Nothing… I was, together with my bitter and hard thoughts that had started that morning during my visit to Toynbee, in the beautifully lit Piccadilly Circus. Suddenly, the light died out. It was for the first time since war, in the evening of the very day I last met Toynbee that the light died out in Piccadilly Circus. Piccadilly Circus, maybe the most lit spot in the Great Britain was then dark. Squeaking brakes of the stopping cars, people running one into another. I do not think panic, discouragement, confusion lasted more than one minute. The people soon recovered, they were again the same Britishers I had always known. But that minute existed. The crisis – of oil and not only that – was real and had warned them. They lived in England, I was just a traveler, but in that very minute neither they nor I were in the Great Britain, but in the world. We were not in the Great Britain; we were in the Universe. In the contemporary world, in the eighth decade, in crisis. A world in which Toynbee had arranged his books in boxes and in which dark suddenly came. In the evening of October 22, 1975, the BBC broadcaster read the latest news: "Today Arnold Joseph Toynbee, 86 years old, passed away in a clinic of York…"

Good night, professor emeritus!

A LIFETIME'S STRENUOUS WORK TO SERVING ROMANIA

The Giurescu house at 47 Berzei St. was an old-fashioned building at the far end of a long and narrow courtyard. However, I did not meet Professor Constantin C. Giurescu there, but in his temporary residence, where he had moved in the 1950s. It was at 4 Monetariei St., a vicarage rising in the far end of a churchyard. It was there that the historian's family lived for twenty years. Just across from the church there is the ex-Museum of History of the Working Class Democratic and Revolutionary Movement, the present Museum of the Romanian Peasant.

I met him in the autumn of 1962. I was a postgraduate student then, studying for my doctor's degree and I had some difficulty in completing my research theme *Romania and the Balkan Entente.* It was a matter of documentation. Between 1934 and 1940 the Balkan Entente had been a mutual-defense alliance between Greece, Yugoslavia, Romania, and Turkey. It was intended to guarantee the signatories' territorial integrity and political independence and also to encourage economic cooperation. The Entente was an open agreement, founded on the principles of national independence, sovereignty, and equal rights between its members, a defender of the territorial *status-quo* as sanctioned by the Peace Treaties in Paris, concluded following World War I. Dogmatic historiography said the absolute opposite: it contradicted the documents revealing the benevolence of the Soviet Union in creating the Balkan Entente. Later on, Soviet Union cooperated with some Entente countries and appreciated their constructive contribution, during the inter-war period, to the collective peace and security, against fascist revisionism and attacks.

I had studied at University that the Balkan Entente was both reactionary and imperialist, and acted against Soviet Union. When I started perusing the archives of the Ministry of External Affairs, I came to gradually understand how far from the documents such enforcement was.

So, I went to Professor Giurescu because I felt like analyzing objectively with him the whole situation: data, documents, arguments. Likewise, he had "lived" the history of Balkan Entente as he had taken part in the general Balkan conferences preparing the Entente. Between 1930 and 1933 he had promoted and supported friendship and cooperation relationships among the six neighboring countries. And, last but not least, he had some books that I needed badly.

Therefore I met great difficulties in studying the Balkan Entente and my questions could not have been passed over by just a *yes* or *no* answer; there were still a lot of things to be solved and I knew I could not label them out, but had to keep looking for the truth in spite of everything. It was the period of Congress IX of the Romanian Communist Party and the general belief was that it would both open the way to several undeniable historical truths and permit *seeking out* the truth about some less clear aspects – an essential premise of knowledge.

I think that I should first tell something about Professor and his way. I visited him several times and he made me the honor to visit me at the office of *Magazin istoric* as he often contributed papers there. More than once he told me about his projects and I ventured to suggest him (I even insisted) that he should complete his *American Journal* and *Memories*. The first thing that inspired respect with him was his calmness. Calmness based on certain self-confidence. Though much older than me (I had studied his *History of the Romanians* when I was a teenager) his attitude was that of a kind colleague who wanted to teach when he was asked to, but eager at the same time to learn, to inquire, to accept an open discussion about divergent points of view. It was an "academic" calmness I could say. Or a classical calmness. The respect he showed to me – he treated me as if I were his colleague – obliged me to "do my homework" very seriously. His knowledge was so vast that he could have easily found a flaw in my arguments.

While the first edition of the present book was in print I had another proof (there were so many!) of Professor's punctuality. It was November 11, 1977 (the very *last* day of his life!) and he had come to the printing house to discuss some technical aspects of one of his books in print at Albatros Publishing House. He had an appointment at 12, and at 11.45 he was already there.

That was just an example, but a lot of his students and colleagues could remember dozens of similar cases of his *punctuality* that had become structural!

But respect did not oblige anyone to agree with him all the time; disputes often *arose.* They arose not broke out. His inner balance – that had helped him to live with dignity in his glorious and hard times alike – had always been intact when the young man and the old scholar brought forward carefully analyzed arguments. And the latter had not the vanity – proper to mean people only – to deny that, in one matter or another, the other might have been right as well. On the contrary, he seemed quite glad to admit, as I informed him about the results of some new research (I studied one problem, he – one hundred), that his old viewpoint had to be shifted a little or even changed.

I'd like to tell something about his love for work and to close up then with the feature that seemed the most important with C.C. Giurescu (and with any genuine historian): his love for truth. For the *whole truth.* Both for its light and for its dark sides. He was confident that the Romanian people – like any other people – had to know the truth, the whole truth about its past. That it should not be "deprived" of truth, as they tried during the aggressive dogmatism. That there is not a trustworthier ally for the people than the truth, without which the very self-consciousness of the Romanians would be endangered. It is history that feeds self-consciousness. He used to tell me that we should never avoid the historical truth. On the other side, he was definitely against aggressiveness in telling the truth (to a smaller extent, that issue was reflected in our contradictory discussions). He would say that historical truth had to be studied as a whole, with shades of difference, with full knowledge of its connections. However it should not be told *anywhere* and *in any way*, but at *its proper place and time.* He had learned the strategy of truth not only from the study of history, but from his own life as well. The truth had to be told in the way he used to tell it: calmly, at a moderate pace, in carefully selected words, far from any excess and exaggeration. That was the way he told it in his books, some of which – very important ones indeed – were published after 1960, and that was the way he told it in his many papers published in *Magazin istoric*. Between 1962 and 1977 he was by far the most active Romanian historian: he published a lot, one book after another, wrote for newspapers, often spoke on the radio, contributed papers to international symposia and congresses. In those years he traveled abroad, in Europe, but mainly in the United States.

The same tact in telling the truth – the whole truth a person can reach no matter how learned he/she is, and the whole truth that could be told in those times – and the same caution in revealing new points of view could be also found in his works published after his death. One of those works, very dear to him, was *Controversial Issues in the Romanian Historiography* published by Albatros Publishing House. The follower of the Giurescu historians, Professor Dinu C. Giurescu, gave me several pages of volume II of his father's *Memories* (unfinished because of the tragic death of its author).

Since I wrote "Giurescu historians" I will introduce some data about Professor Dinu C. Giurescu's grandfather and father. The grandfather, Constantin Giurescu, was born in 1875 at Chiojdu, Buzău County, and died in 1918. He published, among others, *Contributions to the Study of the Walachian Chronicles and Contributions to the Study of the Moldavian Chronicles*. His son, Constantin C. Giurescu, was born at Focşani in 1901 and died in 1977. His vast bibliography includes such books as History of the Romanians, History of Bucharest, A History of the Romanian Forest; and last but not least there is the diary of his imprisonment at Sighet: *Five Years and Two Months in the Sighet Prison* (Editura Fundaţiei Culturale Române, 1994).

Volume II (unfinished) of the *Memories* reports on the period 1938–1947. Those were "years of intense history, of deep implications and huge consequences not only for Romania and Europe but for the whole world. It was the period of World War II. A genuine worldwide cataclysm that spread over land and oceans alike, war left place for a new world – that of *nuclear energy*. It was a period of huge suffering, of unlashing brutal force, reminding that man was no longer the wise being (*Homo Sapiens*) imagined by the idealistic thinkers, but the descendant of the millions of years of prehistory when the club and the stone had made the 'law' – the law of the most powerful one. I was not a *witness* only; in 1938–1940 I was involved in the public life. Therefore, I cannot be a judge at the same time. I confine myself to report facts, to describe people and to point out circumstances. Some of those facts and people will speak for themselves; for some others it is only for the future to judge. However, I hope that the present memories will contribute to that judgement, and I wish my readers the peace of mind required to learn more about a world that does no longer exist."

Constantin C. Giurescu was extremely concerned with the destiny of the Romanians to whom he dedicated more than 10 000 pages of history. It is but natural that in his Memories (excerpts quoted with the kind permission of Professor Dinu C. Giurescu) he speaks about crucial events that took place between wars. Here you are some lines about the attitude of Romania when Czechoslovakia, Poland, and Yugoslavia were invaded by Germany: "In the autumn (1938), king Carol II, accompanied by Prime Minister Armand Călinescu, met Beck, the Polish Minister of Foreign Affairs, in Galați on the royal yacht. Beck had claimed a territory in Czechoslovakia and, as he felt that Hitler would bring forward the issue of the Sudeten Mountains, he had come to persuade Romanians to express their own claims as well. Both the king and Călinescu were very much surprised at Beck's suggestion; the answer – as I learned – was categorical: we were Czechoslovakia's friends and allies; how could we do such a thing? We had the same attitude later on, when the Nazis attacked Yugoslavia and the Horthysts occupied part of Backa. We were suggested then, by Nazis and Horthysts (beneficiaries of the Vienna Award) alike, to do something similar. The answer was categorical that time too. In both situations we answered in keeping with the honor of the Romanian people and followed the old saying: 'A friend in need is a friend indeed'. When both the Polish and the Czechs came under the Nazi occupation we welcomed in Romania all those who wanted to escape and helped them."

Some other paragraphs in *Memories* describe the atmosphere in the spring of 1915, when the Romanians firmly expressed their decision to defend their independence: "When the reserves were called up, the Romanians responded with enthusiasm. The people realized that they had to defend the country and there was no one we could rely on – similarly to other times in our history. Therefore, the young and the old came to put on their military uniform."

In *Memories*, Constantin C. Giurescu blames the legionaries and their ideology. He even gives his own evidence proving the connection between the Iron Guard and the Nazis: "They had funds for elections (1937); besides the money from subscriptions and donations – there were tycoons who were taking prevention measures in case the legionaries would ascend to power, similarly to some German industrialists who had supported Hitler before 1933 – they had foreign funds too, from the Nazis. One of the channels used to introduce these funds into the country was the well-known 'I.G. Farben Industrie', the great chemical and pharmaceutical company established at Leverkusen am Rhein. The go-between was Nae Ionescu, a reader in logic at the Bucharest University. I found that out from him, quite unexpectedly. It was September 1938. I was walking back from the lakes when a car skidded to a halt close to me, into the kerb, and a familiar voice asked: 'Where are you going Professor?' It was Nae Ionescu. I told him I was going downtown and he invited me in. It was a 'Mercedes', a beautiful two-seater sports car, upholstered in red leather. 'Nice car' I said 'is it yours?' 'Yes, it's mine' he answered, 'I represent here the interests of I.G. Farben and this is a gift from them'. It was crystal clear and I did not want to push. We started discussing about his course of lectures at the University."

A special place is held in *Memories* II by the historian's own concerns. "1939. We selected (with Scarlat Lambrino) the digging places – all of them along the Lower Danube: 1) at Garvăn, out of Galați, on the island where the ancient Dinogetia rose; 2) at Enisala, on the rocky hill dominating the Razelm Lake and the Delta, the ruins of three fortresses: Byzantine, then Romanian (from the time of Mircea the Old), and then Turkish; 3) near Măcin, the site of the ancient Arrubium; 4) at Troesmis, the present Iglița, the site of a Roman camp – Legion V Macedonica. (Later on, during the wars with the Marcomanni, the soldiers were sent to Potaissa – Turda); 5) at Poiana, on Siret, in Tecuci County, that would be later identified as former Piroboridava, mentioned by the ancient geographer Ptolemy. Likewise, we assigned the persons in charge of each site: at Dinogetia, Gheorghe Stefan, who was then a professor's assistant, but would follow Lambrino in the latter's position at the University; at Enisala, Grigore Avakian, my ex-colleague at the University; at Troesmis, Emil Coliu, a remarkable researcher who had unfortunately passed away in the prime of his age; at Poiana, Radu Vulpe, who had already dug there and suggested that the settlement could be the Piroboridava mentioned by Ptolemy. Lambrino himself was to take care of Arrubium, where the Danube had almost ate away the settlement. He had to control and lead all the other diggings as well.

We started digging just after the close of the academic year and our unexpected and important results were worth the money spent and also our hopes. At Dinogetia the walls of the fortress started being uncovered. We dug out there a Byzantine hoard consisting of 106 pieces of gold from the reign of Emperor Basil II (976–1025), and of his successors Roman III and Constantin IX Monomachus. The hoard had probably been buried there because of a barbarian invasion and its owner had never come to take it back. Besides the hoard, we uncovered, at Garvăn, Christian testimonies and some other things revealing craft and trading activities – a proof of the ties with the peoples north of the Danube and of the Black Sea and with Byzantium too. At Enisala we found two 14th-century hoards of Romanian coins: one of them was Walachian and had silver coins from the times of Vladislav I and Radu I, and the other one was Moldavian, also silver, from Petru Mușatin's age. Both of them prove the busy commercial life in Dobruja and the circulation of the Romanian coins within the area between the Danube and the Black Sea. We also found there numerous fragments of Byzantine earthenware from the 13th–14th centuries, enameled in yellow and green, decorated with flowers, birds and some other motifs. The French archeologists had already dug at Troesmis in the 19th century, during the Turkish domination. It was there that Coliu found a large jar of heat-fired clay the mouth of which was covered with a Roman flat piece of brick. He did not want to take that brick away all by himself and called both Lambrino and myself to be present at that archeological première. We went to the high plateau of the Roman camp that dominated the Danube and the large plain to take part in removing the brick with due ceremony. The jar held just some remains of grain and nothing else. Coliu was rather disappointed but we had expected that. Both of us knew that such a large jar could have been for grain only. The diggings in Poiana attested the existence of the Roman camp on the site of an older Dacian settlement, Piroboridava.

On September 1, 1939, in the morning I was in a routine inspection in the area. I turned the car radio on and I heard the news: fascist troops had invaded Poland. Therefore, Hitler had started the horrible machine that would kill so many people. The first act of conflagration was short: in 17 days Poland was down and its army, despite its bravery was defeated; what had remained of it came to Romania where so-called camps had been arranged. They were camps in name only as most of the people were free to leave for the Near East or for the Western countries. On September 15, the cars of the first Polish refugees could be seen in the streets of Galați. Mattresses and trunks, all they had been able to take before fleeing, could be seen on the roof of almost every car. The family inside looked almost the same: the woman usually crying, the man looking tired, the fair-haired children gazing at us in wonder. Some of the refugees found temporary shelter in Bucharest, some others in Craiova or in other cities. Almost most of them finally left Romania."

Gradually, Giurescu's professional concerns left space for the political ones… The pressure of the present history on the millennial history…

"Several days following the outbreak of World War II, on September 11, King Carol II summoned the Crown Council, attended by Prime Minister Armand Călinescu, the members of the government, and other political personalities. Some of hem, I mean C. Argetoianu and Gigurtu, suggested an approach to Germany; Armand Călinescu, who was the last to speak, definitely stood for the traditional foreign policy, beside France and Great Britain. At the same time, in answer to the opinions of several participants he handed in his resignation. The king who fully trusted his Prime

Minister, who was also in charge of the Ministries of the Interior and of National Defense, would not accept his resignation. Immediately after the Council, the Prime Minister informed, through his private secretary, also his relative, Radu Lobey, both the minister of France in Bucharest, Adrien Thierry, and that of the Great Britain, Reginald Hoare, about his point of view. The two diplomats sent immediately the news to Paris and to London, respectively. Daladier, the Prime Minister of France, answered that 'this resignation must be stopped by any possible means', as Călinescu was "the only man" who could ensure a continuity of the traditional Romanian foreign policy (Radu Lobey, *Un assassinat oublié*, Le Monde, Sept. 21– 22 1969).

Călinescu's attitude sped up the plan the fascist Germany had for Romania and for its Prime Minister.

The hand that stroke – after ten days – was the Iron Guard. The legionaries had their reason to hate Călinescu, as Corneliu Codreanu, their leader, and some of his followers had been put to death when Călinescu had been Minister of the Interior. On September 21, in full daylight, as the Prime Minister rode home in his car, a cart made the chauffeur slow down and finally stop the car. It was in a less crowded area between the Dâmbovița River and the Ardealul Boulevard, in the new open street connecting Știrbei Vodă and the Military Academy. In that very moment the assassins approached – they had come from Germany, from a special center where they had been trained and equipped – and shot Armand Călinescu and his security man with 26 bullets. The latter could do nothing, not even take out his gun. In the same car, the killers went to the Radio building in General Berthelot Street, where they pushed their way in, immobilized the staff and broadcast their "success". The general stupefaction lasted no longer than a moment. The assassins were arrested just there, in the Radio building; the accomplices were found as well, and they were all killed the very same evening, right on the spot the Prime Minister had been killed in the morning. The bodies were left there for a whole day, so that everybody could see them.

I heard about Călinescu's death from Miloteanu, the secretary general of the Lower Danube Area, whose radio was on when the assassins announced their crime. A terrified Miloteanu came in a hurry to my office and told me what he had just heard. I immediately realized that the crime bore the fascist mark. Their way of acting had always been the same! At noon, when I went home, there was a military guard in front of the gate of my house. A lieutenant told my wife that he had been ordered to stay there. My wife replied that the guard was useless since, if they wanted revenge, they could attack our kids on their way to school. At the beginning of September we had moved – my wife, our three kids, and myself – from Bucharest to Galați. The boys were attending "Vasile Alecsandri" high school, and my daughter, the primary school in the neighborhood (to the greatest surprise of the local notables who could not imagine the daughter of the royal resident attending another school than 'Notre Dame de Sion'). However the guard remained there for about a week.

1940: Out of the twenty-four professors at the Faculty of Letters in Bucharest, in the autumn of 1940, just one had joined the Iron Guard – the legionary movement. The rest of them – important names in the inter-war Romanian culture – had no connection with the legionary regime. It lasted for about five months and during that period the movement did not win *a single supporter*. None of the professors joined that initial follower.

The same about the readers of the Faculty of Letters. Out of them – they were fewer than the professors were – only one, Nae Ionescu, reader in logic, had upheld the legionary ideas.

There were two, maybe three among the assistants. The legionaries were not very successful with them either.

The Iron Guard had attracted some of the students; they were not very many, but they were rather active. However the students having other beliefs outnumbered them. The greatest part of them had joined some other political parties – *țărăniști* (Peasant's Party), liberals, socialists, communists – or were not politically involved. Therefore, I can say, both as a contemporary and as a witness, that the legionary regime (that had come to power in September 1940) had found few adherents among the professors and readers of the Faculty of Letters in Bucharest, and a weak interest among its students. As far as I was informed, the situation was similar with other faculties of the Bucharest University: the legionary professors and readers represented a very small percent.

An atmosphere of tension could be felt everywhere around in the city and insecurity kept growing. Following the executions in the Jilava prison and the assassinations of Nicolae Iorga and Virgil Madgearu, rumor started spreading that others were to follow. Three-zeroed figures were circulated – I heard about five thousand – that included the top of the Romanian society: political (ministers, state undersecretaries, secretaries general, senators and deputies), economic, administrative, legal and cultural personalities. Some of the people aimed at left their homes. I did the same and for a couple of days I was sheltered in the house of an old friend of mine, the secretary of the Faculty of Letters, Marin Popescu Spineni.

In November 1940, another rumor: a weeding out action was aimed at the professors. After a short while a commission was set up and some of the professors were invited in front of it, at the Ministry of Public Instruction. The head of it was the rector of the Bucharest University.

Three such invitations were sent to the Faculty of Letters: for Mihai Ralea, for Alexandru Rosetti, and for myself.

I went there as requested and was invited in the office of the general secretary. The meeting was short, very academic, and the topic was the paper I had written about the ex-Prime Minister Armand Călinescu. The paper had been published in 'Universul' the very next day following his terrible death and had been quoted by some other newspapers in Bucharest. I wrote there that I considered Armand Călinescu a genuine statesman who had always defended Romania's interests. They did not ask me about the volume of Armand Călinescu's speeches that I had published. I could see that the summons had been a mere formality and the decision had already been taken. Later on, after the legionary rebellion, I learned from the photocopy of the meeting minutes that I was to be moved from the University to another state institution. The same copy showed a similar decision for Alexandru Rosetti; Mihai Ralea was to be dismissed altogether from his position.

However the decision of the commission would never be put into practice. In January 1941, the legionary rebellion broke out.

After it had been suppressed, the new minister of the Public Instruction set up another commission, headed by Professor Scarlat Lambrino at the Chair of Ancient History, Faculty of Letters, Bucharest University. The new commission was to investigate the way the previous one had acted. Lambrino's report showed conclusive evidence of the superficial and subjective way the previous commission had worked.

In the first month of hostilities, Bucharest was the target of some Soviet air raids, with few airplanes; casualties were not very heavy. Camouflage and alarm measurements had been taken since autumn of 1939. Alarms had been fixed in different parts of the city, on the highest buildings, to announce the approaching aircraft. As the front moved, those raids stopped; they would be resumed in summer of 1943 and then from April 4, 1944 on, more intense that time.

On August 1, 1943 I was in Breaza; I had delivered there a lecture at the humanist seminar organized by the Professor of Pedagogy from the Bucharest University. At about half past one, as we were having lunch at a restaurant, we heard the loud noise made by aircraft engines. We went out and saw a long line of large airplanes flying at about 150–200 m high. We could even see the pilots' faces. They flew from up the valley and headed to Câmpina. At first we did not realize what kind of planes they were; we thought they were German. But then I saw the insignia on the wings – the five-pointed star framed in a rectangle and I told them: 'They are American and I think they are going to bombard our oil derricks and distilleries'. No sooner had I uttered those words than we heard the explosion of the first bombs dropped over. Many others followed both at Câmpina and at Ploiești-Brazi, but not east of Ploiești, at Teleajen, over the installations of the Romanian-American Company. The bombardment was a total surprise; some of the German commanders of the anti-aircraft gun batteries were missing; they were at the restaurants or strolling around. The punishments inflicted on some of them were very severe indeed. On the other hand, the Romanian mountain corps started fighting immediately; after some-minute surprise the anti-aircraft guns responded. The damage at the oil refineries was important, but it was paid dearly: tens of American planes that had left their base at Foggia, south of

Italy, did not go back. Several crews that had parachuted themselves from their falling planes were taken prisoners. The dead were buried in a cemetery off the Bucharest-Ploiești road, on the right side to Ploiești. As the Americans themselves admitted, it was the bombardment with the most numerous casualties: both planes and people. The prisoners were well treated, better than both they and the Germans had expected.

There might have been the casualties that explained the long break – until April 4, 1944, when the first important bombardment on Bucharest took place. The bombardment, in successive waves, started in daytime too, at about two p.m. The people did not expect such a thing; everybody thought it was just an exercise of passive defense, as many others before. Cotroceni, Grivița, and Steaua were the worst hit districts, and at the North Station they used the system of the bomb 'cover'. Bombs were dropped in other districts too, as for instance in Calea Victoriei on the 'Splendid' and 'Parc' hotels – the latter was the headquarters of the German military mission. Both hotels were completely destroyed and a great part of their residents killed. There were very many victims. It had never happened before, in the whole history of Bucharest, that so many people were killed in such a short time interval – less than two hours. I could not learn the exact figure. A novelist said there had been eighteen thousand victims. The figure circulated among the economic historians was 2500. If the novelist's figure seemed exaggerated, the other one was definitely too low. There were several thousands casualties. Some of the bombs fell on the shelters and killed all the people inside: in Cotroceni, and in Șerban Vodă, Pleșoianu, and Sibiceanu streets. In Sibiceanu St. shelter, 73 dead people were found. In the lounge of the 'Splendid' hotel there were more than one hundred dead people, most of them killed by the blast. Professor I.D. Ștefănescu, who told me that, and his wife were residents of the hotel. They escaped almost miraculously; they stayed on the first floor and were a bit late in coming down. He told me that they had lost valuable things and drawings as his wife had not taken the suitcase already prepared for such an eventuality. She had taken by mistake another one, containing some coat hangers and other trifles. According to the May 1, 1944 manifesto of the Workers' Unique Front, more than

1500 workers were killed at the Grivița Railway Workshops. George Potra told me that about fifty engineers and technicians had died there. A 'pile' of bodies was arranged in front of the Workshops, in Grivița St. and another one near '5 lei' restaurant, in the same street. However, the largest 'pile' was inside the Faculty of Medicine, where the corpses from the Cotroceni and some other districts had been gathered. In the Cărămidarii de Jos parish, about 140–150 people were killed, 75 of which – according to the burials record – were buried in the homonymous cemetery. A woman – Maria Călugăru – and his seven children were killed in one of the houses. The youngest one, just a baby, was buried together with his mother. In Dudești-Cioplea, a district with fewer victims, 21 people died. Several trains in the North Station, loaded with refugees from Moldavia, were also hit. It was a genuine massacre. One freight train in the Bucharest marshalling yard was loaded with documents belonging to the State Archives. They all burnt.

My family and I were all at home, at 47 Berzei St.; Marin, the errand boy from the Institute had just come. When we heard the alarm we all went downstairs, Gib, our setter lavraque included. The basement had a platform of reinforced concrete above it and unless the bomb fell directly on it we were protected. When bombs started falling – we were just 500 m far from the North Station – fear overwhelmed us all. A bomb fell on the house across the street and three people were killed. Pieces of the falling house broke some windowpanes of our house and damaged the roof. I found a whole brick on my desk. At the beginning we thought it was our house. I watched the effect of fear on all of us: our little girl was shuddering near my wife; Gib, its muzzle under my armpit, was shivering spasmodically. Marin, the errand boy told me then: 'Professor, he who says he is not afraid is a big liar'. In a short break between two 'waves' I told my wife: 'If we all escape from this, do you agree to give away half of our belongings to charity?' She immediately answered 'I'll give everything'. 'You'll have to remember your words.' Fortunately, we all escaped after a terrible fear. We fixed our house, although we all knew that such a thing could repeat any time.

The second bombardment, with firebombs too, was eleven

days later, on April 15, 1944. The University was badly damaged: the old wing fell down and the attic of the new building was destroyed by fire. Some of the seminar libraries, among which that of ancient history, containing books by Grigore Tocilescu and Vasile Pârvan, and part of the library of the history of the Romanians, with Professor Grigore Niculescu's donation, were burnt up. The same bombardment completely destroyed the next door building of 'Cartea Românească'. Professor Papacostea's house caught fire from a phosphorus firebomb and it was extinguished with sand – not with water that would have activated the burning. Other raids came, one after another, more or less frequently. They were very frequent, mainly in May; the night raids were American, the day ones, British. The planes of the former, all painted in black were called 'black windows'. They started dropping bombs after launching first the so-called "light grapes' – clusters of parachute-born rockets. They lit everything around, like in the daytime, and the bombs could thus be dropped on the targets selected. The show was terrifying, apocalyptic. The raids were generally announced with fifteen minutes before, when the planes crossed the Romanian border to head towards Bucharest. The 'prealarm' emitted a series of short, modulated sounds; at that very moment any activity stopped; pedestrians started running to the shelters; cars sped up to leave the city. However, they were sometimes too numerous and had to stop because of the bottlenecks. When 'alarm' sounded, the drivers caught on the road either hid in a nearby 'shelter' – houses, group of trees – or they simply fell to the ground waiting for disaster to pass. Those moments were especially difficult: nothing could be done, everything was a matter of luck, and one's life depended on the instant the trigger was acted. I realized that during the April 4 raid, when the bomb did not fall on my house but on the house just across the street; it was destroyed and three people were killed.

The stories below, that took place during the raids, will show what good or bad luck means under such circumstances. Before one of the bombardments – I don't remember if it was the first or the second – in the very instant the prealarm sounded, Lică Rădulescu, the director of the Radiobroadcast Society, called his wife and told her to take their two little daughters and go to the nearest air-raid shelter. A bomb fell down on the very shelter they were hiding in and all the people inside were killed. One could easily imagine the pain of the poor man who realized that he had involuntarily sent his family to death. The next story is about an official at the Ministry of National Economy. The family lived on the last floor of a building in Șerban Vodă St. His wife and their little daughter were at home when the prealarm sounded. They rushed downstairs but, in the lounge, the little girl started crying 'The cat, mummy, the cat!' They had forgotten the cat in the flat. The mother tried in vain to make the little girl understand that they had to go to the shelter. The latter did not want to give up, and started crying and shouting louder. So, they had to go back to take the cat with them. As they were rushing downstairs for the second time, a bomb fell on the shelter and everybody inside died. The rumor spread quickly and it reached the Ministry of the National Economy where the father worked. He ran like mad to his house and to his great relief he saw his wife and daughter at one window of their flat. He could not believe his eyes: his daughter's love for the cat had saved them. (I remember I ran like mad as well, from the place of my parents-in-law to my house after the second bombardment, on April 15. On my way, not far from Rosetti Square, I met Mișu, the kind and competent salesclerk at 'Cartea Românească'. He was all dirty with dust and lime and told me that the old, beautiful building of 'Cartea Românească' did no longer exist.). The third story happened in Dorobanți and Mihai Eminescu streets. The storied building there had solid concrete floors and the shelter was in its basement. The basement had a small ventilation window, at the street level. Otherwise it was very safe. It was bad luck, or evil hour, or whatever it was. The bomb fell obliquely just through the window and killed everybody inside. The people that had remained in their flats were all right, all of them. All these things make one believe in fate, be it good or bad.

The bombardments were not directed to Bucharest only but to other areas as well. They targeted mainly the oil and industrial centers. Ploiești, for instance, attracted all their attention. When the crones in the outskirts of Bucharest heard the prealarm, they used to say 'May God direct them to Ploiești'. Turnu Severin, Constanța,

Iași, and Brașov were bombarded as well. However the raids in Bucharest were more intense as the Capital was the vital political and economic center of the country; the reactions in Bucharest spread all over the territory of Romania.

The air raids strongly influenced the city life. The officials moved to other towns or villages, in general to less important areas so that they might be protected. The rich people left as well. However, the greatest majority of the people remained in the city but their activity was fragmented, interrupted, insecure; everybody lived in a state of perpetual tension; everybody wanted that diabolical situation to come to an end as each day or night could mean death. When the Soviet offensive took place in August, everybody was ready for a great change."

***

Fifteen years elapsed between 1962, when I first met him, and 1977, when he passed away. I can remember him in varied occasions during that time interval. First of all, it was in the house where I first visited him, at 4 Monetăriei St. A room on the first floor, bookshelves all around the walls, a desk, two armchairs, and a small table. Later on, in Berzei St., on the ground floor, in the far end of the yard, a vestibule, a hall, and professor's study on the right: a huge bookcase but not large enough for so many books; a desk with a lamp on it, and some large leather armchairs (maybe the same)… My affective memory often confounds the two houses and I can see him walking around the room, among bookshelves as I am sitting in one of the two armchairs (or were they four: two in Monetăriei and two in Berzei?), not very comfortable since the scientist did not look for comfort but for the essentials of study.

My interlocutor was neither a gossip nor a small talk fan. History was not only his profession, but also his permanent obsession. He thought of history, he wrote history, and he talked only about history. He was not at all interested in common things – not even in, let's say, weather. He valued his time and refused to waste it in vain. He concentrated on historical issues – including the most controversial ones – that completely absorbed him. He wanted

Romanians to be able to face history using history's own arms. The words belong to him. He was the first among the Romanian historians to realize the huge role played by media in spreading the historical knowledge and in changing knowledge into personal belief. Media, he used to say, should introduce the books of history to the young people. C.C. Giurescu reminded me of A.J.P. Taylor, the first British historian who, as far as the 1950s could see the role of television in spreading the knowledge about the past. In the first years of television Taylor had a daily newscast on BBC.

C.C. Giurescu supported *Magazin istoric* with all his heart and soul and contributed papers very frequently. In 1967, when *Magazin istoric* was first published, 35 years had elapsed since the first issue of *Revista istorică* – a magazine founded and edited by Giurescu. He shared his experience – though the circumstances were quite different in 1967 – and he did not hesitate to congratulate or to criticize us, as the case might have been.

I remember the day when he became a member of the Romanian Academy. It was February 15, 1975, in the afternoon. The large assembly hall of the Academy was overcrowded. Besides the members of the Academy, a lot of other people had come to attend the ceremony: colleagues and ex-colleagues, students and ex-students, professors and ex-professors, famous scientists, and even pupils. Professor Giurescu was a tall man, his posture straight. Academician David Prodan (usually a person of few praises) was simply eulogistic. After that, Professor delivered his reception speech, *Romania in the Millenium of Migration*, in loud and clear voice, as emphasizing meanings or the most important words.

"About two centuries ago", he said "the subject of the history of the Romanian people in the dark millenium of migrations was brought up, that is the interval between 271–275, when the Roman army and administration left Dacia, and the last invasion, that of Tartars, in 1241. New documentary materials appeared, mainly following the archeological diggings; studies in history, linguistics, and ethnography were published. Even if the mentioned period has not been completely clarified in each respect yet, there is one very clear thing, to me at least: *the formation of the Romanian people is neither an 'enigma' nor a 'miracle'* but *a normal phenomenon,* similar to those that brought forth the births of the Italians, Spaniards, Portuguese, and of the other Romanic peoples. I have mentioned that with some other occasions as well despite the allegations of certain foreign or even Romanian historians and linguists.

The parallelism extends to the *continuity of all Romanic peoples* on the territories they live today. Has anybody thought of denying or questioning the continuity of the French in Gaul, of the Spaniards and Portuguese in the Iberian Peninsula or of the Italians in Italy? Has any historian ever asserted that the Gallo-Romans left their homes and Gaul itself to pass over the Alps or the Pyrenees and to come back home later, after many centuries? Or that the Spaniards crossed the Strait of Gibraltar to Africa, to come back, hundreds of years later, to their native territory? The simple wording of such questions prove their complete lack of meaning and their foolishness. The same things are valid for Dacia as well. As a matter of fact, up to the turn of the 19th century nobody had ever imagined that the Daco-Roman peasants, shepherds, and craftsmen living on the Carpathian-Danubian territory – with Transylvania as its center – could have left their ancestral dwellings to cross the Danube to the Balkans and to come back home several centuries later. Such an absurd theory had political not scientific grounds and was launched with the aim of denying the rights the Romanian people had over Transylvania – rights based on oldness, number, and work.

Besides the arguments brought by archeological diggings – those in Alba Iulia, at Brătei, and at Noșlac and the Christian inscription at Biertan, all in Transylvania –, besides the extremely important testimonies found in the Chronicle of the Anonymous Notary of King Bela and of the Kiev chronicle, besides the testimonies furnished by the coin hoards and place names, the very study of the Romanian language gives edifying testimony on the continuity of the Daco-Romans on the Carpathian-Danubian territory.

How did our ancestors receive the impact of the waves of migrating people, how did they protect their lives and belongings during wars and plundering? The most frequent answer, both with the Romanian and foreign researchers, is that they found refuge in the mountains.

We have to mention here that it is only a forested mountain that offers refuge and hideout. In a barren mountain no one can hide or subsist. On the other hand, the fir-trees and other conifers that grow in the mountains do not offer too much food. In a fir forest there is no other vegetation than the thick cover of the last years' needles. The situation is quite different with the forests growing on the hills or in the plains – the leaf-bearing forests. In that type of forest light can reach the soil and the vegetation is both varied and abundant. In the beech, elm, lime, ash, oak, poplar, willow, etc. forests a great many plants grow, many of which are edible. There are also some wild fruit trees in those forests; their ripe fruit can be preserved and they are rather tasty. The Romanian forests abound in wild apple and pear trees, in cornel trees – the yellow-bloomed trees the first to blossom – in hazel and walnut trees, in wild cherry trees, and, in many places, in wild vine. The beechnut has an edible kernel and is an important source of valuable oil. The numerous species of mushrooms and agarics, eaten as such, dried, or pickled have always been appreciated.

And last but not least there are berries: raspberries, blackberries, strawberries, box thorns, hipberries, bilberries, and wild gooseberries. On the other hand, there are animals and birds: hares, wild boars, roebucks, hazel hens, mountain cocks, and woodcocks. Let's mention here that the wood clearings and skirts are fit for agriculture and beehives can be put there. Let's not forget the rivers, easy ways for crossing the forests, but also an important source of food, much appreciated by the Romanians: fish. Likewise, forest is an important ally in the battle: it covers the sudden attacks and protects retreats. Many of the important battles of our forerunners were protected by the forest that did not allow an ample deployment of the enemy, thus making up for the disproportion of forces. For instance, the decisive battle at Posada, in 1330, that at Codrul Crasnei, in 1450, won by Prince Bogdan of Moldavia, Stephen the Great's father, the battle at Vaslui, the greatest military victory of the Romanians, that at Războieni, where the forest covered the retreat, at Codrul Cosminului, or at Călugăreni. The Polish chronicler Dlugosz tells about the victory of a Moldavian detachment, in 1422, over the Teutonic Knights, in a forest not far from Marienburg, Eastern Prussia. He wrote that the Moldavians had preferred forest as a 'battlefield' since 'their custom and their nature make them fight more easily under the foliage of the trees' (*facilus ut est mos et natura gentis, tecti fronde et ligno, certaturi*).

I insisted on the hill and plane forests since they were far more numerous in the millenium of migrations than they are today: they occupied about 70% of the territory. Those forests were the first shelters of our forerunners. Fires lit on hills or hillocks announced the danger. When the peasants saw the smoke, they put their children and women in carts, took their cattle and sheep – their most valued wealth – and lost they were in the neighboring forests where the Asian migrants – Huns, Avars, Bulgarians, Hungarians, Petchenegs, Cumans, and Tartars – would not usually enter. They were accustomed to the extensive and free steppe and knew that in the forest they could be attacked any moment, especially at night. The 'retreat to the mountains' was in fact 'a retreat to the forest'. The forest provided shelter during the dark millenium of migrations; it is then that the saying 'the forest is the Romanians' brother' was born. Unfortunately, in the last 150 years, the Romanians have no longer been 'the forest's brothers', but its stepbrothers as they have cut the trees thoughtlessly.

Of course, when the invasions and attacks had come to an end or if a *modus vivendi* with the new rulers could be reached, the people left the forests and started to rebuild their houses or huts burnt down by the invaders. As there was plenty of wood the houses were built in no time.

The tribes of Slavs that came to these regions found here a numerous Romanic population living in the extensive forest lying between the Bărăgan and the Burnaz steppe. That plain forest was crossed by numerous rivers and was spotted with a few lakes and pools. Impressed by the great number of these Romanic people, they called the region *Vlașca*, that is 'the land of the Vlachs' or 'the land of the Romanians', and the large forest in the north of the present Bucharest – Vlăsia, with the same meaning: 'the forest of the Romanians'.

The custom of finding shelter in the forest during periods of war or plunders lasted with Romanians for a long time, even after the foundations of the Romanian countries. A document of September 26, 1617, when Radu Mihnea ruled Moldavia, reads: 'When the Polish invaded our country, all the inhabitants fled to the forests'. A foreign traveler in Walachia during Constantin Brâncoveanu's reign told about the multitude of hill and plain forests and mentioned that all the villages and boroughs were surrounded by forests where the inhabitants could find shelter in time of need.

During the long periods when the waves of migrating peoples invaded their land, our forerunners continued to live and to work *with no interruption at all.*

All along that time, the Romanian communities kept their social, territorial, and military organizations alongside their fundamental agricultural activities, and thus they succeeded to live and to go on.

The Romanian communities were included in the important trading circuits of Europe.

Finally, some words about the political side of the issue. The Slave names of *cnezdoms* and *voivodeships* used for the principalities at the beginning of the Middle Ages clearly prove the evolution of reports: when the Romanians lived together with the Slavs, the former assimilated the latter as they became politically preponderant. They only kept from the Slavs the names of several institutions and social realities.

More than that, the foreign relations kept extending; in the 9th–10th centuries, the Transylvanian princes had connections with the Byzantine Empire, with Moravia, and with the Bulgarian czardom: messengers, representations, and discussions on mutual interests. Later on, in the former half of the 13th century, the Romanian *cnezdoms* and *voivodeships* in Oltenia and in Walachia developed connections with the Magyar king and recognized his suzerainty. Therefore, the Romanian countries adopted the foreign relations characteristic of the mediaeval Europe.

The following *conclusion* can be drawn: during the millenium of migrations the Romanian people was born following the synthesis of two fundamental elements – the native Daco-Getians and the

Roman colonists, in which Slavs had a minor contribution. The contribution of the old Turkish populations was even lesser than that of the Slavs. The process was similar to those explaining the births of the other Romanic peoples: the French, Italians, Spaniards, and Portuguese. The same as all these, the Romanian people has uninterruptedly lived on the territory where it was born, the Carpathian-Danubian territory, and has continued the old occupations of its ancestors: agriculture with all its branches, from grain farming to wine growing, fruit and vegetable growing, cattle breeding, beekeeping, fishing and fish breeding, mining, and trading. Therefore, the history of the Romanian people in the millenium of migrations is not an 'enigma' or a 'miracle', but a normal process. At the end of that millenium, the Romanians, quite numerous and rather prosperous, were divided in the two social classes characteristic of the feudal Europe: the noblemen – owners of land, and the bondsmen – serfs. Likewise, they were organized politically – in *cnezdoms* and *voivodeships* –, militarily, and religiously. Therefore, there existed all the elements required for a superior political organization to develop: the states of Walachia and of Moldavia. They both existed politically with no interruption at all – a unique situation in the South-Eastern Europe – and they finally joined Transylvania to form the Romanian unitary national state, in 1918."

Constantin C. Giurescu concluded his speech and the audience gave him tumultuous applause. He seemed thoughtful, he was contented, and he lived the important moment with his ordinary and well-balanced modesty. It was only his paleness that betrayed his emotions.

1975. He was working for the second edition of *The History of Bucharest* (that was to be published after his death) and we sometimes walked through the Bucharest he loved so much. He appreciated the city, but deplored its defects, mainly its climate and geographical location. He used to stop in front of a building and say: "Look how beautiful it is. We should do more for our city. We should try to keep the important buildings of the old town in the new one. We can't afford to squander away our wealth. It is not that big."

His idea was that Romania was not very rich and it cannot

afford to overspend. He wanted the architects to find the best solutions for preserving the typology of the old Bucharest that was often compared with Paris, Brussels, etc.: "Look at Italy, Spain, Poland, Great Britain, or Scotland. How much the architects worked to keep the old into the new! What would have remained if they had allowed the old houses and castles to disappear? Of course, not all the old buildings can be saved and the city has to be systematized. But it is the architects and constructors' job to try to integrate the new into the old. The Italians for instance have succeeded, and even Ponte-Vecchio is part of the modern life now.

He was open to the truth in his interlocutor's words. Another example. He published *The History of the Romanians*, written together with Dinu C. Giurescu, at the Albatros Publishing House. Several historians, myself included, made some suggestions and he took the most important of them into account in the new edition. However, like any other scientist who relied on scientific precision and probity he could not be easily convinced. And with good reason. He was sure of his theses, as each demonstration was based on documents that he critically analyzed – a thing recognized both by those who admired him and by those who were rather reserved. He could only be convinced with arguments, mainly with the arguments of documents, of historical deeds and data.

However, many of his works include that dose of historical fantasy without which no researcher can formulate intelligent and coherent interpretations of facts. His style, sober, simple, and rich in deeds and data, leaving documents to speak for him makes Giurescu a genuine historical writer. His writing is bright with intelligence. There exists in history, and in prose alike, a certain style that I could call *of confidence*, the very embodiment of which is Giurescu. If I were to use terms from the history of art I could say he was not a romanticist but a realist.

There was neither easy nor comfortable to discuss with him. He was not excessively kind or sentimentalist either. His father had died when he was 17, a circumstance that had not changed his mood for the better. Even if he seemed a hard man sometimes, he was very understandable and he never refused the dialogue. For instance, he finally accepted the viewpoint of the other historians contributing to

Magazin istoric as concerns Capitulations – the old treaties between the Romanian countries and the Porte stipulating the special statute of large autonomy of the former in their relations with the Ottoman Empire.

His father had passed his doctor's degree in the same subject, that of Capitulations, and he had advanced the idea that they were not authentic documents. When *Magazin istoric* resumed the issue of Capitulations in 1975–1976, Giurescu, certainly influenced by his father's thesis, did not take kindly to our effort, in keeping with the 1848 historiography, to demonstrate their historical value despite the fact that the originals had not been found yet. The existence of the Capitulations will be proved – the magazine put forward – by new research in the huge archives in Turkey. (As a matter of fact that has already happened). It is essential – we used to say then – that for centuries the historical statute of the Romanian countries was determined by Capitulations, which were internationally accepted; therefore we had to consider them valid. In the meantime, other reliable works were published, demonstrating the existence of Capitulations and all their consequences. Following long discussions, C.C. Giurescu agreed first not be angry – it was extremely important that a conflict should not rise among us – and then not to launch into polemic. He also agreed with a recheck of the historical arguments. Despite the disagreement over the basic issue of Capitulations – the bivalent character, under the given historical conditions, of our relations with the Porte – C.C. Giurescu was one of the first historians to prove, based on solid arguments, the existence of that specific character. He was a careful interpreter of the Romanian-Ottoman relationships, open to all kind of shades, as he never accepted a "white-and-black" simplification. It was of much help that he lived in Turkey for a long while: he must have had access to very interesting documents there. He and his family came back to Romania at the end of World War II. His cautious attitude to the Capitulations issue, the fact that he chose to wait and to go on researching the historical circumstances instead of involving himself in debate to support his father's thesis, is just another proof that, for him, the objective scientific considerations prevailed over the private ones. Likewise, he gave some lectures on that issue – the Romanian-Turkish relations – in Romania, in Turkey, and in the USA, bringing forth original ideas, supported by flawless argumentation.

"A history of the relations between the Romanians and the Turks", C.C. Giurescu said, "has to start from the 10th century, when the Romanian people, that had already assimilated the Slavs settled in the Carpathian-Danubian area, came into contact with the Petchenegs or the old Turks. In the 11th century the *Petchenegs* were followed by the *Cumans*, also old Turks speaking 'the same language'; the latter remained here until the Tartars came, in 1241. The two old Turkish peoples lived in the Carpathian-Danubian area for *about three centuries and a half* and they were in close contact with the Romanians' ancestors. There exist in the Romanian language place names, people's names and some other words bearing Petcheneg and Cuman influences. Mention should be made of *Bărăgan* and *Burnaz*, the two Walachian steppes (the former means 'snowstorm' and comes from the terrible winds and snows that killed the cattle, either by burying them in snow or by throwing them in the Danube), the town Caracal (*kara kale*: black citadel), the county of *Teleorman* from *teli orman*: mad forest (to be compared with the Ottoman Deliorman, the name of the forest in the south of Dobruja). The Petchenegs and the Cumans were shepherds and cattle breeders and they preferred the large plains, steppes, where their flocks and herds could find food more easily. Nevertheless they settled in the forests too, as proved by the names of Teleorman and of 'the Romanians and the Petchenegs' forest' (*Sylva Blacorum et Bissenorum*) in Transylvania, mentioned in a 1224 document. The mountains *Bucegi* and the peak *Caraiman* have both an old Turkish origin. However, the greatest majority of the place names bearing Petcheneg-Cuman influence are to be found in the fields. These are most probably the names of rivers ended in *–ui*, such as Călmăţui, Covurlui, Dăsnăţui, Gemartalui, Suhului, Teslui, etc. The people's name ending in *–abă* bear the same influence: Tâncabă (that gave the name of the Tâncăbeşti village in the north of Bucharest), Tocsabă (that gave the name of the Tocsobeni village not far from Iaşi), Carabă, a family name found in Clipiceşti village, Vrancea County. The name of Basarabă himself could mean, in old Turkish, 'conquering father' or 'ruling parent'. The very fact that the name of Walachia's founder was Cumanic has nothing special in itself. In the field of people's names the foreign influences have always been very strong. The relationships with the rulers – Petchenegs and Cumans – and fashion, that existed in those times as well, could explain the choice of a foreign name. That does not mean that Basarabă was less Romanian or that his deeds were less important. That is also the case with king Stephen I of Hungary 'the Saint' – his name is of a Greek origin (the crowned one!). There are some words in the Romanian originating from the old Turks: *dușman* (enemy), *toiu* (about middle), *odaie* (with the old meaning of shelter for cattle and isolated dwelling in a forest or clearing), and most probably *cioban* (shepherd).

The next important chapter of the Romanian-Turkish relations is that of the relations with the Ottoman Turks that started in the 14th century and lasted until recent times.

The value judgements on the relations between the Romanians and the Ottoman Turks changed in time: they were harsher or more understanding, according to circumstances, to the way the 'the unfaithful' ruled, to the number of their claims, to the times of war or peace. After the 1877–1878 War of Independence, the historiography appreciated more justly these mutual relations, and to the end of the 19th century the Phanariot age was judged with much less passion.

Far from us the thought of passing in silence over the negative side of the above-mentioned relations: territorial losses or spoliation in times of crises. I think that the whole complex of relations should be investigated objectively, without passion, for a better knowledge of all their aspects and for finding out the positive sides as well.

We have to reveal here the *special character* of the political relations. The phrase 'special political relationships' is largely used today – see the relations between the Great Britain and the United States or between Japan and the United States following World War II – and we think that it can be used for the centuries-long Romanian-Turkish relations. The Romanians realized the remarkable military and political force represented by the Ottoman Empire in the 14th–17th centuries – the greatest force in the southeastern Europe – and, consequently, they knew how to combine military engagements with the flexibility of the diplomatic negotiations, that is with political flexibility. The Turks, in their turn, justly appreciated the Romanians' way of fighting and their realist spirit and established special relationships with them. In this way the Romanian principalities – Walachia, Moldavia, and Transylvania – could resist and exist, unlike the Balkan states which fought, nobody can deny it, but were turned into *pashaliks*. The political existence of the Romanian principalities is of the greatest importance. For a people, the state represents the possibility to develop itself freely, to have its own administration, its own army, and its own economic and cultural lives. Of course, I mean an independent or, at least, an autonomous state, and not a state under foreign occupation or administration.

For a better understanding of these special relationships, we should emphasize their origin and also the periodic alternation between military and political actions.

The Turks did not see in the Danube the northern border of their possessions. They crossed the river in the west of the Romanian principalities and founded the *pashalik* of Buda that lasted for 150 years. They also crossed it in the east and conquered Bugeag and, in 1672, Camenița, in the north of the Dnister. Nevertheless they did not cross the Danube and did not turn the Romanian principalities into *pashaliks* mainly owing to the military resistance of the Romanians that alternated with diplomatic negotiations and concessions. The Turks might have realized that it was better for them if those countries had their own administration; they could gain thus more money and victuals than if they had imposed their not very productive administration.

The history of the Romanian-Turkish relations, starting with the old Turks until the War of Independence, *has to be written again, leaving aside exaggerations and preconceived ideas*. As we will come to know better these relations – due to the Turkish archives – we will be able to appreciate them more correctly, mainly the economic ones. As far as political relations are concerned, we can see that the Ottoman Empire had for us, within the time period 1683 (the siege of Vienna) – 1829 (Treaty of Edirne) one clear advantage: it was an obstacle in front of the two expansionistic empires: the Habsburg and the Tsarist. Otherwise, we could have shared the fate of Poland despite the whole diplomatic ability of our forerunners.

For three decades, Mircea the Old resisted the Ottoman power that was then at the peak of its offensive. He did not take part in the battle of Ankara (July 28, 1402), but he contributed soldiers for one of Baiazid's sons, Musa, who would become a sultan. Mircea was then a kind of arbitrator, an excellent position that lasted until another son of Baiazid, Mehmed I, rose against Musa. The latter died in the battle of Ciamurli, not far from Sofia (July 5, 1413). As two other attempts to support new pretenders to the throne – Mustafa Celebi, in 1415–1416 and Bedreddin in the autumn of 1416 – failed, Mehmed started a campaign against Walachia, in 1417. Following that campaign, Mircea recognized the sultan's suzerainty and accepted to pay a modest yearly tribute – *harach*. Impressed by Mircea's bravery and determination, described by the chronicler Leunclavius as 'the bravest and the quickest among the Christian princes', Mehmed accepted that *harach* and two fulcrums on the left of the Danube, at Giurgiu and Turnu. Otherwise, Walachia kept its whole being and organization: its prince, high officials, economy, army, religion, and social life. The Ottomans were not allowed to settle on the Walachian land or to raise mosques there. They could trade and that activity developed gradually, mainly from the 16th century on. Therefore, Walachia lasted for centuries while the Balkan states disappeared.

The Turks are a chivalrous people; they appreciate bravery and respect it. We think that this very characteristic defined the special relations that existed between Walachia and the Ottoman Empire from the very beginning.

The same was true for Moldavia as well. Alexander the Good (1400–1432) fought against the Turks that besieged Cetatea Albă in 1420 and won the battle. However, his son, Petru Aron had to admit, in 1455, the authority of Mehmed II and to pay a relatively small *harach*: 2000 golden ducats. 'To the noble, and wise, and honorable Io Petru voivode, ruler of Morovlahia, the beloved Christian, I wish you good health', Mehmed II wrote to Petru Aron. 'You have sent your and your noblemen's messenger, chancellor Mihu, who has brought to us your words according to which you agree to pay to my Highness the *harach*, two thousand golden ducats each year. Let it be peace afterwards and the term of the *harach* will be at three months. If you respect that term there will be serene peace with my Highness; otherwise you will know what happens. May God make you happy' (N. Iorga, *Mohamed II's Privilege for Pera* (in Romanian), Anal. Acad. Rom., Hist., XXXVI/1913–1914, pp. 80–81.) It is crystal clear that there existed no other request or condition. Peace was guaranteed in exchange of harach; the state would keep its entire organization with no Ottoman interference. Alexander the Good's grandson, Stephen the Great, fought for 15 years against the Ottoman Empire and he wanted the neighboring country, Walachia, to adopt the same policy. He was victorious at Vaslui, in 1475 – an important victory echoed in Europe – and was defeated the following year in the battle of Războieni, although the campaign was not a failure and Mehmed retreated without being able to conquer a fortress. He won several battles in Walachia, and then lost the two fortresses at the southern border of the country, Chilia and Cetatea Albă (1484). Finally Stephen realized that it was better to reach an understanding with the Ottoman Empire, to conclude peace with them, and to keep thus Moldavia. That was exactly what he did. In 1498, when he started his campaign in Poland, in answer to a campaign started a year ago when his capital-city Suceava had been besieged by the army of the Polish king John Albert, the Romanian prince was helped by Tartars and by an Ottoman detachment, that horrifically pillaged Poland to Lwow.

According to the popular tradition, Stephen the Great, at he end of his life, advised Bogdan, his son and his successor to throne, to get on well with the Turks as they are "wiser and stronger people'. Although this tradition seems to have appeared later – since Stephen had recognized the Turkish suzerainty in the second half of 1489 or the first half of 1490 – it expressed the state of mind of the great Moldavian prince and of his people. His successors followed his advice and Moldavia remained a state in the true meaning of the word: with administrative and military organizations, with its own economy, and with cultural and social lives.

Michael the Brave's reign (1593–1601) offers a last and concluding example of alternation between war and diplomacy. After fighting victorious battles against Ottomans, Michael realized the great disparity of forces and came to an agreement with the Sultan; the latter was glad to accept it and the pasha of Nikopol mediated the negotiations."

***

I was in room 18 of "Al. Sahia" Hospital. One visiting day, at about 4 p.m. C.C. Giurescu entered there accompanied by the distinguished physician G. Rădulescu. Great emotion. Giurescu sat down by me and, instead of the usual "How are you? How do you feel?" he started asking me about my readings, about the projects of *Magazin istoric*, about what I was working at. Then he started to tell me about Alexandru Ioan Cuza, as a European figure. Giurescu had made research in the Viennese archives in order to write the biography of Cuza whom he correctly compared with Camillo Cavour, with Giuseppe Mazzini, and with Abraham Lincoln all three of them Cuza's contemporaries and followers of the great ideals of unity, social justice, and liberty in their own countries. I said that he was a "hard" man and that might be true. But he felt that the best medicine for a modern sick man was to speak with him about his work and about what he would do in a month, a week, or a day, when he would return to his normal life. Normality should replace lament. When faced with obsession of history – of life, as a matter of fact – illness had no power

We also discussed (then or some other times) about the historical ages and about other Romanian princes. He told me something about Brâncoveanu's system of information and I asked him why he did not write something for the magazine. He told me: 'because my father had written once". Some other time he was concerned with "the Thracian curse", having in mind the famous words of Herodotus that had the Thracians been united they would have been the greatest people on Earth. For us, the Romanians, he said, there could not be a greater danger – not even earthquakes, drought, floods, famines, or diseases – than the Thracian curse: all the invasions and all the catastrophes tried both to exterminate and to disunite us. It is only our burning and steady desire of unification that has always saved us and that will always save us in the future.

And there is another idea, a kind of oath: "Let us not destroy the old customs that helped the Romanian people overcome hard times."

He was very proud of his yeoman extraction. He mentioned his roots in almost all our talks. He admired resoluteness, respect, and stoicism. He hated "nylon marriages". He was not an out-of-date man, but he understood by "new man" a man of substance, a classical man, the successor of a system of genuine values. He was not interested in philosophy, but he often referred to the Romanians' life philosophy. Unlike Gheorghe Brătianu – whom he kept in great esteem due to his great and original contribution to the Romanian and European historiography – C.C. Giurescu considered that the Romanians are not the result of a miracle. "Why does everybody say *the Romanian miracle*?" he wondered. "No! The birth characteristics of the Romanians are similar to those of the other peoples in the Balkans or in the West: the French, Italians, Spaniards, or Portuguese. We passed an extremely difficult exam of history, we faced all the invasions, we kept our state (the most important weapon of our survival), religion, customs, language, territory, culture, in a word our civilization. However we do not have a *miraculous* ethnogeny, but an admirable, heroic, yet normal one."

It was November 9. Bucharest had become a building site after the earthquake in March. We started from the editorial office, stopped a moment in front of the Athenaeum, that he called a genuine jewelry of Bucharest, then we started again down Victoria Road, crossed in front of Crețulescu Church, entered Știrbei Vodă St., and then Berzei. He was wearing an elegant gray coat, and was carrying his brown leather briefcase (he never allowed anybody to carry it for him), and an umbrella that served as a stick. He was in excellent physical and intellectual shape – he had just turned 76 – but he told me he was a bit tired. I had to pay a visit in Cotroceni, and professor was going home. We walked past dozens of buildings under repair as a thin cloud of dust was floating all over the center of the city. C.C. Giurescu told me that the night of the earthquake had been a night of solidarity. The character of the Romanians comes to light and shows its entire beauty in the most critical moments mainly. Under normal circumstances there is nothing special with them, but in difficult times their unusual ability to master their own destinies is suddenly revealed. They are heroic. They show solidarity. "Look at this people. Look what they have been able to do this year. Can you see how fast and how well they work? In several years there will be no reminder of the earthquake traces."*

He also told me that he was not afraid of the earthquake, but he was very worried about his relatives, friends, acquaintances, colleagues, and students. He had great plans: he was working for volume III of *History of the Romanians*, for volume II of *Memories*, for the second edition of *History of Bucharest*. In such a busy agenda the word death could not find place.

In 1982, in the United States, twelve American and six Romanian historians dedicated a volume to the memory of C.C. Giurescu. Here you are some words written by the editor, Stephen Fischer-Galați: "I have highly appreciated Professor Constantin C. Giurescu before World War II. We used to 'swot' for our graduation exams on Giurescu's books. Then I met him in 1968, when he first visited the Boudler University and lectured there. Professor was held in high esteem in the USA – where he returned for several times within a decade – since he was a top rank name in the Romanian historiography. He was also appreciated by the American university

world. I thought it was necessary to honor his memory in the USA as well, as a proof of my affection for the value of the man, patriot, and scientist. However, I think it is better to remind you of what I have written in the Preface 'The present volume honors the memory of Constantin C. Giurescu as a man and as a historian. It was conceived as soon as the news of his death reached his friends,

*When C.C. Giurescu told me that he could not imagine that in a few years' time Ceaușescu would order the demolition of the most representative historical districts and churches in Bucharest. The dictator wanted to leave space for a strange architecture that had nothing to do with the Romanian tradition, but was meant to make his megalomania last for ever. Giurescu's son Dinu published in April 1989, in Washington, a document-book, The Razing of Romania's Past (published in Romania in 1994).

pupils, and admirers in the United States. As it frequently happens with collective works, there is a delay in preparing the volume for printing. Owing to the support and efforts made by those who were close to Constantin C. Giurescu, we will be able to print it this month, October 1981, when professor would have been 80. Its pages are a collection of memories and studies about the personality, activity, and role played by Constantin C. Giurescu in the history of Romania. I consider it proper to say here that he did not only place and analyze the role of the Romanians in the world history, but, first of all, he situated Romania within the 20th century history. He did it with authority and elegance'."

I met him when he was 61: a man of about 180 cm tall, with an oval-shaped face and swarthy complexion, large, blue eyes (a genetic gift of all the men in the Giurescu family, he told me once), carefully arranging the cuffs of his shirt out of mere habit. He used to walk with measured, long strides in his study at home, in the street, in the Library of the Academy. Nothing changed in 15 years. He was never in a hurry. He never raised his voice. He hated disorder: in arguments, clothes, in his study. When he entered a room where a flurry activity was taking place he established absolute order with a few gestures and words. There was no reason to hurry, to be superficial. Peace, wise thinking, consideration.

In more than 15 years he had remained the same. That might be why his death was so dramatic. He had been warned (as many of us are) and he ignored it (as many of us do); he had suffered a minor stroke several years before, in the mountains. He had another stroke, several days following our last walk. It happened in the afternoon, while he was working. His granddaughter Marina and his son Dinu found him on the floor, his head on a pile of books. He was writing a recommendation for a historical TV movie. For the great actors the "ideal" death comes on the stage; what kind of death could have been more proper for a great scientist? To die during an intellectual effort, to die while thinking, to die at your desk… It is a privilege. A terrible privilege. Let's not forget that thinking is "nothing but lightning in the middle of a long night. But that lightning is all".

A JOURNALIST IN THE RING

"A mistake in a newspaper lasts a day only. Take care not to think that an article, even an article written by you, can start a war or can change the course of history. Be sure not to think that one of your articles can equal the cable from Ems (the famous cable used as a pretext for the French-Prussian was in 1870). Don't put yourselves on fire. Don't turn yourselves into bogeymen. A history of media without the mistakes in media looks like a Cleopatra with lots of face-lifts. An article in a newspaper is more than you can imagine – or much less. With it you can win or lose the public confidence…"

That was the usual way Mircea Grigorescu used to speak to us at *Lumea* (The World) in 1964–1965. He was one of the few *professional journalists* that had remained from the brilliant pleiad that represented the Romanian journalism. Fortunately, he was a man still in full. His advice reminded me of Mihail Sebastian, whose character in *The Latest Hour* used to say that "a journal lives for one day only".

It was in such days, in such hours of a journal's life that Mircea Grigorescu invested his life and energy, his efforts and his remarkable qualities.

To be a "journalist" does not only mean to keep yourself informed with the latest news, to live, and then to die when the news dies. It means to be able to live as if you were dying every moment, as if you were quite beside yourself. You must be able to separate the perishable things from what is meant to last (even for one hundred years) at about the same temperature. It is to live as if you were in a samovar under pressure, in a battle often dramatically lost and seldom won, in which the awkward combatants run the risk of getting drowned in banality, cheated by the facts with no echo and by their own innocence as well.

It is difficult to find an equilibrium, mainly in a permanent "front line" of a war of attrition, in which the journalist involves willingly, more often than not uncovered, with no other protection than that offered by common sense, a perfect good will, power of discernment, gift – essential components of this profession that has to be learned on the fly.

Mircea Grigorescu entered my life in the autumn of 1963. Or I entered his. It depends from where one looks at the mountain or at the field! There are times in everybody's life when we find ourselves on a narrow, uncomfortable, and unstable platform. From there, from high above, we can see the both ends of the way, one of them farther, the other one very near, one segment covered, the other one still to be covered. But the perpetual movement and the endless change of view and sight do not allow you to know which of the two segments is the shorter, which is "the other one".

I had seen in the journals before and during the war the name of Mircea Grigorescu. I had met it in *Cuvântul liber*, in *Timpul*, and in *Ecoul*. Mircea Grigorescu used to write on the front page of *Timpul* and *Ecoul*: first he was an editor, then a director. I had read several of his articles, but I could not visualize him because I simply did not think that he was still alive. For about two decades his name had disappeared from newspapers and journals.

The team appointed to work for *Lumea* first met in the office of George Ivașcu, the editor-in-chief at *Contemporanul*. At the far end of the table I saw a strapping man, with a hardly-to-forget face, prominent nose, clearly outlined lips, very bushy and dark eyebrows.

I knew more or less the other people sitting at the table. We were about 20 in all. In the first thirty minutes I kept wondering who that man was. Who was the robust man that had come to the meeting with a large black briefcase? (He seemed to have had that briefcase all his life; it was neither new nor old, but it had got a kind of patina.) He was waiting in patience. Finally, George Ivașcu told him: "You will take care of that, Mircea Grigorescu".

Thus I learned who he was. He was taking down notes, and only muttered: "Of course, yes". We made up the team that was to edit the first of the test issues. George Ivașcu appointed an editor in charge for each issue. For the first one, that editor was Mircea Grigorescu and Ivașcu was to be his editorial secretary. At the next meeting, Mircea Grigorescu chose a better place, but it was only at the third meeting, when "his" issue was discussed, that he spoke.

He spoke and many of the people sitting at that table, old journalists (let's mention George Serafin, Florica Șelmaru, Cornel Răducanu, Sergiu Verona, Eugen Pop, Ion Cârje, Felicia Antip, Ileana Nicolaescu, Constantin Florea, Eugen Phoebus) understood that that man knew his job. Mircea Grigorescu *was able to feel* a journal from the very beginning. He had that breadth of instruction that should be the attribute of any modern journalist: he could write the leader, a running commentary, he could edit news or find the best title. Of course nobody is good at everything, but a journalist must master as much as he can of his profession. However, Mircea Grigorescu was an "ace".

He had started to write for a magazine when he was in the 7th grade of "Sf. Sava" High School. The first issue of *Revista literară* (Literary Review) came out in January 1927. Mircea Grigorescu was its editor-in-chief. I could find there – in embryo, of course – Grigorescu's style of laying out, a style that I greatly admired when we worked together. The then 7th-grade-pupil Eugen Ionescu, the future member of the French Academy, contributed the poem The *Night Show* – an inspired exercise of tenderness.

Although I knew almost nothing about Grigorescu's professional biography, in that very night he won our respect forever.

He showed us then, almost imperceptibly – and from then on, for many times – how we should lay out the pages of a journal. He was excellent in titling (he produced 8–10 titles for an article until he found the best one) and in alternating the pages within the body of the publication. Last but not least he knew that one must know everything. Starting with that evening of October 1963, I watched with fascination as he laid out magazines or magazine pages, wrote notes and series, commentaries and scientific papers (he was passionately fond of science and of technical-scientific revolution), feature reports and external chronicles. I also watched him as he read and corrected the galley proofs, cut the press cables of the agencies, stuck photos. He was always in a hurry and sometimes walked kilometers within Casa Scânteii between the editorial offices of *Lumea* (The World), *Contemporanul* (The Contemporary),

Flacăra (The Flame) and the printing house. He was constantly moving, yet he was perfectly calm and amazingly quick.

As a matter of fact I met two Mircea Grigorescus. The former was in permanent alertness, incessantly looking for news, ready to throw an article in the waste bin if another subject seemed more important. He was careful both about *what* we tell to the public and also about *how* and *in what way* we do it. That Mircea Grigorescu was a man of perfect concentration – he was able to focus on his editorial work for 24 hours a day if necessary. He was also one of the very few journalists who never wasted a minute when he was working. He had something to do every moment. When everything was ready and in good order he left. He never remained an extra hour when he had nothing to do at his office. He told me once that he had understood the meaning of time even since he had been a junior journalist. He had come to work for *Adevărul* (The Truth) when he was less than 20. He was received by Tudor Teodorescu-Branişte who was writing a paper; the latter stopped just for a moment and asked him "Tell me, young man, do you know the *Railway Timetable*?" Mircea Grigorescu answered promptly: "Yes". Branişte was somewhat taken aback. Had he liked the young man's boldness? Anyhow he gave up checking the answer. That was not important; the young man's attitude was. "You have to know the *Railway Timetable*", the director told him, "because if you miss the morning trains you can compromise the newspaper. You have to get the journal ready, so that it can be printed, wrapped and sent to the station in time for the earliest trains."

Mircea Grigorescu "burned" all his life. The majority of days and nights of his life were dedicated to just one aim: the journals he was working for, that he made up, that he intensely loved should catch the trains. They had not to miss – literally and figuratively – any train.

Mircea Grigorescu told me one late night in the spring of 1969 about another station and about another train. On December 29, 1933 the stationmaster at Sinaia station called to tell him that legionaries had killed I.G. Duca. He succeeded to send a cable to an important press agency in London; any phone or telegraph connection was interrupted afterwards.

The other Mircea Grigorescu was a delicate, quiet man contemplating his own life and that of his interlocutor with a permanent smile, sometimes affectionate, some other times ironical. With a kind and soft man, delicacy is but natural; it does not appeal as something special. But if the man is a "hard", telluric appearance with a tempestuous nature that stares at you and says: "journalism is not a weak man's job", then the delicacy seems a kind of special gift. I do not think he was cynical and I cannot help agreeing with his words "Journalism is not a job for the people who come to work just eight hours! Media stands in the front line of life. It is the hard ones that can resist here".

That is why he never asked you to work. In an extremely civilized manner *he asked you* to be a journalist. And I did not know him as a director or editor-in-chief, but as an editorial secretary, commentator, or part timer. Sometimes the journalist simply vanished to leave place for a rather shy man.

I saw that side of his nature when faced with two persons: his mother (who lived to a venerable age) and his only son. His mother was bursting with vitality and that helped her live for almost 30 years with a terrible disease. I can remember that any time when we left the office he used to stop and buy doughnuts for his mother. He did that every day, irrespective of the nerves and thunderbolts at the office, irrespective of his tiredness and concerns.

His attitude towards his son, Mircea Grigorescu jr., was simply touching. Young Mircea was rather frail and his father was permanently concerned because of him, but he was also very proud of everything his son accomplished. Naturally the father was careful not to reveal his feelings, but he sometimes simply did not succeed in doing that. Before his death (he might have intuited it) he had a tender gesture towards me.

There was a difficult moment during our collaboration I have to mention. Otherwise, his gesture cannot be understood. In 1969 I asked him to help me with *Magazin istoric*. He agreed and he found an attractive layout for the magazine. Actually, he and the other editorial secretary at *Lumea*, Radu Dobre, invented it in 1969–1970. We improved it later. We worked very well together, I respected him, accepted him, liked him, admired him. I went on with my part time work at Lumea as well. But once he did something he had no right to do. He simply vanished, for three days, with the dummy copy of the magazine. In May 1969 – when we were preparing the July issue – we could not find him. He was nowhere. When he finally came I asked him: "What happened?" He did not answer much at the beginning. "Where is the dummy?" He took it out of his famous black briefcase and gave it to me. I was simply dumbfounded; the delay was important. I took it and told him: "From this very instant we will never work together."

Mircea Grigorescu was not on the payroll of *Magazin istoric*. He worked as a part-timer and his name was mentioned in the journal.

He looked at me in wonder: he simply was not able to understand how such a thing could happen to him. I can never forget the perplexity in his eyes, which turned into irony (he thought it was a joke); then he started to look daggers at me. He took his briefcase and left. Very quickly. Of course, we passed beyond that situation, but the encounter had been dramatic. I tried to explain my attitude; he seemed to have been waiting for my explanation and accepted it. I told him: "Well, Mircea dear, I could have died because of your foolish act. For three long days you disappeared with the dummy, just before the deadline. You did not even call me to let me know what to do. The journal had to be printed." "I couldn't help it" he answered. "I believe you", I said "but I had no choice then. I acted in the only way I could." "What way?" he asked. "The way Mircea Grigorescu would have acted", I replied.

He liked my explanation very much and he accepted my invitation to work again for us. We resumed our previous relations and we both called the episode mentioned above "*remembrance of things past*".

One day he came to my office, took a small box out of his briefcase, and gave it to me. It was a tiepin that I had liked very much when I had seen him wearing it. "Dear Cristian, it will be perfect with you" he told me and left very quickly. I was very touched. I looked for him and I thanked him. Then I started pestering him again with questions about his health, his blood pressure; I asked him again to write his memories. I could say that

Mircea Grigorescu was like a bull in the ring. The values of his blood pressure were incredible. He had had three or four strokes, one of which very severe. I visited him then at his place, at 8, Dr. Nanu Muscel St. in Cotroceni. He was furious with himself that he made his family and his friends sad with his disease. But he was not frightened; there was no trace of panic with him. As a matter of fact he was a very brave man. After that stroke he refused to stay in bed more than a week and the recovery was spectacular. His unusual vitality had won. I remembered then what the English historian Anthony Seldon wrote about Winston Churchill. Seldon told that in the evening of June 23, Churchill offered a dinner in the honor of the Italian Prime Minister de Gasperi. In his witty speech Churchill reminded another Latin "guest" of the British land – Julius Caesar. Several moments later, as the guests were leaving the room, Churchill fell down on his chair. His son-in-law, Christopher Soames took the old man to his flat. Churchill had had a stroke. Despite the doctor's recommendations – it was Lord Moran – Churchill insisted to take part in a meeting of the government the following morning. It was an imprudent act, yet full of courage.

I had tried several times to make Grigorescu see a doctor. It was impossible. He was not able to change anything in his way of living. "If I can't smell the ink on the rotary printing press I am sure to die" – he used to say after his severe stroke in 1974.

I think that for about ten or fifteen years he was the most prolific Romanian journalist. He was an editorial secretary of three magazines: *Lumea*, *România literară*, and *Magazin istoric*. He had put down in a notebook (kept by his family) that between 1973 and 1974 he worked part time for no less than twelve journals, magazines, and other periodicals (*Lumea*, *România literară*, *Săptămâna*, *Flacăra*, *Tribuna*, *Ateneu*, *Teatrul*, *Urzica*, *Apărarea păcii*, *Almanahul literar*, *Almanahul Flacăra*, *Almanahul Magazin*). He also had radio and TV features – about four a week: political commentaries, sport reports, travel notes, etc. I asked him to write his memories. He promised, he tried… He left behind very few original works. Several essays were published in *Flacăra* after his death.

I thank his family for granting me the permission to quote

some lines of his notes all of them revealing future projects. Here you are the list entitled *Memories of a Journalist*, prepared for some magazine. “The social and political feature within 1920–1940 – the first journals published after World War I and their ink; the renaissance of the idea of national unity at a wider social-political level; proper democratic media – *Adevărul*, C. Mille (after Beldiman), B. Brănişteanu, Const. Graur, Iosif Nădejde (the last one had directed his steps to journalism); several actions: *Stânga*, *Cuvântul liber*, *Reporter*, *Lupta*, *Bluze albastre*, *Albatros*, *Adevărul*, and *Dimineaţa*, Adevărul literar şi artistic. Printing houses in Bucharest – printing houses that had published progressive journals and books; the on-the-spot reporter at the trial of communists in Craiova; the birth of the modern feature in the Romanian journals – Brunea-Fox, C. Băleanu, Badea Marinescu, Geo Bogza, Miron Radu Paraschivescu, Al. Sahia; poets-journalists, journalists-poets: T. Arghezi, Camil Petrescu, Geo Bogza, Miron Radu Paraschivescu, George Călinescu, Gh. Dinu.” Some other notes: “A problem of the *world – the quality*”; “new + quality make up the substance of the society of tomorrow, of the revolutionary, socialist, communist, and humanist society in the best sense of the words.”

Before quoting the last sentences found among Mircea Grigorescu’s papers, I’d like to quote here a TV commentary that has never been published; I found the telegraphic style in it extremely inspiring:

“Departures… Arrivals… All our life seems a long voyage, a series of arrivals and departures at the end of the waiting intervals.

Sometimes, to depart means to enter bag and baggage a dream of illusions and hopes. Some other times to arrive means to write the very first line in a feature.

What happens between arrivals and departures, between these events connected between them as if they were the first letter and the final period in a fairy tale? We do not know and we will never learn. That is not important for the reporter who only wants to grasp the boisterous excitement of these landings, the tired whistling of these locomotives in their final station. They all bring with them hundreds of stories – of some other reporters. For us, the camera takes only the pure excitement of he who is waiting and the smile, conventional sometimes but warm, more often than not, of he who comes.

For the rhythm of arrivals I have preferred plane to trains. I have chosen the crystal palace of the 'Bucharest-Otopeni' airport since it is new and beautiful. I filmed it during the day, with its heteroclitic liveliness, but I will go to see it at night when it becomes a huge organ of lights. It is then that huge silver butterflies, ruby flashing from their foreheads come from the unseen sky.

Nowadays trains might be more discreet. They have given up their plume of smoke and tufts of steam seldom surround them. I do not know why they seem tired as they enter the stations and keep sobbing when they come to the platform. There the locomotives stare at us as if trying to tell us how their voyage was, if there was rain or if sunshine caressed them.

Some other features are already packed and wait in the luggage. How many thousands of indiscrete stories, how many poems of intimacy, and how many ordinary facts are nicely arranged, folded up and pressed in that suitcase. Or, more dynamically, just thrown helter-skelter in the worn out briefcase – the beginning and the end of millions of the everyday life voyages and stories.

The luggage is useful but not compulsory; it grows, multiplies, covers us, moves in pyramids along platforms, and concentrates in piles in the waiting rooms. Let's remember the buses. Most of them pass unnoticed by improvised stations. A pillar with a fading name written on it. Some others are treated with more hospitality. Exactly one hundred years after the first train had arrived in Bucharest, the Filaret station was turned into a bus terminal. Filaret is a station of lost memories. The reporter becomes melancholic here. A tear on the platform of a deserted century…

The vibrating atmosphere of arrivals gradually melts in the waiting rooms, under the glass roofs of the railway stations. It's the time of inquiries. The train from Cluj has arrived; when does the Iași one leave? She has arrived early in the morning for her journey to Măneciu and is knitting a shawl that will be ready by the end of the voyage. Planes are somnolent; trains seem to sleep along the railways.

The traffic controller knows everything or he can find anything in the *Timetable*. Does the express train stop in Mizil? Of course, yes. And in Râmnicu-Sărat? It stops for a whole minute. Some departure pieces of advice: sit forward in the train, sit backward, and don't forget to write to me. Time passes slowly, but each minute is recorded. There is a quarter of an hour dedicated to the snack brought from home or served out on the airport terrace, at the airport.

There are two "faces" in each station; it depends if you come in or out. The former, with fountains, busses, and streets where the travelers lose their identities. The other one, with trains, planes, hasty travelers, and piles of luggage. There is an ordinary city face and a mysterious one, the starting points of the ways to horizon.

The platform separates people into two worlds. Some of them stay here, with us; the others leave to write, moment by moment, the features of their lives. Homesickness and love stay as well. A kiss. It is too quick. A longer one. It seems never to end. But moments are flying away.

For a while, the rhythm has changed, the movements are brisker, and everybody is looking at the clocks.

A severe-looking, professional speaker announces on the TV screen that the plane is ready for departure. At the end of the platform the stationmaster gives the starting signal. The engine operator is ready; the fireman has disappeared in the depths of the locomotive.

A baby has just started the first voyage of his life. Another traveler is late; he seems confused as if he could not find his carriage.

Now everything is put in line.

A new, intense moment. The light has changed too. It is the beginning of the voyage. It is no longer ours. Have a nice voyage. We are at the North Station in Bucharest. Our voyage is coming to an end. You can hear the vibration of the jet engines running hot, in wild harmony, like a hymn of force and an invitation to speed.

There remains only the short moment for saying 'good bye' and the gesture that we'll remember till the end of our voyage.The feature of life, obsolete and original at the same time, is interspersed, as in movies, with arrivals and departures."

The following pages are the last ones in his notebook.

About *landing on the Moon*. "Joy intermingled with sweet hope, that moment in the childhood when you first come to understand that you have dreamt.

The dream from the Moon, broadcast with no substance, immaterial, a thought at 400 000-km distance seems to have changed nothing.

Yet, the people's flight to Moon and their presence there have broadened the horizon, opened new thoughts – together with a more and deeper trust in technology, in science, and in philosophy.

People *will look* at the sky in a different way. These people of the 4th dimension – the astral one – and of the 7th sense, of … (the word is missing in the manuscript).

Electricity meant a new future for mankind. Similarly, the expansion in the extra-terrestrial space will create a new spirit – a psychology of a man completely free of superstitions. I mean millions of people who think rationally of the space, not only the élite.

The Apollo program is coming to an end. Are there no longer brave people who want to learn more about the Moon? I am sure there are. The program will soon be ampler."

Some wonderful words about *forgotten memories*: "I have to look at pale photos. To look at crooked furniture. To listen to some ridiculous music. To read a quarter of an old newspaper. To be in a train that passes by a silent station, in a year that is not very warm but neither is it rainy. To look at the houses, a few houses at the end of a straight street with old trees that are not beeches, limes, nor chestnut-trees as I remember them to have been."

About *himself*: "Never before has gravitation seemed so heavy to me as now when I am 70."

And then the "news in brief" about Mircea Grigorescu's death.

He died because of a stroke in a market of the city he had traveled all over, he had known so well. He died in the Amzei market place, in the very moment he was buying a newspaper – *Informația Bucureștiului*. He had had a small talk with the street vendor: "Where are you from?" he asked the man. "From Râmnicu Vâlcea" the vendor answered. "What are you saying! I'm from Râmnicu Vâlcea as well…"

And down he was the newspaper grasped in his hand. The farmers laid him down on a counter and lit a candle for him.

Ironically, he had to lie there covered with some copies of the latest issue of *Informația Bucureștiului* until the ambulance came. But there was nothing to be saved.

In that very day, poet Adrian Păunescu, the glory of whom Mircea Grigorescu had heralded, published in his *Flacăra* magazine a nice poem, a liturgy in tears in the memory of the journalist.

Radu Popescu together with Aurel Baranga passed by the Amzei market place at noon as Mircea Grigorescu was still there under a shield of newspapers. The fatal day was February 18, 1976.

Later on, Radu Popescu, the famous publicist, wrote: "Mircea Grigorescu used his many gifts, his intelligence, and his huge power of effort, if not in a perishable field (theatre for instance), then in an ephemeral one. The activity in the media and the journalist's endeavors, irrespective of the field of writing and of the scope of the journal, are ephemeral since the interest for the facts recorded vanishes with the day, week or month that succeeds in stopping them for a while but to which they are subject as well. 'I call journalism what today is less interesting than yesterday' Gide said. From this point of view and from the point of view of his death, the journalist is the most unselfish man in the world, the most altruistic, and the most modest. Mircea Grigorescu was like that and he behaved like that. He was deprived of ambition and of vanity and his modesty was close to humbleness.

He had an 'instinct' of the public, of the public opinion, similar to that of Ford or of other famous people in the field of cars or of electric devices. That instinct incessantly pushed him to improve and to refresh the journal by new, inventive, and bold formulas meant not to flatter a dull and mediocre reader but to stimulate and to attract him to superior media. Mircea Grigorescu had dreamt of all kinds of newspapers and magazines, dense and fascinating 'bombs' and it was not his fault if he could not make them.

There was no technical or editorial stage and there was no specialty or column unfamiliar to him or that he was not glad to deal with. He was a complete journalist not only because he knew, and did, and could do everything, but also because he liked everything, he was interested in everything, and he was passionately fond of everything.

He was also a complete journalist not only because he was at his ease with any aspect concerning a journal, but also because he permanently kept his eyes, mind, and soul focused on the whole of it. He was a gardener concerned about his garden, not about a certain path or a certain flower, an architect for whom a building meant the basement and the roof, the main stairs and the attic, the carpeted and mirrored rooms and the back stairs or the annexes as well. Alongside the great development of journalism a saying started being circulating '*Le journalisme mène partout, à condition d'en sortir*' meaning that as it had become 'the fourth power', media was opening way to glorious careers and to maximum honors. If in a circumstance or another Mircea Grigorescu had had to follow one of those ways he would have been the most unhappy man in the world, he would have fought against it by all means and would have become, for the first time in his life, a savage."

Mircea Grigorescu did not start to tell immediately. He used to study you first. He had much experience. First of all you had to gain his confidence. Then, in an atmosphere of human and professional confidence, you had to find the proper moment. It usually came late in the evening since any journalist has nightlife. Even if he trusted you or the best moment came he was still reticent in telling you anything or anyway.

He told me, for instance, that he had accompanied Titulescu in several European tours. He told me about the birth of Balkan Entente, he remembered the chill day in Athens when the agreement had been signed. He told me admiringly that Titulescu had a special gift of creating moments of suspense. He had also another gift: to talk to the journalists. Several years before *Magazin istoric* published a short text – found by historian George G. Potra – the shorthand report of a speech the great diplomat delivered in Geneva, at the journalists' Club. What Mircea Grigorescu had told me years before was supported by Titulescu's speech.

He told me then about the role Titulescu had – together with the delegates of the other signatories of the Little Entente – in outmaneuvering the plans meant to create a directorate of Europe, the plans of Mussolini taken over by Ramsay MacDonald, Prime Minister of Great Britain. Grigorescu remembered that Titulescu had invited to the ministry several editors he knew, conferred with them, and told them before they left: Well boys, launch, in any possible way, the attack against that project. They want to take hold of our land. They want to put Europe under the trusteeship of four countries: Italy, Great Britain, France, and Germany and to create a directorate that might decide instead of ourselves. Farewell to Versailles, farewell to peace treaties, farewell to any opportunity of assertion of the small countries!

The Romanian democratic newspapers, together with those in Yugoslavia and Czechoslovakia – Romania's allies in the Little Entente – started firing.

In their *Cuvântul liber*, historians Ion Ardeleanu and Ion Muşat remind the younger generations of the Romanian personalities who rose for defending the freedom and independence of Romania: Tudor Teodorescu-Branişte, Demostene Botez, D.I. Suchianu, Victor Eftimiu, Scarlat Callimachi, Şerban Cioculescu, I. Felea, Geo Bogza, Gala Galaction, Şerban Voinea, F. Brunea-Fox, C. Titel-Petrescu, Al. Philippide, B. Brănişteanu, Ion Clopoţel, Miron Radu Paraschivescu, T. Cristureanu, Dorina Rudich, George Macovescu, Lucia Demetrius, Sidonia Drăguşanu, Ştefan Voicu, L.D. Pătrăşcanu, A. Joja, P. Constantinescu-Iaşi, Eugen Jebeleanu, Ella Negruzzi.

Before *Cuvântul liber*, Mircea Grigorescu had worked for *Stânga – linia generală a vremii* (The Left – the General Direction of the Age), first published between Nov. 13, 1932 and March 19, 1933 where M. Ralea, P. Pandrea, M. Roman, M. Grindea. I. Felea, T. Herseni, P. Comarnescu, Demostene Botez, Tudor Teodorescu-Branişte contributed.

In the pages of *Cuvântul liber*, a genuine university of the Romanian modern journalism, Mircea Grigorescu defined his options in the years before the most difficult and the most dramatic period of all. The open letter Mircea Grigorescu wrote to Hermann Göring on April 27, 1935 in *Cuvântul liber* was a kind of anticipation of the verdict of history itself. His very risky attitude was similar to that in November 17, 1934 when he exposed the aggressive fascist mentality by revealing the political conspiracy of the German *chargé d'affaires* in Romania, Pochhammer, forty years before sensational archive documents proved it.

Mircea Grigorescu was the first journalist that told me more about the activity of the Students' Democratic Front, very influential within the 1935–1938 period. He remembered the demonstration in the afternoon of January 23, 1936 and also the meeting in the following night – both expressing the students' options in the fight against fascism, for democracy, independence, and progress. Mircea Grigorescu said that Gogu Rădulescu, the then president of the Students' Democratic Front, had told him that the organization was under communist influence although its members had other options as well. The journalists were deeply moved not only by the combative spirit of the students, but also by they way they showed their gratitude to the democratic journalists who had supported them. The hundreds of students coming down Calea Victoriei to the Matei Millo Street stopped in front of *Dimineața* and *Adevărul* offices and printing house to express their feelings towards Tudor Teodorescu-Branişte and towards other democratic journalists. The gesture was very appealing.

Mircea Grigorescu also told me about the day Romania had entered the fascist war. He was there when the event was made known to the main leaders of the Romanian media. On Saturday night, June 21, all those managers and editors-in-chief were summoned to the Government headquarters and were announced that General Ion Antonescu would make an extremely important announcement. In reality, Ion Antonescu was then on his way to the north of Moldavia. After several hours' delay, Mihai Antonescu, the vice-president of the Government and also Minister of Propaganda came and briefed them. Gentlemen, Romania will join Germany in the war against Russia and the Romanian army will start tomorrow morning on the side of the German one. Bolshevism will be destroyed. Gentlemen, Romania will regain its territories lost following the Soviet Dictate of June 1940. This war is sacred and Romanian media should consider the importance of the moment. Our brothers on the other border of the Prut River have suffered too much. They are waiting for us, let's not disappoint the Romanians' hopes. That was General Antonescu's proclamation.

Uproar started and lots of questions were shot. Mircea Grigorescu did not say anything. At the end of the meeting each of those present was supposed to go to his journal and to direct the Monday issue (June 23) in keeping with the new line. Mircea Grigorescu went to Ică Antonescu and pointed to a wall map; "Mister Mihai Antonescu, have you looked at the map?" "Yes" Antonescu answered. "Have you seen the map of Europe. Do you think it can be changed?" "Germany, with its endless power" Antonescu replied "has got three quarters of Europe. It will be able to make Europe look different." "Well. I've just asked you if you had a good look at the map. Look at it!" "I'm looking". "And what can you see?" "I can see that Germany…" "No Sir, look beyond Germany (and he pointed to Russia). How could you imagine that such a country, with all its resources, people and territories could be occupied?" "Mr. Grigorescu we do not want to occupy that country. That's Hitler's problem..." "Well, but don't you think that Romania is making this evening a move with hard to appreciate and expect consequences?"

Of course, Mihai Antonescu called Mircea Grigorescu to order then. (The documents in the archives reveal that Mircea Grigorescu – together with other democratic journalists – tried to influence the public opinion in the direction of his belief, a fact easily noticed by the fascists who reported in Berlin about him.)

When he was the manager of *Timpul* and of *Ecoul* he allowed a great number of democratic journalists or communist sympathizers to write for the two newspapers. Subtle analyses of the world aspects were often included in their pages. Grigorescu's antifascist and democratic attitude was also manifest in *Adevărul*, *Stânga*, and *Cuvântul liber*. He was a dear friend of numerous journalists, writers, and printers. On August 29, 1941, poet Miron Radu Paraschivescu wrote the following words on the copy of his *Cântece ţigăneşti* (Gypsy Songs) that he offered to Grigorescu: "To

Mr. Mircea Grigorescu with my deepest and most constant friendship and with the belief that he also knows that friendship can be either *integral* or it cannot be at all." The pages about war in *Timpul* and in *Ecoul*, together with other papers about arts and culture are historical pages written by democratic journalists; they are a great victory against the Romanian official censorship and against the German censorship as well, since Romanian was practically an occupied country. Those papers spread the ideas of the antifascist resistance with a lot of courage, intelligence, and subtlety.

That was Mircea Grigorescu and that was his patriotism. That was his way of showing his belief in the Romanian democracy. Unfortunately, he died before 1989, and was not able to see the renaissance of that democracy.

It is time now for a story that best reveals Mircea Grigorescu's life and courage.

Mircea was a counselor at the Press office affiliated with the Government in the period 1941–1944. After 1947 he was accused (although he had proved his democratic attitude all along Antonescu's regime) of having worked for the 'fascist dictatorship'. He did not wait for the trial to take place and left for the mountains where he found refuge. There he became a shepherd. From time to time he used to come to his house in the Cotroceni district, at 8 Dr. Nanu Muscel St. where he had lived all his life. One autumn day in the 1950s a police raid was organized in that street while he was at home. Somebody called Mircea Grigorescu to tell him about that and the journalist grasped the nettle and adopted the most film-like solution. He took off his fleecy shepherd coat, put on a dark gray suit, a coat of the same color and a hat over his head. The very moment the first two policemen were in front of his house he went out of the gate and told them in a hurry "there's nobody here, I've already checked. You may go on with the other houses", and away he was in the most "policeman-like" posture in the world. Obviously, none of them dared to question him. And nobody ever thought that the "chief" was the very man they might have been looking for.

There is also another story related to his coming back to

Bucharest for good. To the end of the 1950s the communist repression grew weaker and Mircea took the opportunity to go more often to the Obor market place with his dairy products. One day, a French guest in Romania (the famous French dissident Roger Garaudy, at that time a Communist leader) asked somebody working for the Press office at the Ministry of Foreign Affairs: "There was a great democratic journalist. What has happened to him?" The state machinery geared up to find him and Mircea Grigorescu "appeared" miraculously in 24 hours. In the meantime he had sold and smuggled wool, had bred sheep, and he even owned a soft drinks stall.

Ironically, his "collaborationist" file was clean and a lot of cultural personalities had given evidence. People's Court acquitted him. A relative of Eugen Ionescu and of Lola Bobescu, Mircea Grigorescu used to tell me that a journalist needed *names* abroad willing to remember him when necessary.

Thus, he had come back to his dear universe; George Ivaşcu, another ex-political prisoner brought him to *Lumea*.

And now, the last story about Mircea. It was the afternoon of August 22, 1944. Mihai (Ică) Antonescu had entrusted him with the mission of leaving to Geneva, via Istanbul, to connect Grigore Gafencu there and arrange together a European press conference, favorable to Romania, with a view to preparing Romania's going out of war. (Obviously, that was the decision of Marshall Antonescu's government). The minister of the Foreign Affairs opened the secret safe and took out some piles of Swiss Francs that he wanted to give to Mircea Grigorescu for his mission. "It is too late", Grigorescu told him. And he reminded him of the meeting of June 21, 1941. "Russians can no longer be stopped and Germans can no longer be saved. Let's try to save us from here, from Romania. I am sorry, but I cannot leave."

MARCH 1939:
TURMOIL IN THE FOREIGN OFFICE

In the morning of February 9, the royal carriage drove the envoy extraordinary and minister plenipotentiary of Romania in London from his residence at 1 Belgrave Square to Saint-James' Palace. At 11.45 King George VI was to receive Virgil Viorel Tilea's letter of accreditation. The presence there of the foreign secretary, Lord Halifax, was an unusual thing that revealed the importance of the event. In such occasions, Foreign Office was usually represented by a secretary of state. During the meeting that lasted till after 13, the Romanian minister showed the British king that in the case of Romania "it is not the domestic situation we should worry about but the pressure of Germany." Likewise, he warned, "if Germany subdues Romania economically, the German potential will increase by 200%".

Tilea was appointed in London both owing to his relations in the business and political circles in the city where he had studied (he had graduated from the London School of Economics) and on account of his friendship with King Charles II. Therefore, in that very first meeting V.V. Tilea echoed the concern of the Romanian official circles about the fate of the Romanian independent state, founded on December 1, 1918. In March 16–21, in less than 45 days since the audience in Saint James' Palace, Tilea's interventions in Foreign Office would generate a diplomatic turmoil concerning a would-be ultimatum Germany had issued to Romania. The so-called "Tilea case" was dealt with both by Romanian (Gheorghe Buzatu, Viorica Moisuc, Gheorghe Zaharia, Al. Gh. Savu, Eliza Campus, Ion Calafeteanu) and foreign historians –Andreas Hillgruber (German), Sidney Aster (Canadian), David Funderburk and Paul B. Quinlan (Americans), Elisabeth Barker, Simon Newman, Martin Gilbert, Richard Gott, and Elisabeth Wiskemannn (British), Philippe Marguerat (French). I have quoted here the best known ones who have insistently written on that topic in the latest 25 years.

The serious concerns of the Romanian government had been sent directly to the British king and to his foreign secretary.

The dangers threatening Romania's independence, sovereignty, and integrity were important. Totalitarianism and revisionism were aiming at the very freedom of the Romanian people.

Several of the numerous actions taken in that period for defending Romania's independence were linked to Tilea's name, whom I met one October evening in 1970.

Besides some diplomatic reports I had read, what else did I know about V.V. Tilea when I rang the doorbell of his flat in Kensington? I knew that he was one of the most dynamic Romanian capitalists in the interval 1920–1930 and one of the youngest politicians (he was a member of the Nationalist Peasants' Party) between World War I and World War II. He was born on April 6, 1896 in Sibiu, in a well-established family. He studied law and economy in Bratislava, Vienna, Cluj, and London. In 1918 he was the Secretary of the Romanian National Council in Vienna, and in 1919–1922 he took part in the Romanian delegation to the Paris Peace Conference. Soon after that, he became cultural and press attaché of the Romanian legation in London. He was one of the most active under-secretaries of state in the Romanian Government. Likewise, he was a deputy in several legislatures, was one of the leaders of the National Peasants' Party and – as a journalist – wrote a lot between the two world wars. So, he was a journalist like myself. During Antonescu's regime his whole property was confiscated and his citizenship suspended by a decree; in February 3, 1941, the punishment, notified by a decree, was confirmed and got an enforceable character.

So, let's come back to London in 1970 and to a several-hour' discussion about the "Tilea case". Psychologically, it was quite natural and justifiable that Tilea had made a kind of fixation about his "case". I cannot say that he was overreacting but, as he had been on the crest of the wave of the European politics, he was still obsessed with his finest hour. In 1939 he was 43 years old. Our meeting took place in 1970 but the clock had stopped for him 31 years before.

Tilea received me in his small apartment on the 2nd floor of a Victorian house, at 28 Redcliffe Square. He came to meet me in a wheelchair. Following a stroke his legs paralyzed; he had just recovered a short while ago. Architect Barbu Călinescu, the son of Armand Călinescu, ex prime minister of Romania, who had introduce me, left us alone. Tilea was quite elegant and both his voice and his eyes were full of energy. He nostalgically remembered Alba Iulia and the unforgettable year 1918, he spoke about the Peace Conference in 1919, and I could see that he was acquainted with the latest books about the history of the Romanian foreign policy. However his thoughts were dominated by the events of March 1939. Based on my notes, on the documents and the journals of that time, and on the books dealing with that topic I think I can structure the "Tilea case" (the West German historian Andreas Hillgruber called it a case) into a prologue, three acts, and an epilogue.

PROLOGUE

Tilea told me the reason why he had been selected and sent to London in 1939. He was not a diplomat. Leaving aside the period in which he had been sent to the Paris Peace Conference as an expert and a short mission in London (1923–1924) he had never worked at the Ministry of Foreign Affairs. But:

1. he was on very good terms with King Charles II;
2. he was a friend of Armand Călinescu, king's counselor and minister;
3. they were both members of the Peasants' National Party;
4. he had studied in London;
5. his social position and material independence were guarantees for the British Establishment.

Therefore, Charles II and Armand Călinescu decided to send Tilea to London since he was rather well known both to the British public opinion and to the influential circles (Tilea had founded and had led the British-Romanian Association). He wanted Great Britain to reevaluate its political and economic position towards Romania, that was to support Romania's independence and integrity.

ACT I

Tilea came to London at the beginning of 1939. He was eager to concentrate on a rapid development of the Romanian-British relations, but he had some other special missions. The Romanian officials had realized that hard times were coming and that the revisionist and aggressive tendencies of the European fascists were a menace to Romania.

Tilea read for me a copy of a telegram about the way he had been received by King George VI. After the accreditation letters had been presented, Tilea immediately approached the subject of the German menaces. Following the tour King Charles II made in 1938 in several European capitals (not a very successful tour) the officials in Bucharest understood that new steps had to be taken to ensure Romania's international position. King George VI was extremely receptive and promised that Great Britain would do its best to support the Romanian efforts and to help Romania protect its independence. Tilea told him: "Your Majesty, we do not need words, we need facts".

In the meantime, in Bucharest, Romanian-German negotiations were carried on, extremely difficult ones indeed; Tilea had been informed about them. During February and in the first half of March 1939, Tilea tried to draw the attention of as many influential people as possible that the things kept degrading and, consequently, Romania could be in great danger. "During those weeks I had political, financial, cultural, and artistic guests almost every day" he told me. "I kept trying to persuade them and to make them support us; in fact I wanted to make them open their eyes."

ACT II

On March 15, in the morning, Hitler, in spite of all his promises and in spite of all the treaties he had signed in Munich, invaded and occupied the rest of Czechoslovakia. The next day, Tilea received from Bucharest, by a roundabout way, a message meaning "green light". The decision-makers in Bucharest, Tilea told me, knew that the new borders of Germany meant that aggression was closer and closer.

Tilea's words strengthened partly what I had already known from the historical sources. Additionally he told me that he had had a confidential understanding with Charles II and with Armand Călinescu. Later on, in the spring of 1984, Barbu Călinescu told me that he had discovered the personal code of his father who had mentioned that understanding.

When Tilea left for London, he agreed that if Romania had ever been in difficulty the king and Armand Călinescu would send him a message that would give him a blank check. Tilea was free to do what he considered to be the best for Romania.

In the same day when Tilea was presenting his accreditation, the English minister in Bucharest, Sir Reginald Hoare sent a report to Lord Halifax about the significance of the government made up on February 2, 1939. Sir Reginald wrote there that the main aim of the new Romanian government was to promote Mr. Călinescu by creating for him the new position of the government vice-president. At the same time Călinescu had remained minister of the Interior and of National Defense. Therefore, Călinescu, the most prominent personality of the new administration became its official leader, as well. On March 6, Hoare announced the Whitehall that Armand Călinescu had become Prime Minister after the death of the patriarch Miron Cristea in Cannes. The referent of the Foreign Office wrote on the ciphered cable received from Bucharest that Călinescu, in his double quality of minister of the Interior and of National Defense, was the main responsible for the policy against the Iron Guard. The king and his new Prime Minister had established ways of contacting Tilea that skipped the Ministry of Foreign Affairs, where Grigore Gafencu was in charge.

During our talk, Tilea clearly revealed his dislike for his ex-chief, but he was not able to prove the latter's "conciliatory attitude".

On March 16, 1939 he had received the confidential "green light" message and following it Tilea took the responsibility of his own actions.

Later that day he went to Foreign Office and asked to be received by a higher rank diplomat. Sir Orme Sargent, a state undersecretary received him. Tilea told him that Romania was on the verge of its disintegration as a state since Germany intended to turn it into a German protectorate.

Starting with the evening of March 16, the turmoil in the diplomatic circles in London kept growing. Let's remember it had already started when Czechoslovakia had been occupied. The following day Tilea received the famous cable no. 17 180 from the Ministry of Foreign Affairs in Bucharest. He was asked to go to the Foreign Office and to explain that the Romanian-German negotiations are in an extremely difficult moment and to warn the British officials about it. Tilea asked urgent audience from Lord Halifax the foreign secretary and from other high officials in Foreign Office: Sir Alexander Cadogan, Sir Robert Vansittart, and Sir Orme Sargent. "I told them about the deadly menace against Romania" Tilea told me. "I spoke about the pressure and the claims Germans raised during the economic negotiations in Bucharest. They were very close to an ultimatum, I could say. On March 17, I clearly asked Lord Halifax what would happen if Romania were the victim of the German aggression. I raised the problem of the German ultimatum to all the other British diplomats I talked to that day. Following the occupation of Czechoslovakia, Wohltat, Hitler's representative in the Romanian-German economic talks in Bucharest, had become more and more threatening. Therefore I asked from the Whitehall a clear answer: "Can or cannot Romania count on the British support in case of Hungarian or of Hungarian-German aggression.

Faced with my insistent questions, the British officials – also informed by their diplomats in Romania and by King Charles II himself – reacted, in everybody's opinion, promptly. That reaction was mainly due to Sir Orme Sargent, Sir Alexander Cadogan, and Sir Robert Vansittart who were in conflict with the 'conciliators' and did not want to yield to the Nazi Germany."

"In the Foreign Office of that time" Tilea told me "there were five, six, seven, even eight different directions. Of course, Lord Halifax and Premier Neville Chamberlain had the last word. However, there were a lot of people who did their best to promote Anthony Eden's policy, ex-foreign secretary until 1937, of antifascist orientation, who resigned in protest against the fact that he had been refused that direction. Foreign Office asked all the British ministers to point out, in their declarations, that Great Britain was interested in the southeastern Europe. More than that, they called Birmingham, where Chamberlain was due to speak in the evening of March 17. Prime Minister was kindly asked to introduce some words in his speech about the interest Great Britain took in southeastern Europe and about the resistance against German aggression. The tragic fate of Czechoslovakia would never be shared by the other countries in that area."

Based on careful corroboration of sources, the American historian David B. Funderburk showed the role Romania had in making London adopt a new tone in its policy. [Since I could find only a Romanian translation of Funderburk's book I will give below his main ideas. A.C.] When he met Sargent, Tilea wanted to know if Romania could rely on Great Britain in case of German aggression. More exactly, Tilea told him that, based on certain information, Germany would soon offer Hungary part of Romania, with the final aim of creating a German protectorate over the whole country. However there was more than that. Everything started when Tilea told Halifax, on March 17, that the Germans wanted a monopoly on the exports to Romania and a diminution of Romania's industrial production in the best interest of Germany. The Romanian government, Tilea said, considered that those threats were *not far from* an ultimatum. However *The Times* and *The Daily Telegraph* did not underline the shade of Tilea's declaration. The extreme simplification of Tilea's words roused exaggerated reactions and the obvious concern of other governments. The French reaction, for instance, was one of suspicion and Prime Minister Daladier warned the French government that the very day Germany had control over Romania's oil resources it would be able to fight war against the whole Europe. The general opinion was that Tilea had exaggerated the proportions of the threat and the menace of the German domination as expressed during their negotiations with Romania. As a matter of fact his words were misinterpreted or were exaggerated. Nevertheless, taking into account the Romanian-German agreement of March 23 and the subsequent relations between Berlin and

Bucharest, Tilea's alarm was not altogether unfounded. King Charles II reiterated Tilea's fear and informed the British minister in Bucharest, Sir Reginald Hoare, that Hungary, Germany, and Bulgaria could invade Romania any moment. More than that, Alexandru Cretzianu was sent to London "officially to guide Tilea because they did no longer trust him". In fact, Cretzianu's mission was to inform the Britishers that Tilea had told the truth. Therefore, Tilea had expressed the natural reaction of the Romanian government, with no trace of the indiscretion or hysteria attributed to him later. The way the British officials received Tilea's appeal proved their concern too and it has to be considered within the Czechoslovakian crisis in mid March 1939. Much more important than Tilea's so-called exaggeration or the misunderstanding of his report was the reaction of the British government. The archives of the British Cabinet reveal that, to a certain respect, Tilea's opportune indiscretion influenced the British policy. Germany having occupied Prague had already irritated the sensitivity of the members of the government and, consequently, the alarm Tilea gave could be motivated. Tilea's intercession with Sargent and Halifax on March 16 and 17 had been decisive for the political change of direction in the British government that started with Chamberlain's speech on March 17.

These are the main ideas synthesized in Funderburk's book.

ACT III

The other side of the coin. On the one hand, the German-Romanian economic treaty was signed in Bucharest on March 23, 1939; on the other hand, Tilea had been discredited. Grigore Gafencu, the minister of Foreign Affairs made a public statement according to which Tilea had overstepped his authority and there had been no ultimatum; the relations between Germany and Romania were quite normal.

Therefore – if I were to use Tilea's words – utter repudiation. It was dramatic, even in 1970, to see Tilea – half-paralyzed – blushing as he remembered those events. There had always been animosity between himself and Grigore Gafencu. But after March

17 a clash took place and then the breach that lasted until the end of their lives. Gafencu died in 1957 and Tilea in 1973. As long as they lived there was declared and total antipathy between them.

"Can you see? He showed his total disagreement with me in an extremely tactless manner. He was totally undiplomatic and made a fool of me all over Europe. I could understand that there were higher political interests. All right. But what was the point in making such a fuss since he knew very well that Romania's position had to be protected by all means. More than that. He called me to Bucharest. He didn't say that he was going to dismiss me. He said that he wanted me home 'to confer with me', but everybody knew that that was a call to order."

"Of course" Tilea went on "I did not go. An exchange of cables followed between Gafencu and me – I have them all here."

He took out a ring file. Everything was in perfect order and all his documents were filed.

"I went back to Bucharest much later, at the beginning of April."

In the meantime Tilea had had flu, an epidemic that had hit London. In Bucharest he met the king several times and Armand Călinescu once. None of them reproached him anything. It was an obvious proof, he told me, that both the king and Armand Călinescu had agreed with his action. In fact they had started it.

"I came back to London and I went on with my mission, of course under more and more difficult conditions because of the German offensive and because of the fact that Great Britain had to suffer the consequences of its own reconciliation policy. Armand and the king had other more important problems to solve than to blame me. What will Romania do in the future? How could we defend ourselves? Those were real problems. But I was disgraced before the media and before the diplomatic corps. It is true that part of the politicians understood that it was just a subtle political action…"

Irrespective of the exactness of some details, it is the general significance of the affair and its consequences that made important the events that focused on Tilea: they worried Sargent, Halifax, and Chamberlain and a visible change in the British policy started immediately.

Funderburk considers that the Romanian-German economic treaty made the Nazi actions even more suspect in the eyes of the Western countries. Two days before its being signed, Chamberlain and Halifax had started preparations for a new guarantee system. On March 22, the French Minister of Foreign Affairs, George Bonnet, met Halifax and they laid the bases for the guarantees to be offered to Romania and Poland. However, for Romania the decision was coming too late.

The occupation by the Germans of Bohemia and Moravia on March 15 and a possible threat for Romania, together with "Tilea affair" was the last straw for the Britishers. In response to the German actions, Chamberlain's Cabinet tried to adapt their policy and way of thinking. Rearming of the Great Britain was quickened alongside with the introduction of the compulsory military service. Germany's action against Czechoslovakia drastically reduced Chamberlain and Halifax's confidence in the Munich Agreement. Besides, the problem of Romania (the "Tilea affair" and the Romanian-German economic agreement included) made the British government guarantee the independence of Poland. The guarantees given to Poland on March 31 clearly showed a fundamental turn in the foreign policy of Great Britain towards Germany. That tactical change had occurred during the previous fortnight when the whole attention had been focussed on Romania. The ground for the commitment to Poland might therefore lie in the fall of Czechoslovakia and in the further problems raised by Romania. The British attempts to issue a declaration supporting the political independence of the Eastern European countries might prove the above assertions. Chamberlain himself, while considering guaranteeing a Polish-Romanian alliance was surprised by the news of an imminent attack on Poland. Therefore, they offered one guarantee only, on March 31. The core of the whole issue, as seen from the British and French sides, was the conviction of the West that the help offered to Poland was the key for the protection of Romania, the more so as they considered the attitudes of the two countries versus the problems of the Soviet military assistance.

The threat hanging over Romania, mainly that of a German-

Hungarian invasion in Transylvania, following collapse of Czechoslovakia, convinced the Britishers to offer guarantees to Poland, on March 31, and two weeks later to Romania. Following the conclusion of the Romanian-German economic treaty, the Western countries considered that the "immediate" threat against Romania had been removed, or at least postponed, since Germany had attained most of its aims diplomatically. Gafencu himself emphasized that "the pact ensured for Romania peace and calmness at the beginning of an extremely serious international crisis that would destroy the most small and middle-sized European countries."

That was why the Western powers focussed their attention on Poland, considered a crucial element, and on protecting Romania. It was obvious that following the Czechoslovakian crisis, the defense of Poland could no longer be separated from that of Romania. Mention should be made that a defensive alliance treaty had already been in force between Romania and Poland since 1921. A day before the announcement concerning the guarantee given to Poland, the governments of Great Britain and of France approached both Warsaw and Bucharest with regard to the mutual guarantees. In the case of Poland, the help was conditioned by a promise to grant assistance to Romania.

The Great Britain offered guarantees to Romania following the impression that an invasion was imminent, taking into account the situation in Czechoslovakia and the "Tilea affair". (Some more lines from Funderburk's book.)

EPILOGUE

Martha Bibescu largely dealt with the Tilea episode in her memories. It seems that Martha Bibescu and Gheorghe Tătărăscu, the Romanian ambassador in Paris, realized how difficult the situation was for Romania. They alerted the Western governments and political circles, but no use was made of the incriminated word "ultimatum". Tilea kept on maintaining till the end of his life that he had been authorized to say what he considered proper about the difficulties and the grave situation Romania was facing.

Lately, Romanian and foreign historians alike studied all the circumstances connected to that diplomatic case of European scope, maybe the most famous in 1939, and reached the conclusion that there was an "ultimatum" in its content only, not in its form. Germany's economic and political pressures – corroborated with the military menace following the invasion of Czechoslovakia that brought closer the fascist danger were so strong that Romania was obviously facing an ultimate situation. The months to come proved that Tilea's steps were well grounded.

Tilea's intervention had varied consequences. Unfortunately they were not very efficient as far as the defense of Romania was concerned. However, the guarantees given to Romania in April 13, 1939 by Great Britain and by France were partly negotiated with Tilea, and partly the direct result of his act of March 16–17, 1939. They were decided upon in the meeting of the British Cabinet of March 18, dedicated almost entirely to Romania.

Likewise, the rejuvenation of the economic and political relations, the fresh interest of Great Britain towards Romania, materialized by mutual visits, delegations, intense economic and financial relations, loans, and arms deliveries originated in Tilea'a intercession.

However, there is one more important consequence acknowledged by the foreign historians. Tilea was the last one to blow the whistle for the British policy.

After the war, the "Tilea case" became a more and more relevant topic in the history of the Romanian and European diplomacies. Although almost all actors and witnesses of that moment passed away, the diplomatic annals and memories revealed new details of the so-called "incident" of diplomatic "indiscretion" in the spring of 1939. Besides the Romanian minister in London, V.V. Tilea, there were other personalities involved in a way or another in those events: King Charles II, Premier A. Călinescu, Grigore Gafencu – Minister of Foreign Affairs, Mitiță Constantinescu – Minister of Finance, Gh. Tătărăscu – the Romanian minister in Paris, writer Martha Bibescu, some other officials in Romania; also the main members of the British government, and other conservative leaders, among whom W.

Churchill and A. Eden. Likewise, Tilea made known the international situation of Romania to many other foreign diplomats in London: to the Russian representative, Ivan Maiski, with whom he had discussed a lot about a possible Romanian-Soviet cooperation with the Western powers; to Joseph Kennedy, the USA ambassador; and to the ambassadors of the countries forming the Balkan Entente. The governments in Berlin and Rome could not ignore the "Tilea case", the more so as the Romanian minister disturbed the Nazi diplomacy. Corroboration of the present sources shows that Tilea's intervention had alerted many European political and diplomatic circles and that it was object of serious concern in many capital cities.

Up to the end of his life Tilea maintained that his message had been an important step. Not many historians doubt about it today. When I met him in London, he told me that although the government – more exactly the minister of the Foreign Affairs – had disavowed all knowledge of the matter in less than 48 hours, his intercession was fully supported by a confidential message sent to the British leaders by King Charles II who insistently asked British support for defending the independence and integrity of Romania.

Princess Martha Bibescu, an expert in Romanian policy and also in the European diplomatic backstage, recorded those events. Martha Bibescu came to London a day before Tilea's intercession. On March 15, the day in which Hitler occupied Czechoslovakia, Tilea called her and asked her to come to London sooner. The following day they talked again. That time in London; Martha Bibescu had listened to his plea. They met on March 17, 1939 the day when Tilea was due to see Lord Halifax.

"Tilea came to me at about 9.30. We talked a lot. He was extremely agitated and seemed very unhappy. 'I've got terrible news from Transylvania. The Germans are close to our border and they claim us to give up industry and to remain an agrarian country. Otherwise they do not guarantee our borders. Gafencu has lost his head… Nobody is able to keep calm. All our armament (made by Skoda) is still in Czechoslovakia and the Germans have taken hold of it. We've got into a muddle!'

It is just a question of hours in his opinion. Transylvania will be snatched away and will be put under the leadership of a German general and of some Hungarian count. Tilea speaks with much pain and his despair sounds genuine. I promised him that I would do my best during my stay."

Notes from the following days.

"Victor Cazalet, a deputy in the House of Commons came to see me. He promised me that he would do something.

The Vansittarts promised they would meet Tilea here for dinner. Vansittart insisted that we should be alone with Tilea since he did not want anything to leak out. He asked Tilea about Germany's economic ultimatum, about the 22 divisions ready to invade Romania, about the German violence…

To my great surprise, Vansittart said 'I'll call Maiski' and so did he. From my cozy drawing room he called Russia on the phone. Maiski answered and they arranged an appointment.

'Can you see how these things go on?' Sarita [Vansittart] whispered.

The truth was that in the afternoon the Cabinet met in Downing Street to decide on helping Romania. The news that Bucharest had rebutted the ultimatum irritated the Prime Minister, although an economic ultimatum is no less serious than a political one. Romania had to give up its industry and to content itself with agriculture. *Georgics*, *Bucolics* happiness, Heaven!

Tilea told me that Chamberlain was in danger, that his political death could not be avoided and that Parliament wanted Halifax at the head of the Government. Likewise they ask for introduction of military service.

And to meet these aims, the people here want to use Romania." That was the end of Martha Bibescu's notes about Tilea in her *Political Journal* published by Editura Politică (Politică Publishing House) in 1979.

Mention should be made here that Sir Reginald Hoare, the British minister in Bucharest, informed London that a secretary of the German Embassy, intoxicated with too much champagne, committed suicide after having tittle-tattled in a bar about the ultimatum Germany gave to Romania.

Tilea also showed me one of the photocopies he had from

Foreign Office. It was a note made by a Foreign Office official on the basis of a cable sent by Sir Reginald Hoare. The note wrote that what Tilea had said in London seemed closer to reality that the words of the Romanian minister of Foreign Affairs. Although it was difficult to understand why the Romanian king had chosen to disclose in London an information that he was keeping secret in his own country. However, in March 18–20, Charles II had ordered intense military preparations, able to resist German threats.

When the diplomatic turmoil generated by the "Tilea case" had calmed down, the Romanian government furnished fresh examples that explained Romania's fears and its concern to protect its independence.

On May 5, the British minister informed that on May 1, 1939, at the Congress of Corporations, the Romanian Prime Minister had made a speech about Romania's decision to resist any foreign threat and pressure. Three weeks later, the British diplomat informed Lord Halifax about the meetings between the German minister in Bucharest, Dr. Wilhelm Fabricius, and the Romanian Prime Minister. A. Călinescu told the British diplomat about the accusations of the German minister, according to whom Romania had contributed to the encirclement of The Reich. The Prime Minister said that Romania was encircled as well, but he was not unhappy because of that. He added then that, to the Romanian government's great surprise, when Czechoslovakia had been occupied there had been there posters in Romanian, calling population to calm and order, and he emphasized the contradiction between such posters and the German-Romanian relations.

In his report of April 28, 1939, Hoare appreciated that the Germans had been impressed by the recent behavior of Romania. (He meant the mobilizations in the spring of 1939 and the firm attitude of the Romanian government concerning the national sovereignty and the territorial integrity). He considered that the Germans knew that if Romania had been attacked it would have destroyed its oil industry before Germans could have taken hold of it.

In one of his reports, Sir Reginald expressed his opinion on the Czaky-Mussolini-Göring meeting in Budapest and also on the fact that Romania should be encouraged to remain independent, even if part of its oil resources went to the enemy. He considered that Romania would have been overwhelmed if it had entered war in a first stage and despite all British effort it would have been simply thrown in German hands.

Hoare noted that Czaky, the Hungarian Minister of Foreign Affairs, was pretty sure that neither Romania nor Yugoslavia would ever join the Axis. Hoare agreed with the Hungarian Minister's foresight that the British were struggling to offer concrete support (for instance, anti-aircraft defense) to the Yugoslavs so that the latter could go on. In that way, Romania could express its wish and gradually pass from a correct and passive neutrality to an increasingly favorable one that could be concretely translated by selling its produces to Great Britain alongside a propensity to sabotage its own economic arrangements with Germany. Finally, considered Sir Reginald, when Great Britain and Turkey had got control of the situation, Romania would by all means be ready to broke up with the Axis.

On May 19, 1939, the British diplomat sent to Sir Alexander Cadogan, the Foreign Office state under-secretary, a "for his eyes only" note saying that Germans started worrying whether they could trust Călinescu for fulfilling in its letter and spirit the economic agreement of March 23 and whether they should keep or better eliminate him. Sir Reginald considered that neither the king nor the Government wanted to do anything that could provoke Germany as they would try to avoid being pushed to a total economic dependence on Germany and to stop too many German specialists coming to Romania. The British diplomat considered that he saw in Călinescu the best man able to focus the national resistance. The latter was an ambitious man and, based on his bad relations with the Iron Guard, he knew there was no future for him in a country dominated by Germany.

The above opinions, expressed in April and May, were confirmed by the neutrality adopted by the Romanian government under Armand Călinescu at the beginning of the war. That neutrality together with the hospitality and support offered to the Polish Government, army, and population severely spoilt the relations between Romania and the fascist powers.

Today, several decades latter, when we already know the efforts made by Romania to keep intact its integrity, independence, and peace, and following the evolution of the "Tilea case" I could not think of a better title for the epilogue than "The posthumous celebrity of a Romanian diplomat".

THE YOUNG LADY WITH ROSES

I met Martha Bibescu quite late. Actually I have never met Martha Bibescu.

It was in 1971, when Martha Bibescu was about 85, that I saw a manuscript that had remained unknown until then: her notebooks, in French, from 1939, 1940, and 1941. Everything I had known about her vanished when I first read those notebooks. They were the starting points of Martha Bibescu's *Political Journal* (that I published in 1979 together with Nicolae Minei) and of my decision to write a book about the life of that woman belonging to the Romanian upper class in the first half of the 20th century. Along the years she often showed her arduous patriotism, and more often than not expressed her disgust at the legionary movement or at the Nazis. Her fine spirit manifested not only in ballrooms or in easy talks – since she was beautiful and intelligent, a brilliant lady indeed – but mainly in her books revealing her love for her people and for her native land. Between 1915 and 1940, as an unofficial ambassador of Romania, she was an outspoken critic of revisionism, fascism, and communism as trying to help her country defend its independence and dignity.

As I have already mentioned I have never met her. After having read her notebooks I made up my mind to suggest her to publish fragments of her diary in *Magazin istoric*. I wrote to her. In her letter of April 14, 1973, Martha Bibescu replied: "There is nothing I'd like more than to see the pages you mentioned translated in *Magazin istoric*, an excellent publication". Of course, the fragments were important, but the selective translation of her notes made in the above-mentioned interval was much more important as we had in view an entire book in Romanian. I had to go to the Great Britain and I had arranged to make a short stay in Paris and visit her at her place, on the bank of the Seine, at 45 Quai de Bourbon. Unfortunately, because of flu I had to delay my voyage for a week. The very first thing I made when I was in Paris was to call her. She answered in an irritated and categorical voice "Well sir, I have been waiting for you for eight days and you have not even bothered to call and tell me you are going to be late. You are the first man in my life I have been waiting for so long".

She was about 85 and I had my reasons to believe that men had not let the beautiful and intelligent lady wait for them. However, her words proved that she had not lost either her spontaneity or her humor. I tried to apologize but she did not allow me.

"Yes, I repeat I am looking forward to working together for publishing a book about those sad years. As you probably know, I like Chateaubriand very much, but I do not want my Journal to be a kind of Mémoires d'outre tombe. And you are not very quick when it comes about meeting ladies… Let's say I could forgive you but the circumstances force me to punish you; in two hours I'll be leaving for Brussels. I have been invited for an anniversary of the Belgian royal family and you can realize that I cannot say no just because a young gentleman was late for… not eight minutes but eight days."

Low-spirited as I was I apologized once more and gave her my address in London. If she was ready to forgive me she could let me know if I could pay her a visit on my way back from London. To my greatest surprise she wrote that she would meet me on December 6 or 8, 1973, at 17.30. So she was not that angry after all.

On December 7 I was in Paris and on 8 – in an unusually cold Sunday – I went for a stroll on the bank of the Seine, not far from the Saint-Louis bridge, where the river hugs the islet with the same name. I passed several times by the impressive 17th century hotel where Martha Bibescu lived. The sky was perfectly blue and, although it was not dark yet, the full moon was lighting the spires of Nôtre-Dame, Saint-Jaques, and Saint-Chapelle. At 17.30 sharp I was ringing at the door of her flat. There was no answer. I rang again. Silence. Again, longer that time. Nothing. I climbed to the third floor and a gentleman came out. He told me "Princess died ten days ago. In a moment". Death had not arrived late to the meeting.

The gentleman – Ghika Comănești – asked me if I wanted to meet his wife, Martha's daughter – Valentina Ghika Comănești.

I happily agreed. I offered my condolences and I started discussing about the journal. We came to an understanding pretty soon. Later on I found that there was a copy of Martha Bibescu's journal in a castle in Florence with a special mention: "It will be read after five hundred years". Let's hope that the young researcher in 2473 will be in time for that meeting.

In June 1984 I got the permission of Paris Bibliothèque Nationale to consult her journal covering the World War I period. (Her heirs had sold by auction the most part of her manuscripts.) The pages were typewritten, like those I found in Bucharest, and reveal the same arduous patriotism, a genuine communion with the Romanian land, and understanding with the secret sufferings of the Romanians in the territories occupied and with the pain caused by war).

Until when all her notes are processed and the story of the fascinating lady is written we can study her more than 40 volumes, or tens of other books where she is the main character or just mentioned. Maria Brăescu, the author of an excellent book *Romanian Interferences in Martha Bibescu's Work* (in Romanian, Ed. Minerva, 1983) told me that in 1972 Martha Bibescu had mentioned her projects, all of them historical writings: the second volume of *La Nymphe Europe*, entitled *Une famille transeuropéene* was to be followed by *En Dacie heureuse*, which was almost finished. There was another book, *Napoleon vu par l'Europe* and a volume containing her correspondence with General de Gaulle. All these and many others are spread in different private or official archives in the USA and in Europe.

Let's discover together a part of the writer's soul by reading the daily notebooks Martha Bibescu wrote in 1940–1941 (in French) and the numerous notes, some elliptical, describing the dramatic suffering of George Valentin Bibescu in his last years of life. The moving pages are interesting not only for Martha Bibescu's readers but also for all those who want to know more about the famous Romanian aviator, and for all those who want to become familiar with that epoch and with its people. George Valentin Bibescu's disease started immediately after the tragic summer of 1940, when Romania experienced terrible moments of international isolation and of serious internal crises following the setting up of the legionary dictatorship and Romania entering the Nazi influence. The notes are written in a lapidary style and I bracketed some explanations when I felt like it.

Posada, Sunday, September 29, 1940

White night.

Dogs. The dogs howled the whole night! Early in the morning George came by my bed, fully dressed, ready to leave.

Very worried

"I've spat blood. I've got galloping consumption like my mother.

I beg him not to leave the house, to stay in bed, to take care of him. "You shouldn't work so much", I say. "What would you eat if I don't take care of the factory?" he asked me. I try to cling to him but he let go of me and leaves. He mentioned my "wound" [the bullet in 1927].

I called Ion [George Valentin's butler] and said "Prince told me he had spat blood all the night". Ion answered "That's true, I've found blood on his handkerchief" and added "He's very ill but he doesn't want to take care of him".

I'm very frightened and call Valentina [Martha and George Valentin's daughter] and we agree to call Professor Ciucă from Predeal. We have to go to Mrs. Petroni, who knows him, to get his address. The first serious warning. I was very worried not only because of his paleness but of his voice as well.

When he left he told me, hinting at his health or at his work "I can't stop now. My children, you still need me…"

Posada, Tuesday, October 1, 1940

George's disease.

Professor Ciucă. George was gladly waiting for him but then he grumbled because the professor, who had fallen ill with typhus in order to save the mankind in his own laboratory, could barely stand. He made a serious effort to have lunch with us at Posada today. In the afternoon, George and he retired. Professor Ciucă would make him some very serious tests in Bucharest.

In the evening, George tells Valentina "Where on Earth have you brought Ciucă from?" Obviously, Ciucă, a famous scientist, disturbs the thaumaturges that think they can cure George with injections with mysterious serums, hormones, the silver needles from China used by Dr. Costinescu, etc. George is very tired, sad, and in a bad mood.

Mogoşoaia-Bucharest, Sunday, November 24, 1940

A terrible day. George's disease. It has been lasting for four months.

I've come to him [in the Bibescu house, Robert de Flers St.] after the church.

He was in his room on the first floor, in great pain.

Hypotheses: cancerous tumor in his lungs or consumption. The house is twice profaned. The legionary persecution and George's disease.

Mogoşoaia, Monday, November 25, 1940

The good somebody you don't love does to you comes like an evil, the evil somebody you love does to you is delicious."

George is very down. He insults the doctors. I look at him and tell him with all my confidence "You'll be well soon. Your wonderful health. Remember your mother who used to say 'George is as hard as an acorn'". "Yes", he answers sadly "like a rotten acorn".

The atrocious mystery of his disease.

Mogoşoaia, Wednesday, November 27, 1940

The legionaries killed Iorga.

Weather is beautiful.

Doctor Mamulea at Mogoşoaia. We decide to ride George to the Elias Sanatorium.

I went to Professor Danielopolu, the same old friend.

The terrible verdict of Doctor Iliescu: “Condemned”.

… A summing up. Several months’ time: Paris occupied, London demolished, the horrible earthquake, George’s life threatened with death, with prison, maybe with something more terrible [see the visit I paid to Zozo Stursa]; robbed by my private archive, my activity ceases, George’s disease has got its hideous name – cancer of the lungs!

I can’t believe.

I hope and I pray with my entire hope that everything will be all right.

Mogoșoaia, Thursday, November 28, 1940

George! George Valentin!

I repeat his name in a low voice.

When I was 20 I thought I would soon leave him and I used to say “One day I will take my hat and my long walking stick and I will go somewhere far, far, far. How much wrong have we done to each other! How much sadness! We haven’t done that to anyone else!

More sadness than joy.

I used to make him repeat “Tell me I am making your life, your home, and your garden more beautiful!” And he obediently repeated.

Mogoșoaia-Bucharest, Friday, November 29, 1940

At about 11.30 I entered the Elias Sanatorium. A rather uppity doorman asked where I was going. I answered “To Professor Danielopolu”.

He showed me the way in professor’s office on the first floor. Professor received me with great kindness. He asked me “Do you want to see George?” “Of course” “Come with me. I’ll show you the way.” At the end of the long passageway. Room 16.

I enter together with Danielopolu. What a tragic sight!

George in bed, like my brother George before, his hair disheveled.

He was having breakfast.

He nodded a greeting.

The hard sadness of a silent dialogue.

Danielopolu warned me that they wanted to start blood transfusions. But they had to wait. "He has albumin, poor thing!"

Mogoșoaia-Bucharest, Thursday, December 12, 1940

Professor Auler [a famous oncologist] comes from Berlin. He comes to see Iunian [Grigore Iunian, politician, The National Peasants' Party] who has a neck cancer. Professor Auler will deliver a conference as well. We meet him and Danielopolu is glad to discuss with him about this mysterious case.

Mogoșoaia-Bucharest, Friday, December 27, 1940

An unknown intern: Doctor [Gheorghe] Comșa [between 1950–1975 a physician at "Alexandru Sahia" Hospital in Bucharest]. A vertebra is caught. Pains. A new radiography tomorrow. It must be sent to Auler in Berlin.

Mogoșoaia, Saturday, January 4, 1941

White snowstorm.

George's disease.

He told his butler "I have something that bites my chest".

My heart breaks with pain. My soul is simply ruined.

George: very weak, his red cells die. He raves. He whispers about the air line Lyon-Paris. He asked if it was opened. I said, "Yes".

Bucharest-Elias, Friday January 10, 1941

Delirium. He sees apparitions. He laughs, whispers: "Don't believe what they say… All is nonsense".

Yesterday afternoon, at about 4.30 George asked me: "Is it difficult to leave for Villejuif?" [The famous hospital in Paris]. "Not at all". He said it in another intonation. He answered his own questions. He asked Vladimir Ghica with a strain in his voice: "Can you understand me?"

Yesterday, in his delirium he said: "Ten percent soda. Orange juice – as much as I want. That has knocked the tricycle over."

On January 9: "I haven't betrayed my country. If I had done it I would have deserved to die. My children (that was the way he called Valentina, our daughter, and me), you have to do me a favor. Later." He stopped talking and turned his head to the window. Then he added with a sigh "I'm talking nonsense." And then in a more categorical voice: "At 60 I'm finished" [G. Bibescu was born on April 23, 1980).

He spoke in a very clear voice. The words were well selected. The voice was the same.

Today, a new blood transfusion. Donor: Valentina.

Bucharest-Elias, Saturday, January 11, 1941

Nine in the morning. He told me with a sigh of exasperation: "Everything presses me, pinches me, jams me."

How nice is he speaking... His politeness, his extreme politeness.

This morning he asked me twice: "Have I said 'Good morning' to you?" I assured him "Yes, my love."

Bucharest-Elias, Sunday, January 12, 1941

Yesterday he started being better. Pulse 96 instead 168. Blood pressure 15. It is a miracle.

Counter-consultation. His doctors, Professors Danielopolu and Simici [Dimitrie Simici was a famous specialist in internal medicine]. The two interns, Isăcescu and Mănescu, and the nurses find that the sickness regresses...

Bucharest-Elias, Monday, January 13, 1941

Tomorrow, a doubting Tomescu will make another

radiography. They want to know. Danielopolu doubts about the diagnosis. Lung cancer? Today George told me with a tone of intimacy that has always moved me: "You have huge qualities and huge defects!" He keeps my hand and adds: "I've been working all my life. Now, I'm working at that"(meaning his disease or, maybe his healing).

Matei and Marian tell me about the rumors outside.

I am not interested in anything but his pulse and pressure that is almost normal, 15.

Danielopolu is extremely kind and gives me a side-room next to George's room. There are two beds, one for Valentina, the other one for me.

Since January 7, this is the first time I can lie in a bed. It is very hard, like all the other hospital beds, but I find it terrific. Several times during the night I get up to follow George sleep. His breaths better.

Bucharest-Elias, Wednesday, January 29, 1941

It was bitter cold. Minus 19 degrees.

The physicians doubt. They doubt whether their diagnosis is the correct one. The number of red cells is increasing. A miracle. Another miracle. George started to eat. From the teaspoonful of water they forced into his mouth he has passed to orange juice, through a rubber tube, and from that to milk that he drinks assisted by a nurse. Then the glass of yogurt, custard, coffee. And then a soft-boiled egg, and Porto wine.

So many miracles with a man everybody thought dead 20 days ago.

Bucharest – unfortunately Elias, Thursday, January 30, 1941

White frost. It snows again.

The day before yesterday George said: "I made my contribution to subjugate the air and I suffer from lack of it now." He was looking at the oxygen flasks.

He was still under the impression of his intolerable suffering when he had not been able to breathe because of the shock produced by the first transfusion.

Bucharest – unfortunately Elias, Sunday, February 9, 1941

Yesterday they hung a large map of the Mediterranean on the whole earthquake-damaged wall on the left of George's bed, in front of the window. It is a rather rough German map, in violent colors, but that can be useful.

George said as he showed the Mediterranean area to Marina and myself; "That's my garden".

He flied around it or crossed it in his plane for so many times. I flied too with him from Brandies to Athens, from Athens to Crete, from Crete to Alexandria, from Cairo to Abajdos, from Cairo to Marsa Mateu, from Marseilles to Barcelona. Some other times I flew along to meet him, from Mariqnona to Ostia, from Ostia to Syracuse, from Syracuse to Tripoli, from Tripoli to Tunis, from Tunis to Palermo, then to Naples, then to Rome.

He was very inspired when he said "My garden!" That beautiful garden he had offered to me…

George looks tenderly at "his Africa" as lying on the hospital wall. Once he said "Benghazi" with so much tenderness as if he would have called a gazelle. Called by him, the gazelle would have come and I would have allowed her to.

Unfortunately Elias-Mogoşoaia, Monday, April 7, 1941

Leaving. With George's full agreement. With everybody's approval, but mainly with the feeling of escape, a secret escape in a way, but immensely longed for. I don't think I'm dreaming, I am dreaming.

The leaving preparations have been kept secret until the very last moment. Nobody outside, not even Marina knows about it.

After an early breakfast I helped George to put on his clothes – shirt, tie, hat that make him look like a man again. A still sick man, but a man.

When he came to Elias he was in agony, unconscious, his mouth open, his eyes closed.

"Oh, God! I haven't deserved such happiness! This departure. This coming back..."

Mogoşoaia, Tuesday, April 8, 1941

Nice weather. In the morning, Professor Simici comes to Mogoşoaia for the first time. He is delighted. George is flattered. Mogoşoaia is very dear to his soul.

In the evening he was sad. He was looking in the distance at the lakeside in front of him where the willows had started to blossom.

He told me in a very soft and remote voice: "hen hawks have nestled in the fir-trees".

His eyes are as quick as ever after so many months of suffering and disease.

His words moved me deeply. So did his eyes. His large eyes in the emaciated face. His melancholic expression.

You could say he was a prisoner who regretfully looked in the distance at the free beings, at birds.

You could say that it was a Farewell to his previous existence. He seemed to see the hen hawks nestle for the last time in fir-trees.

Mogoşoaia, Good Friday, April 11, 1941

He is in pain again. There have been no pains since he came back to Mogoşoaia.

It is depressing.

He is in pain again.

It is cold. It is raining. A proper weather for the Good Friday; a sad delight.

George starts to say again mysterious words, like for instance: "At night everything decreases, the thorax included.

Then, after a long silence, as I turned the bedside lamp on, he told me: "Thank you for the way you are taking care of me."

Those words, uttered for the first time after so many days and months, almost injured me. It was quite natural to take care of him.

He has no reason to thank me. I haven't thanked him for Bizet St. [Martha Bibescu had a stroke there and her husband saved her.]

Later in the night he told me somehow playfully: "I've worked so much all during all my life that I'm entitled to suffer now."

Mogoșoaia, Sunday, June 29, 1941

Our wedding anniversary. It was Sunday too, 39 years ago.

I was afraid I would make George sad, so I kept all my thoughts for myself. It was a kind of presentiment. He hates old age, he forgets birthdays and anniversaries; it might be a kind of protection instinct against lapse of time.

In the evening I offered him a large piece of Turkish delight that he ate with great pleasure. "Such a piece of Turkish delight is better than a beefsteak," he said. Then I could no longer resist and told him "It is my present for our wedding anniversary. Thank you for having eaten it with so much pleasure."

He looked at me, then looked at his legs and said in a very sad voice: "Something like a husband!" I answered with great difficulty: "You are alive, alive. That's all. The only thing I pray to God is to keep you alive for me."

Mogoșoaia, Monday, June 30, 1941

Great pains. All the great pains have come back. My heart breaks.

Mogoșoaia, Tuesday, July 1, 1941

Yesterday he started removing all the flowers from his room. I remember having done the same when I felt ill in Bizet St.

This morning he told me: "Take the roses away. Their smell is too strong."

And I gathered them with a terrible pang in my heart.

A little later, after a long silence he told me gently: "Thank you for the way you are taking care of me". I started crying and said, "Why are you telling that? Do you forget the way you hold me for seven long hours when I had that stroke in Bizet St.?

He turned his head on the pillow and told me "You've thanked me hundredfold". His words made me suffer.

Doctor Stoicescu came in the afternoon. He saw George and looked in perplexity at his legs. Then we came out on the veranda and he told me: "He is passing away". Dr. Isăcescu asked as if he had wanted me to hear that: "Is it a matter of months or of days?" Stoicescu bent his head and answered "Days".

Alarm and bombardments at 8.30. I came out on the veranda for one minute and the next moment everything was over. I returned in a hurry to George's room.

I was sitting close to him; he was lying on his right side. Suddenly he put his hands together in a gesture of desperation I had never seen with him. A feminine gesture. He said in a strong voice: "Oh God. What have I done to deserve such a suffering?" Then he calmed down. He asked me to give him his handkerchief and a glass of water. He kept telling me: "My little Martha. Matou, my dear".

Tears, tears, tears.

I do not even bother to hide them. I started telling him how good he was, what an obedient patient he was. He had always been so polite towards us all. He had been so brave during his illness, as brave as ever. That he had been an example for all of us; he had been kind, considerate, and very brave.

Mogoşoaia. Wednesday, July 2, 1941

George, today at 10.20. Agony. Death.

Fine, his last word, was the answer to Isăcescu's question: "How do you feel?"

Everything I have written about you this day, George, when my life comes to an end together with yours.

Shocking and gentle, revealing and sad, all these notes remind us of the famous writer and historian Cornelius Ryan and of his courage in facing darkness.

With George Bibescu, ex-president of the International Aeronautics Federation the "idea of his Romanian land was deeply rooted in his own being", as Pierre Paquier pointed out. To the end of his life, when he was very ill indeed, George Valentin Bibescu could find the power to say; "The German radio rashly announces their victory […] Arrogance, imprudence, and boast, similar to 1914, when the battle of the Marne made the hopes of France revive."

Let's close with respect the pages of the *Journal* and look at other areas of the writer's life.

There are several books and magazines in front of me. Books written by Martha Bibescu, magazines with fragments of her work. Written pages and photographs. A young woman, there is no photo of her at an older age, an ever young lady, who wrote in the preface of her first book *The eight heavens* (published in 1908 in Paris): "Although I am nothing but worthless clay I have lived together with the rose for a while". She is surrounded by roses or close to them in all of her photos. *The Eight Heavens* opens with the following lines: "The sailing vessel coming from the east has stopped by our vessel. The water is gray tonight. Long clouds darken the horizon. The sun has not set in the sea. Who has given these flowers to me to kiss them? They smell and they are delicate and nothing seems more ephemeral than this smell and this delicacy". I browse the book – one of the few translated into Romanian (besides *Izvor, the Land of White Willows*; *Lord Thomson's Destiny* and, more recently, *At the Ball with Marcel Proust* and *Political Journal 1939– 1941*). I glance at some other lines, about flowers as well: "If you live to think of roses, you will become a rose yourself; if you live to think of the passionate nightingale you will be a nightingale".

Did she think of roses all her life? Could I call her "the lady with roses?" She is known to have been a great lover of flowers. Photos show that she liked roses most of all… Here she is, extremely beautiful, wearing a fur coat and a tall toque, on the cover of her *Journal* (Ed. Politică, 1979). A fur muff hides her hands and a bunch of roses rests on her elbow. In Magazin istoric of December

1977, on page 42, a still young lady wearing a fox fur on her shoulders looks at us; on her right, on the large sash of the window a huge vase with roses; one of them touches one of her shoulders. The lady with roses. Yes, but it is more than that. You will see why.

After she passed away I found numerous sources that mention her, I found new documents or volumes revealing her personality, or I met people who had met her and dealt with her role in the history of literature and in the public life of Romania or of Europe. Of course when one wants to write about a writer, the writer himself/herself furnishes the most important data. Martha Bibescu's work is very rich indeed. But, with this writer, the study of her work is not enough. Her correspondence, the criticism of her work, and the testimonies of the people who had known her are equally important. Likewise significant are the gossip columns published in the decades when she was either in the limelight or behind the scenes of the political life. I found out that the names of the writers, artists, journalists, kings and queens, literary critics, officers, aristocracy, and intelligence service agents Martha Bibescu knew might make up an original index card that could cover about three quarters of a century of Romanian and international public life. Martha Bibescu published her first book less than one hundred years ago. Today, I guess she is at the beginning of an important posthumous literary career. The new proofs are two biographies dedicated to her by Ghislain de Diesbach in Paris: *La Princesse Bibesco. La dernière orchidèe*, and by Christine Sutherland in London: *Enchantress-Marthe Bibesco and her World.*

As Martha Bibescu was internationally very well connected, the Romanian government sent her to Turkey, in 1944, to negotiate peace with the Allies. One year later, when the Red Army entered Romania she left the country by a RAF plane. She needed then ten years to take her daughter and her son-in-law out of a communist prison. Martha Bibescu died in Paris in 1973. She had lost her fortune and fame, but her sharp intelligence had remained the same. She once answered to a leftist wondering that she took up the minorities' cause" "I'm an aristocrat, so I belong to a minority".

Posterity will never forget her. Quite the opposite. The Martha Bibescu foundation established in Romania will perpetuate her memory.

... May 25 1982. Location: General Direction of London Transport, 55 Brodway, just in front of the Scotland Yard new headquarters. I had an appointment with Sir Peter Masefied, director general of the London Transport. At 14.30 sharp, a tall and stout man welcomed me. He looked a little more tired than he was when I last saw him, two years before. In the meantime, Sir Peter had taken over the leadership of the Caledonian Airways. He told me that for the sake of his older passion, aviation, he was going to leave his first job. Then he opened a safe and took out the preprint copy of his *To Ride the Storm – the Story of the Airship R-101*. Before showing the book to me, Sir Peter told me its story.

Before getting on the giant dirigible R-101 that was to take him to India, on October 4, 1930, the British Minister of Aviation, Cristopher Birdwood Thomson, Lord of Cardington, gave a manuscript to his secretary who had seen him off to the airport. It was his memoir. In the very last moment the minister gave up taking the manuscript with him since he had realized that busy as he was he would not have had time to reread his text or to write new pages.

A short time following taking off, on October 5 at 2.00 a.m. the large plane fell down not far from the point called Crève-Coeur, close to the French town Beauvais, in the Allonne forest. The British minister and the other 48 people died.

The secretary brought the manuscript to lord Cardington's office and left it in a room where Peter Masefied (ex vice-president of the Council of the Admiralty Museum, ex-war correspondent from the *Sunday Times* in 1940–1943, then counselor of the lord of the private Seal) lived at the end of World War II. Among some dusty papers, Sir Peter found part of the old manuscript, read the text and, impressed by the tumultuous life of its author, made up his mind to gather some more data and to met people who had worked with C.B. Thomson in order to write his biography.

***

Thomson was a specialist in the Balkan issues and, in 1915–1917 the British military attaché in Romania. He was also a great friend of the Romanian people to whom he dedicated his volume of memories *Smaranda* in which, according to Ramsy MacDonald, ex Labor Party Prime Minister, Lord Thomson showed his "love for Romania".

In a paper published in the Romanian journal *Viitorul* (The Future), I. Gh. Duca revealed some less known details about Thomson, a friend of Martha Bibescu as well.

"It was during the neutrality.

In the allied legations and in the circles of the nationalist opposition there was agitation, intrigues, and incriminations. 'Brătianu is obstinate, Brătianu does not want to take action. The things can no longer stay this way. Brătianu must be forced to make up his mind.' Pressure was everywhere, more or less obvious.

In those days of utter concern, a new military attaché was sent to the British Legation, Colonel C.B. Thomson. A distinguished, tall, very lean man with a typically British figure. Energetic features and piercing eyes, betraying melancholy. He spoke French quite well, with a strong British accent, but he was rather taciturn. When he told his opinion about something he did it with unusual independence of thinking and of wording.

To the general surprise, Colonel Thomson's voice was dissonant in the atmosphere of rush interventionism characteristic of the circles favorable to the Allies.

'Brătianu is right' he used to say. 'You must not enter without conditions or without guarantees. An immediate action, at any cost, would expose the country to the greatest danger. And it would not be of much help to us. Instead of threatening him we'd better try to persuade our governments to meet his requirements. In this way the intercession of Romania could be beneficial to the development and to the end of the war.

The stupefaction was general.

Who was that officer who instead of following orders takes the liberty of having ideas?

The French legation did not try to hide their irritation; the Russian one was obviously dissatisfied, the Italians protested glibly, the opposition muttered imprecations, and respectable Sir George Barclay, with his eyes full of jovial naivete, wondered why War

Office had sent such a subordinate an assistant to him.

But for the inborn respect of the Britishers for any honest and sincere opinion, Sir George would have asked War Office to recall the strange military attaché. However, Sir George was very loyal and the logical and convincing arguments of his military attaché seduced him. Consequently, he tried to persuade his colleagues. So, little by little, the indignation died away, the pressure diminished.

In Paris, London, Rome, or Petersburg, the Bucharest legations pleaded for Brătianu's point of view. In this way, the British military attaché did an important service to Romania and if his words had been listened to we would have been spared great misfortune in the first part of the war.

I frequently met Colonel Thomson in those sad and unfortunate days. He felt that the Allies had not done all their duty towards us. And besides the sincere compassion for our fate he felt indignant remorse as well.

In August 1917, Colonel Thomson left us. I can remember him in the Iași station, leaving together with Robert de Flers and with Duke de Luynes. That time was tragic and the separation rather moving.

My emotion was mixed up with a feeling of curiosity. What would be Thomson's future? It was obvious that his intelligence, culture, and his paradoxical spirit made him a too strong personality to share the fate of his colleagues and to live for the rest of his life in a garrison or in a striped position.

When we could resume our contacts with the Western countries, I was happy to learn that Colonel Thomson had reached high and influential positions.

Back to London, Thomson started to collide with his superiors, because he showed them without hesitation their mistakes as far as war was concerned. War-Office sent him in disgrace to the Egyptian front. There Thomson distinguished himself quickly. He was the first British officer to enter Jerusalem. He was then appointed in the council in Versailles, where he played an important role in the last months of the war.

He did not agree with the conditions set for signing the peace treaty and he did not hesitate to tell his opinion. The plenipotentiaries of his country might have listened to him! For us, the Romanians he was a resolute and warm friend.

Once the war was over, General Thomson resigned from the army and dedicated himself to the politics that attracted him much more than the monotonous military life.

He became a member of the Labor Party. The start was very difficult. The House of Commons did not seem ready to open its doors for him. In 1924, when the Labor Party was able to form the first Labor government, Mr. MacDonald offered Thomson the Ministry of the Air. More than that: as the Prime Minister needed some representatives in the House of Lords, he thought of Thomson who thus became 'Lord Thomson of Cardington'. General C.B. Thomson was asked to inform the House of Lords about the title he wanted to choose. Usually, a new lord does not keep his family name, but he takes the name of the place where he was born, the name of the place his family originated, or the name of one of his estates. As Thomson had no personal fortune and no estate, and as his family lived in the colonies and had no connection with any particular place that he could adopt for his new title, he considered that 'Lord Thomson' was the only logical and possible solution. However, the Chancellery needed at least a name with aristocratic assonance besides Thompson.

Thomson had got then a salutary idea. He asked the department offices to give him the list of the aviation fields all over the United Kingdom. It was there that he could find, to his great satisfaction, among so many complicated and ugly names, the harmonious and sonorous name of 'Cardington'.

The solution had been found: Thomson's name would be 'Lord Thomson of Cardington'.

A curious coincidence: it was from that aviation field of Cardington that Lord Thomson started his last voyage. It was in the same Cardington that the carbonized and impossible to identify body of Lord Thomson was buried together with the other 48 victims of the accident.

Lord Thomson was born in India and he died on his way to India he had not seen for so many eyes and to which his melancholic eyes kept looking with nostalgic emotion.

During the retreat, Lord Thomson, in his quality of the British military attaché, had the mission to set our oil derricks on fire. During that operation that silhouetted Dantesque images against the sky of the invaded Romania, another member of the House of Commons, Colonel Norton Griffiths, assisted Thomson.

Another strange coincidence. The same week Lord Thomson died crushed and carbonized in the catastrophe of the large British plane, Colonel Norton Griffiths disappeared – suicide or assassination – off the Alexandria coast, in the blue waves of the Mediterranean.

When 'Zeppelins' attacked Bucharest, in September 1916, a bomb fell down on the house where Lord Thomson lived, in Luminei St. He was sleeping quietly and deeply, when the bomb exploded in the very next room.

The furniture flew to bits, the ceilings fell down but Lord Thomson miraculously escaped.

The following day he showed us the house and made jokes about the German planes that dared touch his British self.

Ironically, Lord Thomson survived the German planes to be killed by a British one.

Thomson played a greater and greater role in the leadership of his party. Minister of the Air for the second time in the present government, an appreciated speaker in the House of Lords, a good friend of Mr. MacDonald – Lord Thomson's career was in full progress. It was rumored that he would be the future Foreign Secretary and he would be India's viceroy one day.

In the meantime he was happy, as a Secretary of State of the British king to show all his interest to a united Romania. That was why his unexpected death in the catastrophe of R-101 wakes dear memories and well deserved gratitude in our souls.

We'd like to put some flowers over the ashes his body was turned into… The flowers of the Romanian gratitude."

***

Let's come back now to my meeting with Sir Peter Masefied in 1982. He showed me the almost 600-hundred book that was to be launched on June 15 by Kimler Publishing House. The first page reproduces a letter written by Lord Thomson to Princess Bibescu, on August 20, 1930, a few months before his accident. "I have always liked R-100", the letter opens. Lord Thomson goes on saying that entering storm and surmounting all obstacles has always been his ambition and he hopes to achieve it during his voyage to India.

In his Preface, Peter Masefied writes that there exist, according to Bernard Shaw, two tragedies in life. The former is to fail in getting what you want; the second is to succeed in getting it.

Christopher Thomson had got both of them. The present book is the story of the devotion to a cause and of the attachment to one of the most charming and gifted women of her time: Martha Lucie, Princess George Bibescu, says the Preface.

The book reproduces two photographs of Martha Bibescu – one of 1905 and one of 1929. There are dozens of references (in Lord Thomson's letters and in other documents) to the friendship between Lord Thompson and Martha Bibescu. To the end of our meeting, Sir Peter told me that a larger part of the second volume *Catch the Sunlight* would be dedicated to the relationship between Martha Bibescu and Lord Thomson.

Martha Bibescu had been a member of the Belgian Royal Academy since 1955, succeeding Anne de Noailles in that position. On February 19, 1977, after her death, the seat was occupied by Mircea Eliade who mentions in his opening speech: "I have made up my mind to emphasize a less known, but equally important aspect of her work: the way she interpreted the European spiritual tradition. As we shall see, Princess Bibescu anticipated certain discoveries of the contemporary historiography, mainly the priceless value of the popular cultures and [...] the life giving function of the European historiography, meaning that any genuine historical research reaches the conscience of the European cultural and spiritual unity."

In his speech, Mircea Eliade revealed what Martha Bibescu herself had revealed in her *Izvor, the Land of White Willows*, a fundamental work showing her ties with the Romanian land. "In fact, Martha Bibescu had discovered a very old rural civilization, rooted in the Neolithic and enriched by more recent cultural contributions", Mircea Eliade says. The famous historian of the religions continues: "having discovered that inheritance of prehistory, and knowing the daily deep and secret life of the Romanian peasants she did no longer doubt their creative capacities". (Académie Royale de Langue et de Littérature Française. Séance publique du 19 février 1977. Réception de M. Mircea Eliade, Bruxelles, 1977, p. 19).

In 1916, Martha Bibescu led a hospital for the wounded soldiers in Bucharest, then under German occupation. She was thus an important source of information for the Romanian government that had taken refuge in Iași. Zoe Bengescu, the daughter of one of Queen Elisabeth's ladies-in-waiting and Titu Maiorescu's niece, wrote in her diary on November 1, 1918: "In the latest days we have been very worried because of Martha Bibescu's, our manager, arrest. It seems rather mysterious. [...] She is such a dissembler. However, it is obvious that she is both very beautiful and very intelligent. The rest depends on time and on circumstances [...] She looked very worried when she left."

The new documents published in Magazin istoric by Ion Dumitru-Snagov certify Martha Bibescu's intelligence and determination in helping Romania during those very hard times.

Decades later we will find the same "very intelligent" and active Martha Bibescu, a ruthless enemy of rascals. Her sarcasm in speaking about the fascist leaders and their acolytes is quite annihilating. Here you are her comment on the story of Sheila MacDonald (the daughter of the ex-British Premier, James Ramsay MacDonald, one of Martha's closest friends) who had visited Germany in an attempt to persuade the members of the *Hitlerjugend* to join the British young people in an action of ... defending peace. "She was having lunch in a students' canteen, somewhere in the outskirts of Berlin, when a uniformed SS entered with pomposity and handed her a letter sealed with the Reich emblem. Hitler was inviting her to tea, in that very day. Before answering, surprised (and scandalized) she called the British Embassy to ask what she had to do. 'Go by all means' they told her, and the girl went although she did not feel like it.

When we commented on that visit we could not help deploying, both of us, the dictator's fatal stupidity. He had believed that he could take advantage of the girl's presence in Germany, although she had only come to meet students of her age. Hitler did not succeed anything but to disclose his insanity. He knew that Sheila was the British Prime Minister's daughter but he did not know anything about the wall separating the family of a British minister and the respective government. A victim of ignorance and of confusion dominating his mind, the absolute master of Germany imagined that a cup of tea offered with a trembling had (as Sheila had noticed) could solve anything and could persuade the girl.

Hitler started a long monologue and told Sheila, who had not asked anything, that he would not invade Czechoslovakia – yes! no! never! Nor Austria – yes! no! never! He overwhelmed her with explanations, with anticipated exculpation in a very high voice, complaining of all those who blamed him of having bad intentions...

When he ended his monologue, Sheila rose and stretched her hand, a gesture that obliged him to do the same although he had started raising his arm for the Nazi greeting. The girl left, fully aware that she had listened to the discourse of an insane man who could no longer control himself. Why had he felt like lying on her in so many respects? Because he had studied at the school of Bismarck who had warned 'Tell the truth and no one will believe you'. Hitler lied because he wanted to be believed."

In 1938, Martha Bibescu saw the Nazi dictator in Rome.

"Today, my young companion and I leave Rome for Athens. We have seen everything: Frascatti, Tivoli, Villa d'Este; Rome and everything that is not in Rome – even the arrival of Barbarossa (allusion to the German emperor Frederick I – 1122-1190) who, during these hard times has had to content himself to a small black moustache.

I will tell you about the Eternal City turned into a temporary city, full of fireworks and sparks that died out in an instant, of faded wreaths and carpets taken away as soon as the earthquake was over. *Terremoto*! A Neronized reception! The general rehearsal before setting Rome on fire.

I watched the arrival of the new master of Germany from behind the curtain of the room in which Napoleon's mother had died as I thought of the old Corsican woman who had been both Niobe and Cassandra of the Bonapartes."

The same year, Martha Bibescu saw the corpulent Reichsmarschal Herman Göring in Berlin, at the Congress of the International Aeronautic Federation. "Marshall Göring who made us visit, among other things, his room of thinking (Denkzimmer) in Karinhall is one of the leaders who does not think at all. To think is unhealthy and dangerous. He says: 'As soon as I hear the word Geist (spirit) I feel like taking out my gun'.

He is perfectly right, from his point of view. It is the spirit that will defeat them [the Nazis] after all."

In 1944, she answered the question asked by an Englishman who wanted to know when she started to believe that Hitler would lose. "...If you want to know the exact day, on September 20, 1939 [...] when the Polish government and everything that had remained of the marshals, ministers, diplomats, aviators, and princes of Poland withdrew to Romania, to be followed, after a short while, by the commander-in-chief and by the President of the republic himself."

That day she left for Greece and saw on the Băneasa airport the Polish military planes that had found shelter in Romania. The Government presided by Armand Călinescu opposed the Nazi pressure and refused to extradite the Polish refugees and their military technique to the Nazis. On September 21, the day following Martha's departure, the legionaries assassinated Călinescu by order from Berlin.

Following George Valentin Bibescu's death, Martha left Romania for several times between 1942 and 1944. For seven months she lived in Istanbul where she tried to arrange Romania's getting free from under the Nazi domination. "On April 2, 1944 I was again in Mogoșoaia to warn the people [Romanian politicians] that they had to sign the armistice the soonest possible. Two days later, I had to persuade my family first and then all the others who had come to see me that the future of Dacia, mutilated and torn as it was, would be different some day, when we had overpassed long and painful ordeals."

Martha Bibescu greeted enthusiastically the day of August 23,

1944. “The boors [the Nazis] were driven away and defeated, the ‘body and soul’ Nazis [the Legionaries] ran to their masters in Berlin trying to find shelter there; others forgot to take their famous green shirts from the laundress.”

Academician Al. Rosetti highly appreciated her. “Despite the immense cataclysm generated by war and by unpredictable events, a heroine has appeared, who strongly believes in the triumph of Light over Darkness.”

A character that cannot be missed by any chronicle between the two world wars, Martha Bibescu strove to support – in Romania and abroad – the Romanian historical interests. The role she played in her epoch was best epitomized by *Times* in the leading article *The Brave Princess from Romania*, published several weeks following her death. The author, Clarence Calhoum, a high official at Foreign Office appreciated that Princess Bibescu “has served her country by everything she knew to be”. Unfortunately, we will never know what she really meant for the European political life of the 1919–1940 period. “She was permanently asking something for her country and incredibly frequent she got what she wanted. She mainly succeeded not to let anyone forget about Romania and its problems”.

I could find no better conclusion for this chapter than Martha Bibescu’s own words. “Nothing could turn me into an exiled in France.” Although she was buried on the banks of the Loire River, not far from the Castle of Ménars, Martha Bibescu, through her love, talent, and devotion to her country, is a proud daughter of Romania, to which she belongs.

THE ACTS OF THOMAS

We often met and I saw him play dozens of times, but I have never considered of writing about him. When I was very young I had signed interviews with great actors, but those times were long ago. On the other hand, he liked history, but I am not interested in people who like history; I focus on those who make and write history. And then why Toma (that is Thomas in Romanian) Caragiu? Why do I feel like saying anything I know about him, resuming the few occasional lines I could write immediately after that unnatural and hideous March 4, 1977, and trying to explain again and again how much I admired him? Admiration? It was more than that. He was very dear to me.

Toma Caragiu was not only a great actor; he was also a man of a rare dignity, generosity and strength of character. That might be why nobody can forget him. More than 25 years have elapsed since his death and his presence in movies, on television, in books and on the radio proves that he is still alive in the public memory, that people need to meet him. Toma has remained a private interlocutor in the thoughts of each of us. However I do not want to speak about our thoughts, I want to speak about my thoughts only. Toma Caragiu is an obsession of mine. Maybe I feel a strong desire to write about him because I was one of the last people who heard his voice. I should be a hypocrite if I denied that that thing "marked" me. How could anyone forget the voice of a man who called you half an hour before his death, to speak to you about his plans for the future? The more so as the man was Toma Caragiu who died such a death! A death that has – surprise! – a "future" beyond it; a future we are living today.

The short interval in which we were rather close and the long years when I was captivated by his fascinating and lucid way of acting taught me, most of all, to respect Toma. He was extraordinarily rich because he neither counted his possessions nor did he enumerate the gifts he had been endowed with. He did not enumerate his defects either, suppose he had had some. He had no time. He was an actor; therefore he had to act. He had to prepare in detail each part, to arrange each masque for his face, to make his words and gestures on the scene convey what he really wanted to say. And he always wanted to say something; he had his own message that he conveyed in the only way a great actor could convey his message: acting well, acting perfectly. Could that message be put into words? I do not know. However, it embodied an immense love for people and a special kind of hatred. Hatred was an embarrassing, even boring feeling with him, but he knew that it was not proper to muffle his blessed hatred against human stupidity, obtuseness, meanness, against the innocently smiling wretchedness, or against the daily anomalies that so often hinder or prevent good intentions.

Toma, the citizen-artist, was a defender of noble causes. He always sided with the good; otherwise, his life would have been nonsense for him. It is very difficult to speak about him in the past. He did and he still does. We could not imagine for an instant only, that that exceptional man, one of the best actors of the Romanian Theater is no longer with us. That he does not, with his arms, mind, or heart, help us in the unexpected battle of reconstruction and in so many battles to follow? He who was at large in the thick of the nobles battles, he who did not spare any effort, he for whom Romania was the most beautiful of all fairies.

How could have I imagined that the short call at 7.45 p.m., on March 4, 1977 was his farewell call? He had called me half an hour before. He had invited me to visit him and I had to say "no"; I had to meet someone else. (It was another actor and, as I knew him rather susceptible I did not say any name). We had talked quite a lot – and his voice was as sthenic as ever; and his jokes as intelligent as ever; and his tenderness, and encouragement, and concern were so convincing. He told me what he had done during the morning. He had been at Titu to see an old friend – Doctor Viorel Chiriță – whose voice – attention! – had sounded rather sad the evening before. When he was sure that the doctor was all right, a bit tired maybe, he came to Bucharest a little after 6 p.m. I asked him when he would act again in *A Lost Letter*: I wanted to take my mother to the theatre and I needed two tickets. He said that on Sunday, March 6, at 10 o'clock in the morning and promised me that he would call me later. He phoned at about 7.45. He told me that it was OK; that the next evening he would be on a TV show; that he was thinking about a new tour abroad. Then he "flashed" for me some sequences of his new TV show directed by Alexandru Bocăneț. No one who did not meet him could have imagined his capacity of evoking. He could build a whole show for you, using quite a few sentences, several inflections of his voice, some pauses between words or between syllables. He was magnificent. Then he insisted again (and I had to say "no" again): "Well, why don't you come?" I did not go; Bocăneț did.

How could have I imagined that Toma would never answer his phone 16 61 48?

Years have passed. Manase Radnev (who introduced me to Toma) and Teodor Caranfil who profiled Toma on TV, Geo Bogza, Valentin Silvestru, Radu Cosașu, and Lucian Raicu with their excellent portrayals, Ion Miclea with his "Caragiu's memorable world" make me write about some aspects they did not evoke. To write about the long (and much too short) way of the artist to eternity.

First of all about his passion for history, I have already mentioned. He was not much interested in the historical phenomena, but in characters. He had read a lot and he wanted to know as much as possible about the lives of the heroes (positive or negative; more often than not positive and negative at the same time) populating history from the Antiquity until the present times. He enjoyed discussing about the politics of the bygone times and he succeeded in creating the best effects (owing to his considerable histrionic talents) when he evoked past events. Of course he could see that his listeners were watching him with bated breaths and he chose the best subjects he could interpret and those in which he was most interested. For instance, French Revolution. He acted different parts in a new play, *Danton*, he had just created for us and he was in turn a Jacobin, a Girondist, and a Montaniard. However he was not some Jacobin, or Girondist, or Montaniard, but he was Toma Caragiu the Jacobin, or the Girondist, or the Montaniard. He succeeded in being himself and someone else each time. And he made fun of himself when he watched Toma Caragiu acting the part of a revolutionary at the end of the 18th century. As he acted he could understand better and made you perceive historical meanings you had only guessed before.

Some words about his silence when he was listening. You started speaking, calmly or hastily, and he looked at you, watched you speak, and suddenly his eyes filled with a huge wonder. In his eyes you could see yourself speak. Then you had the feeling that everything you say, no matter what, is so insignificant and so ridiculous (compared with *something*, with a certain *something* disclosed by his amazed, distrustful, and finally stupefied eyes) that both of you started roaring with laughter. Well, what was that *something*? You had uttered common-sense words and he had no intention to contradict you. Why then did you have the feeling of the uselessness and of the comedy of your words?

What was that admiration of his (because it was admiration) that gradually turned into stupefaction and hilarity? Had anyone entered the room? Who? Where did he get from those eyes that annulled you, made you fly to heavens, and burst into guffaws at the same time? Was he aware (like Gogol, for example) of the inutility of words, of any kind of words versus the complexity of life that refuses *to be put into words?* Or, the very fact that you preferred to blabber instead of keeping silence and perhaps of thinking made him split his sides with laughter? You could see in his eyes that laughter grew, and grew, and grew: a grain, a drop, and a mite of laughter that gradually became a waterfall, an almost apoplectic explosion. I had the same feeling when I saw him on the stage, playing in comedies as well as in drama: it seemed to me that he was going to explode. Quite the opposite, when he was at home, he made no effort at all, he was calm, he seemed lonely, rather penitent I could say. Until when he made you explode with laughter under his eyes. Then he started to laugh as well: a non-conformist laughter, a laughter "in itself" that made fun of the whole automatism of our daily lives. His laughter expressed an entire world; it could neither be equaled nor mistaken for.

Toma Caragiu belonged to the category of actors that could

have died on the stage. When he started acting he was fantastic. The infinity of shades in his voice, the great diversity of nuances in his way of speaking, of looking, of walking were as many secret weapons of Caragiu. I was afraid that the thousand-volt electrical force he accumulated in his body when he acted could eventually generate an explosion.

Toma Caragiu was – like so many masters of laughter – a sad man. However, he subjected his sadness and never fell into self-indulgence. He, to be sorry for himself? Unbearable! He knew life and he was aware of its traps; he was not naïve. I do not know how he had been as a young man; he might have been a joyful person. I met him when he was 49 (he was 52 when he died) and he was then irreconcilably sad. His sadness was austere and dignified – a deep, and noble, and manly sadness. It was that sadness that generated his poems. And his answer to *his* sadness and to that *of the world* was his laughter. He entered eternity with his laughter and with his poems that concealed that laughter.

My head
is very large
it is larger than the unlimited
half of the Moon
it is imbecile
and knotty as well
the fault is mine
and of the darkness
I should cut it off
for a while
(you fool, my mother-in-law
will say sometimes!)
I want to rest
at least till spring
the burden is too heavy
believe me

I can no longer carry it
I complain
like Christ

on the Cross
my head is too heavy
anybody can see it
and I'm ashamed
Mother, I can swear
that I'll cut it off
'cause nothing can be said
more easily
than the truth

***

it is only You God
that can hear
my low lament
my flute is old and ill
I've got it from Thermopile
it's there that I was first defeated*

I remember Toma acting in Aurel Baranga's play *The General Interest*. I met the author quite often that period and he was in a state of febrile satisfaction. As if he could not believe it was true! And Baranga was more than demanding a man. "He is a total actor" Baranga used to tell me. "Can you understand? A total actor. I cannot think of a better actor. And I don't mean my plays only." After the first night, Baranga, who had seen a lot during his life, wept. He was crying with happiness and emotion: "I could kneel before him and kiss his hands for what he has done with my text."

Geo Bogza, who wondered "How will we welcome 1978?" best epitomized what Caragiu meant for the Romanian theatre, film, radio, and TV? How, indeed? The first New Year's Eve without Toma. I remember the 1975 TV program for New Year's Eve when Caragiu and Anda Călugăreanu were the front persons. As a matter of fact *we all* were then the front persons. After so many years, whenever I watch that program or fragments of it my feelings are as

*Poems and Other Confessions (in Romanian), Dacia Publishing House, Cluj-Napoca, 1979.

fresh as ever. Then, we all were Toma Caragiu. He was each of us! He took us with him and made us welcome the New Year together.

Our friendship lasted for three years. Thirty meetings at his place, at mine's, around the city. Thirty shows in which I saw him act. There were, I think, several dozens of films. And I watched him on TV about several dozens times too. And other several dozens times when I listened to him on the radio. I feel Caragiu will always overwhelm me. I cannot forget some moments we spent together.

He was a great lover of animals and of nature. In his small house in Periș I met Toma together with his dog, Puși. Whenever I went there I witnessed extremely tender scenes between Toma and his poodle. Toma ran together with him, spoke to him, and slept in the same bed with him. As it often happens with dogs and their masters, Puși had borrowed something from Toma's way: it had become very expansive and started acting. And with such an appetite!

Puși, perhaps the only witness of Toma's tragic end, became, following March 4, the saddest dog I have ever seen.

Dogs that destroy ugliness! It is only Toma who could have had such a magnificent vision.

Eighty thousand dogs
of Alaska
have answered the order
and started
to chew
the rottenness of the world
one hundred and thirty thousand
hungry dogs of Alaska
started
by the order of law

I also remember what he told me in the last winter of his life. It was January 1977. One evening as he was going to the theatre a man stopped Toma and told him he did not like his rather long hair.

The stranger stopped in front of him and did not allow Toma to pass. The latter asked him to let him go, explained that he had to act that evening… Nothing. Suddenly, Toma slapped that man in the face and ten minutes later, perfectly calm he was on the stage.

And another story. He once came to my birthday anniversary. “My dear” he told me “I haven’t brought you any present. But I’ll give you my necktie.” He took out his tie and gave it to me. It was December 25, 1976. Whenever I come close to that tie (I wear it each March 4), I have a feeling of piety. And each time I can hear his voice: “You behave like a child, my dear! You *are* a child!”

Again, the memory of the last phone call, when he phoned for the second time, at about a quarter to eight, to ask me again to pay a visit to him. What would have happened then if he had learned about my little lie? I can almost hear him say “Well”, but such a dramatic “Well” that I would have given up anything else to go and see him. Finally I promised him we would see each other on Sunday.

That Sunday has not come yet; but it will!

A FIERY SPIRIT

File no. 2055/1952

Bucharest Court of Justice, Popular Republic of Romania, Penal College I

Penal Sentence no. 1040

Public Session on March 21, 1953

On March 4, 1953 the case was tried of Gheorghe Ivașcu and of Constantin Salcie, guilty of plotting against peace, as stipulated by art. 2 letter c in Decree 207/1948. The Court continued the debates in the meeting of March 6, 1953 and the judgment was adjourned for further consultation until March 21, 1953 when it pronounced the following judgment:

THE COURT

On the present penal cause,

Following the public prosecutor's charge no. 507, on September 20, 1951 at the Bucharest Prosecution Department, War Crimes Office, prisoners Ivașcu Gheorghe, aged 40, office worker, born in Certești, Tutova County, living in Bucharest, at 6, Lt. Victor Manu St. and Constantin Salcie, aged 45, office worker, born in Salcia, Teleorman County, living in Bucharest, at 105 Colentina St. have been sued at law for crimes against peace as stipulated by art. 2 letter c in Decree 207/1948, sanctioned by art. 4 in the same Decree.

The prisoners are accused that, as writers, they were drafted into the States-General, the Propaganda Military Department, where they contributed papers to the *Soldatul* (The Soldier) newspaper and to the *Sentinela* magazine backing the aggression against the Soviet Union in support of Antonescu's fascist war.

Prisoner Gh. Ivașcu was a professor's assistant in the Letters and Philosophy Department of the Iași University. He came to Bucharest in 1940 and, from February 1941 till August 12, 1944 he contributed papers to *Vremea*, a weekly serving Antonescu's regime.

During June 1941 he was drafted for 45 days into the States-General, the Propaganda Department, at the editorial office of *Soldatul* and *Sentinela*. He published several papers in line with the Nazi propaganda, praising the Nazi regime and slandering the Soviet Union.

As a part-time journalist at the *Vremea* weekly, the prisoner published several papers between 1941 and 1944, in which he backed the war against the Soviet Union, praised both Antonescu's regime and the Nazi regime in Germany, showing it was incumbent on Romania to be by the side of Hitler's Germany and against Soviet Union. He showed his absolute confidence in the power of Hitler's Germany, able to establish a new order in Europe where Romania had to play an important part, but it was Soviet Union that blocked the way.

Thus he published in *Vremea* papers nos. 606 of June 22, 1941, 610 of July 20, 1941, 622 of September 12, 1941, 615 of August 24, 1941, 642 of March 22, 1942, 653 of June 21, 1942, 657 of June 19, 1942, and 652 of June 14, 1942. All the above-mentioned papers could be found in the collection of the Romanian Academy and their copies were attached to the file.

The prisoner said that he had written the papers for *Soldatul* and *Sentinela*, publications spread among the soldiers on the front, while he had been called up. The managers of the Propaganda Department used to tell what they wanted the journalists to write and then they checked up any material before having it printed.

The witnesses Ghimbăşeanu Matei, Velcescu Ioan, and Nicolaescu Gheorghe gave evidence that, to a certain extent, the activities of C-tin Salcie and Gh. Ivaşcu had been influenced by the fact that they had been called up to write for the States-General during the war.

Prisoner Gh. Ivaşcu said in his defense that he had fled to Bucharest and contributed to *Vremea* because the legionaries had been hunting after him. Likewise he had been pursued by the Political Police and by Antonescu's regime that wanted to send him to the battle line. Therefore he had had to embark on that activity, but he had been all the time in connection with the progressive circles and with the resistance groups. During 1943–1944 he was one of the editors who had contributed to the underground *România liberă* (Free Romania).

Prisoner Gh. Ivașcu also showed that he had succeeded in writing his papers in *Vremea* in such a manner that the members of the progressive organizations could realize the truth about the military operations.

According to the testimonies of the witnesses Gh. Călinescu, Gh. Vlădescu Răcoasa, and Jean Hefter, during Antonescu's regime, prisoner Ivașcu kept in touch with the progressive circles and with the resistance groups and he was an editorial member of the underground *România liberă.*

However, the above-mentioned facts cannot exonerate him, since the prisoner's duplicity made a contribution to supporting and continuing war. The particulars of charge in this case are that the prisoner served the Nazi regime, backing, both in writing and by word of mouth, the war.

The fact that he signed his papers in *Vremea* with the pen-name "Paul Stefan" while keeping in touch with the progressive circles and harboring progressive ideas does not make any less important his crime.

The prisoners' activities under the above-mentioned circumstances are crimes against peace, as stipulated and punished by art. 2, letter c of December 207/1948.

Likewise, according to the testimonies of the witness Iorgu Iordan and to the articles the prisoner wrote in the *Manifest* magazine, Gh. Ivașcu, then a professor's assistant at the Department of Letters in Iași, had a progressive activity before Antonescu's regime.

Following legionaries' pursue, Gh. Ivașcu took refuge in Bucharest where he started contributing papers to *Vremea*, the officious organ of Antonescu's regime.

It is true that the prisoner went on keeping in touch with the progressive circles and he was one of the editors of the underground *România liberă.*

As the prisoner is shy and lacking strength of character, and he was afraid of being sent to the battle line he made a compromise and contributed to the above-mentioned publications and to *Vremea.*

However, there are several extenuating circumstances pleading for the prisoner.

Considering the stipulations in art. 107 ff.

For the above-mentioned reasons

In the people's name

DECIDES

Prisoner IVASCU GHEORGHE, aged 43, living in Bucharest, at 6 Lt. Victor Manu St., born in Certeşti, ex-county Tutova, an office worker, with no registered capital will be sent to prison (under an extremely severe regimen) for five years and his real property will be confiscated.

Read in the public session of today, March 21, 1953.

POPULAR REPUBLIC OF ROMANIA
SUPREME COURT

President's Office
No. 10/2781/954
of Aug. 24, 1954

To

SUPREME COURT, PENAL COLLEGE

According to art. 413, pen. pract. I demand the correction of the sentence in the criminal case no. 1040/953 delivered by the Bucharest Court of Justice, penal College I, concerning prisoner Gheorghe Ivaşcu who was sent to prison (under an extremely severe regimen) for five years on the charge of crime against peace.

The Court of Justice lies its decision on six excerpts from the papers published by Gheorghe Ivaşcu in *Sentinela* and *Soldatul*, and also on several excerpts published by *Vremea.*

However, the decision is baseless since it started from some excerpts and the indictable papers were not examined entirely.

This way of acting led to wrong conclusions and generated false evidence.

This activity is in contradiction with the prisoner's intention to contribute in writing and by word of mouth to the support and continuation of the war of aggression and, consequently the charge according to which Gheorghe Ivașcu perpetrated such a crime is absolutely unfounded.

For these reasons I ask that the above-mentioned sentence should be canceled and the case should be sent to the Bucharest Court of Justice for a new trial, according to art. 406 pen. pract. so that a correct verdict can be reached.

MINISTRY OF THE INTERIOR

FORMATION No. 0951
Bucharest I
Office Sector P.T.T. Tudor Vladimirescu district
POB 61
No. 68 721
January 15, 1955

Ivașcu D. Gheorghe
6 Victor Manu St.
23 August district

In answer to your request to give you back the things held in Jilava, please send us:

• a detailed description of the mentioned things, their quality and wear included;

• their equivalent value in case those things can no longer be found.

Signed

I first met "prisoner" Gheorghe Ivașcu at the end of the 1950s, when he came from the United States where he had made a documentary visit to learn about the American election system. I called him on the phone and invited him to a radio program; he refused rather tactlessly. However, in the end he accepted to meet the people at the foreign affairs department for an exposition-lesson. Then, I met him several years later in a lift at the Europa Hotel in Prague. Both meetings were very short. Anyway…

George Ivaşcu's fame (increased by the years he had spent in prison) filled me with admiration, but also with a kind of fear at the same time. However, in September 1963, when we started working for *Lumea* (The World), I could feel his sarcasm, so well known among his colleagues. I did not know then that the sarcasm was one of the weapons he used to disguise the bitterness of so much humiliation and suffering endured during the prison years. The documents that open the present chapter about *my teacher of journalism* have never been published. It was rather difficult for me to get them from his beloved daughter Voichiţa Tessa Ivaşcu who treasured them together with some other things that had belonged to her father. Ivaşcu's sense of decency hindered him from communicating them, but I think they are worth being known for a better understanding of the fact that life is not white, or rose, or black, and not even gray; it covers all the palette of colors and of shades of colors.

My story starts with the moment I became part of the team trying "to give birth" to a Romanian journal of foreign policy named *Lumea* by George Ivaşcu, in memory of a similar journal published by Jean Hefter, an old journalist, in Iaşi between the two world wars.

It is difficult for me to render today the state of frenzy that characterized the whole team gathered to work for *Lumea*. (The general atmosphere at *Lumea* was also mentioned by Felicia Antip, Paul Niculescu Mizil and by Professor Virgil Nemoianu at the Catholic University in Washington DC in some of their works.) However, I think that the moment deserves much more than that.

First of all, our enthusiasm was generated by the moment itself. For many long years in Romania the comments on foreign policy could be read only in the Romanian edition of the Soviet journal *Novoe Vremea* (New Times). All of a sudden, we, who had known nothing but the "Party's word" and the voice of *Novoe Vremea* had to launch a Romanian journal. It was 1963. Mrs. Felicia Antip published some things about our life at the editorial office,and Mr. Niculescu Mizil about those circumstances as seen from the top of the Romanian Communist Party leadership. I should like to tell something about the way the things were perceived by the journalists on different papers, on Radio, and Agerpres, the more so as several of those journalists could get information from the very leaders of the Communist Party. (I have to mention here that in the time interval 1948–1989 everything had to be endorsed by the Party. The first provision governing the nation was *the communist party is the leading force in Romania.* I think that this should be the starting point of any analysis of totalitarianism and of the state-party communist system.)

According to the new political line of getting freedom of action from under the Moscow "tutelage", Gheorghe Gheorghiu Dej and his loyalists considered that a more independent international orientation was extremely important and, consequently, a foreign political journal was a must. The same had happened with *Viața economică* (Economic Life) conceived and managed by a refined intellectual, Costin Murgescu, a member of the Romanian Academy of Science.

In 1963, the time had come for *Lumea*, a journal conceived and managed by George Ivașcu.

The second reason of our enthusiasm was our manager himself. George Ivașcu had plunged into the activity of creating *Lumea* with all his ambition, with all his journalistic gift, with all his charm able to conquer not only women, but also hard to move people. It was a game he wanted to gain by all means. The very moment the task had been entrusted to him, all his journalistic instincts and all the experience he had gathered during almost thirty years became alert and he had only one aim in life: to succeed, to be the best of all. He had already been editing *Contemporanul*. If he had succeeded with *Lumea* he would have been the strongest editor-in-chief in Romania, with his two weeklies. Although he was a member of the Communist Party, his ideal was the Romanian democratic papers published between the wars, and his secret dream was *Le Monde*, later *L'Express*, *Le Nouvel Observateur*, and *The New York Times* to a certain extent.

Where was he actually coming from? He was born in a modest Moldavian family: his father had been a worker and his mother a seamstress. His father died when he was still in high school. In 1933 he graduated from the Iași University in modern philology. He was the president of the Society of the Letters and Philosophy Students and then vice-president of the Association of the Iași Bachelors of Arts. He approached communists. He met Lucrețiu Pătrășcanu who persuaded him to edit *Manifest.* Ivașcu accepted, but the paper was suspended and he was arrested for a short while. In 1936 he was a substitute professor's assistant at the Chair of Romanian Philology led by Professor Iorgu Iordan; in 1938 he became the editor-in-chief of *Glasul* (The Voice) in Iași. However, the great meeting took place in 1939 when he became an editorial secretary of *Jurnalul literar* (Literary Journal) edited by George Călinescu to whom he had been very close all his life. The legionary police arrested Ivașcu several times in 1940, the last time in November. When he had been set free, he left for Bucharest where he went into hiding till January 1941, after the legionary coup. In March, Professor Rosetti recommended him for the post of a substitute teacher at "Gheorghe Lazăr" High School in Bucharest.

In June 1941, he was drafted and started working for the papers mentioned in the documents opening the present chapter.

Following August 23, 1944 he started contributing papers to some cultural magazines and to George Călinescu's *Națiunea* (Nation), was a director in the Ministry of Information, then he was arrested, sentenced, and sent to the Channel.

Ivașcu, like many other young people in Romania or in the world, was attracted by the communist ideal and then had to pay dearly, both psychically and physically for his early adhesion. Nevertheless, when I met him and started knowing him better, I realized that he had no connection either with the ideology or with the system. When we started working for *Lumea* he talked to us as if he had been a journal manager of 1933, not of 1963. He was a little over 50 then, and his intellectual performances were at their most; both *Contemporanul* and *Lumea* were his "toys" and he would not have been able to live without them.

From the first editorial meeting, at the beginning of September 1963, and several years after that, we were part of *a show* each time we met. He was both the director and the main actor, and we answered him, contradicted him, retorted, or rejoined. Within a well-established hierarchy, the team spirit prevailed and one could resist there only if one had something to say. Our editor-in-chief did not want *extras* but *journalists*. The meetings there were quite different from all the other meetings of the kind. Everything was discussed openly and freely, sometimes shocking, and if outsiders happened to be there they would leave in perplexity.

Ivașcu mentioned "the party indications" with quite a transparent mimic and asked our opinion about the way of orienting our papers as a specialist, not as an ideologist. He used the word "forum" to speak about the party. "What else do the forums want, Sir?" was a frequent question among his assistants. Under Ivașcu's magic rod, the team at *Lumea* succeeded to inform the Romanian reader about what was happening in the world, in a professional manner and with the least possible ideological hints. One of the greatest battles he fought was to send his people abroad, to get informed there, and to have contacts, to know something about the editorial work in other cultures. I do not think I will annoy the reader if I list the names of the journalists making up the first team at *Lumea*. Ladies first: Florica Șelmaru, Felicia Antip, Ileana Nicolaescu, Anca Voican, Liana Enescu, Rodica Georgescu, Rodica Dumitrescu; the seniors: Cornel Răducanu, George Serafin, Constantin Florea, Mircea Grigorescu, Ion Cârje, Sorin Mladoveanu, Sergiu Verona, Mircea Ivănescu, Darie Novăceanu, Eugen Pop, Ștefan Augustin Doinaș, Eugen Phoebus, Roger Câmpeanu, Radu Dobre, Ștefan Bănciulescu, Eduard Spiegel; and the juniors: Mihai Matei, Cornel Vlad, Radu Varia, Radu Pascal, George G. Potra, Mircea Fodoreanu, Ilie Șerbănescu, Virgil Nemoianu, and Ionel Cloșcă.

Some of them have become international names (like, for instance Radu Varia, arts history and critic), or glories of the Romanian culture (Ștefan Augustin Doinaș and Mircea Ivănescu), or names in the public relations fields (Sergiu Verona), or in the United States academic world (Virgil Nemoianu). Ilie Șerbănescu was a minister. Many of them became editors-in-chief. Some others passed away much too early. Each of my colleagues at *Lumea* has borrowed something from Ivașcu's spirit and irrespective of the fact that they admit it or not they were under his spell.

How did he succeed to impress, surprise, or subdue you?

First of all by his intelligence. His quick thinking and his power of association were remarkable. His questions about a subject followed one after another like the rapid fire of a machine gun. During the famous contents meetings he used to ask you all the possible questions about your proposition. And, God forbid if you had not done your homework. We used to discuss the contents in the morning, after 11 a.m., in the afternoon, or in the evening. Until he had not been completely enlightened on each detail of the contents he did not rise from the long table in his office at *Contemporanul* (just across the rooms occupied by *Lumea*). Each of us could say anything we wanted, but our remarks had to be to the point. For all of us who had worked in the media, but had not been familiar to those unorthodox meetings, the pleasure was simply "perverse". I think I could call those contents meetings at *Lumea* "genuíne bathes of intelligence".

After the meetings, Ivașcu was again silent, taciturn, hurried. I can remember what he answered when I reproached him for having lost one of my papers: "It serves you right! I've told you to make copies of all the papers you give to me."

When he called somebody alone, Ivașcu was very kind and considerate. The conversation was easy and extremely pleasant. Leaving aside his cynicism and sarcasm, Ivașcu became almost imperceptibly your confidant.

However, his supreme argument was his professionalism. Ivașcu used to read each line in the three journals he had been editing since I had met him and he also used to visualize each space on a page, each title, and each letter font.

And, above all, he corrected all the grammar mistakes in our articles. He was terribly meticulous as far as comas were concerned (he had been a teacher in high school for so many years). Of course, he did not want to teach us Romanian; all he wanted was the papers in *Lumea* (that's what I know) to be linguistically accurate. He simply refused to receive articles written in a loose or slipshod style, bad wording, or those that did not follow the usual conventions of spelling and punctuation. He used to call us and we discussed the paper or the fragments incriminated. He was a bundle of nerves then. He only accepted you to come with new materials, new information, and new topics. He did not allow you to be wrong. The worst for me was when I failed to interview Haile Selasie, Emperor of Ethiopia, who had been in Bucharest for two days. He made a scene in front of my colleagues and accused me of incompetence. Thus, in a few hours' time I removed all obstacles and although I had to suffer later for my attitude, I succeeded beyond my hopes to get the interview. When it had been published, Ivașcu congratulated me and gave me a bonus. That was his manner of acting. The collection of the *Lumea* issues is the written proof of the success of several journalists in a time when freedom of the press was just a dream. However, owing to Ivașcu we started being a part of the family of the great foreign press. There were few canons and rules Ivașcu obeyed at *Lumea*.

His refrain at the meetings at *Lumea* was "the journal has to look at the world without ideological glasses, without apprehensions and without preconceived socialist ideas. We have to look like Titulescu, *à tout azimout*." Of course, Ivașcu had learned through his connections with I.Gh. Maurer and with the Ministry of Foreign Affairs about the new directions, but he pushed. Little by little he wanted us to outstrip the socialist press and if possible to break loose from it.

Ivașcu's lectures were part of our instruction. After having shown you how to "make" an article he did no longer watch over you. What made him different from all the other editors-in-chief I had known till then – leaving aside Murgescu and Dona – was the fact that he was at ease with any journalistic genre, he knew the best way each page should be arranged, and the exact place for each photo. Besides the famous Mircea Grigorescu, an old friend of his, Ivașcu was very closed to Cornel Răducanu and George Serafin. Irrespective of the countless "storms" between them, Răducanu and Serafin were his permanent concerns until he left *Lumea*. As his deputy managers, they knew his weaknesses and what he thought better than we did. His mixture of shyness and cynicism, and his capricious nature must have hindered him from showing the two journalists how much he appreciated them. Distinct personalities, class journalists, sensitive and highly cultivated men, totally honest,

Răducanu and Serafin must have regretted the "Ivaşcu moment" as long as they worked for *Lumea* after he left. And they must have remembered our famous meetings, when the imprecations and nervousness were but shades of color added to our efforts joined to turn world into a better one.

Ivaşcu's departure from *Lumea* and then from *Contemporanul* and his transfer to *România literară* turned our relation into friendship.

My feeling is that the years spent at *România literară* were, by far, the darkest in his existence. I do not want to compare them with the prison years – about which he used to speak with huge disgust – but I could see his sadness, vulnerability, and annoyance when he worked for *România literară* and I suspected that he suffered a lot. He had been almost famous for his roars of laughter, a sardonic and full laughter, an expression of delight, intelligence, and irony. He who had made fun of political situations, never of people, hardly smiled in those years. He was permanently concerned and gloomy (because of varied reasons) and, above all very tired (the causes were biological, political, and private). A taciturn Ivaşcu – that was, for many years, the director of *România literară*.

I saw that "new" Ivaşcu week by week, and it was from that special mood of his that our friendship was born. We had never been very close when he was my editor-in-chief at Lumea or when he worked for *Contemporanul*.

Ivaşcu loved *Contemporanul* and I could say he identified himself with it. He was also very fond of *Lumea* that reminded his of his youth at *Timpul*, *Vremea* and *Ecoul* (during the war). I am sure Ivaşcu was flattered to be the director of România literară, was ready to love it, and he loved it with abnegation, he was proud to edit a modern weekly of the Romanian writers, that could join the European literary magazines.

However, Ivaşcu's sadness had deep roots. First of all, the very fact that Nicolae Ceauşescu appointed him in that position. Ivaşcu was too intelligent a man not to grasp the skilful maneuver. At the same time he could not afford the liberty to say "no". His naivete (that sometimes characterizes the very intelligent or cynical people) made him believe, when he had taken over *Contemporanul*, that they had done him justice and that the communist party wanted to reward him for the years spent in prison. He had seen in his appointment to *Lumea* an acknowledgement of his professional value. Then he understood that România literară was a "punishment" for the political license he had made at *Lumea* and at *Contemporanul*. Ivașcu had got a prodigious memory and he was always ready to accept the supremacy of the great values, but he was merciless and even vindictive with all those who offended or attacked him.

After having gathered a genuine elite at *Contemporanul*, from Gelu Naum to Nichita Stănescu, from Zaharia Stancu to Marin Preda, from George Călinescu to Tudor Arghezi, and from Moisil to Daicoviciu, the director of *Contemporanul* became an "undesirable". The reasons were quite well known: he had been the director of the cultural magazine for too long; the great influence *Contemporanul* had among the public opinion; and the political liberties he had taken by publishing, among others, the apparently innocent "tips" signed al.b. that contradicted Ceaușescu's economic theses. Al.b. was Alexandru Bârlădeanu, a member of the Political Bureau of the Communist Party. Al.b's tips could no longer by published, the control over the magazine became more drastic, and Ivașcu started to understand. Under Ceaușescu he was not allowed to do what he had done during Antonescu and during the Nazis. That was why the leftist journalists George Macovescu, Ivașcu, Gh. Dinu, and Miron Radu Paraschivescu were so much disappointed. *During the war*, despite the *military censorship*, they had managed to publish papers supporting the anti-Nazi coalition and the Western democracy. Now, they realized that the new political regime they had credited forbade them to disobey the Party line and the dictatorship of the proletariat. The liberty of expression kept narrowing considerably following the moment August 23, 1944. Ivașcu, a rebellious nature used to think like that: well, sir, if I am devoted and honest with the regime, let me write what I want and how I want it because that is my job; don't come and lecture me because you are not good at anything. He used to tell me the same things when he spoke about the "forums". Ivașcu had kept his rebelliousness during his years at *Contemporanul* and at *Lumea* and tried to transplant that spirit to *România literară*, but the conditions were harder there and the Party extremely hostile. I could not say that Ivaşcu was an outspoken critic of the regime or that he was a dissident (I wonder how many they really were!). He consciously sacrificed himself, like so many others in varied cultural fields, for *România literară* to exist. The editorials he was ashamed of and the concessions he had made to the Ceauşescus were his autodafé. Ivaşcu felt that he had been obliged to choose between *Lumea* and *Contemporanul*, so that he could no longer go on with his "liberalist", "intellectualist" or "elitist" games. (One of those who understood Ivaşcu's situation was Professor Nicolae Manolescu. Following 1989 he wrote several editorials evoking the ex-director of *România Literară*, a fact that highly honors him).

I'd like to add here some lines written at Ivaşcu's death by the controversial, and talented, publicist Dan Zamfirescu, a friend of Ivaşcu's (although there existed a kind of a conflict between them sometimes). "The most overwhelming feature in George Ivaşcu's personality was his wonderful sense of friendship. One could write a genuine eulogy of classical friendship by simply speaking about George Ivaşcu. I have never seen anyone more ready to remain in the shade of some friends of the same generation and to serve them beyond his own safety by virtue of that very feeling only. Likewise he was a "people-maker", the third one in a series opened by Maiorescu, meaning that he helped and encouraged the gifted young people aspiring to a career or a destiny in the Romanian culture. In his company the most unassuming beginners felt important, and the day when they were invited to enter his editorial office was a kind of acknowledgement.

The very presence beside George Ivaşcu was a privilege, a gift of life, and a joy that explain the total devotion of his decades-long collaborators on the publications so much needed by our culture.

It was not only his peerless journalistic craftsmanship that, by a simple stroke of pen, brought to light the precious grain and taught you how to write in the future, and it was not only the warmth of his soul, controlled with irony and self-irony, with a kind of pretended cynicism under which one could guess his Moldavian sentimentality. More than anything else there was his huge energy and his endless diplomacy that prompted his actions and destroyed all the obstacles. He spent for himself not even the tenth part of what he did for a whole generation. If, one day, a volume is dedicated to him, similar to that recently dedicated to Blaga by Ionel Oprișan, everybody will be able to see the stature of the man who has left us to occupy his place in the sky, beside the people of his kind with whom he has to share what is meant to them. Beside Arghezi, Sadoveanu, and Călinescu, but also beside all those he has given a new life to in his book."

I do not want to speak here about the books he wrote or about his university life, as I do not know them well. But I have to mention his own words in defining himself: "A retrospective view of my public existence would discover, first of all, a militant journalist. Yes, I recognize that journalism was not ephemeral for me, but something very different. I have never left journalism willingly and the short eclipses that exist in my activity are not my fault."

One of the most difficult things at *România literară* was that he could not make the magazine as he wanted to – the best mirror of the Romanian literary life and information about the literary life abroad. Not only writers, but numerous journalists and artists as well contributed to *România literară*. The physical feeling of watching the birth of the magazine out of his hand and under his hand was almost obvious with Ivașcu. Roger Câmpeanu, the extraordinary editorial secretary of *Contemporanul* and *România literară*, knew exactly how that demiurgic act took place.

I can only tell what happened at Ivașcu's home, at 62 Aviatorilor Blvd. I used to go there late in the evening and sit on one of the chairs at the long table in the dining room. The Florentine table was full of texts, journals, and books. It is such a pity I never took a photo of that table that meant *România literară* in full swing of its creation. With the glasses on his nose, his face concentrated as if wanting to lunge in fencing, and the pencil moving quickly on the proof reads, Ivașcu at work seemed to play an intricate role. One could hardly imagine more legible and elegant handwriting. His nervousness could only be guessed by the way he pressed the periods and commas on the paper: as if he had wanted to reach the center of the Earth with his pencil. Ivaşcu did not write easily and he was permanently unsatisfied with what he produced. I seldom saw him contented. The few papers we published together were written under great strain. That was quite natural since Ivaşcu knew exactly what an article, a running commentary, some piece of news, a commentary, an editorial, an essay, a pamphlet or a column should be.

I acknowledged him the most accomplished journal-maker in those years. He, Mircea Grigorescu, and many other journalists between the two world wars are the masters of the modern Romanian journalism and they should become examples for the young people who invaded the Romanian media following December 1989.

The evenings I spent at Ivaşcu's place were dedicated to two topics only: reality and history; *România literară* had always been the favorite one. Ivaşcu used to listen daily to *BBC*, then to *Paris*, *Voice of America* and, of course, *Free Europe* and *Deutsche Welle*. Sometimes we listened together. Many times he called me late in the night for an extremely important piece of news.

His mind was in permanent search. The most irritated he was the least he could understand the malformations of our daily life. Ivaşcu had remained all his life a wonderful intellectual of village extraction stuck in the inter-war period. His intelligence and talent helped him to adapt himself to the new climate, but his structure had remained at the stage when he, according to Florica Şelmaru, "had entered the Bucharest editorial offices and Capşa dressed up, wearing yellow gloves and a felt hat".

A chronicle of his relations with the "forums" could be one of the most fascinating readings on the totalitarian press. He devised all kinds of schemes in order to succeed where there seemed to be no alternative: gave up names, annulled columns and sections, attacked foreign radio stations, etc. The exhausting negotiations echoed sometimes at the Central Committee of the Communist Party. Constantin Mitea, Petre Ispas, Mircea Muşat, or Ion Ardeleanu highly esteemed him and showed him all their understanding. But *România literară* was being forced into a corner in the 1980s. The protection of the people and of their names had become a kind of a crusade. Manolescu was always in danger. Ivașcu helped him more than a father could have helped his own son. I remember him telling me hundreds of times: "I simply don't know what to do. How could I save Manolescu?" Ivașcu pledged in every possible way, ranging from the emphasis on Manolescu's value to a possible revolt of the students if his column disappeared from the magazine. Nobody will ever try hard enough – and why should anyone do it – to reconstitute the whole network of subterfuges found by many of the directors and editors-in-chief during the communist regime to save the few "clean" pages. Compared with us, Ivașcu had an important biographical advantage. He had known the war censorship when he had worked for *Timpul*, *Ecoul*, and *Vremea*. I remember his emotion and pride whenever he showed me copies of *Vremea* or *Timpul* where they had introduced some democratic ideas under the very nose of Antonescu's or German censors.

One evening, in 1982, we started to classify the difficult periods in the Romanian press. The inter-war period was a free one, even if states of emergency were declared sometimes – a journal could be legally suspended, fined, or sued. But journalists wrote what they or the owners of the papers wanted. Following February 10, 1938, when Charles II imposed his personal authority, many publications were forbidden, but there still existed a certain liberty of press and of points of view. When General Antonescu acceded to power, the hard-right press proliferated and censorship was enforced. Following the defeats of the legionary rebellion and the outbreak of war on June 22, 1941, military censorship was enforced. However, the press of that period succeeded to filter through a few free ideas. August 23, 1944 brought along a new press and democratic newspapers, and communist journals as well. A new censorship, the Soviet one, started soon to suffocate the Romanian press.

In 1948–1949, the censorship system was finalized: all media started being rigorously controlled by the General Direction of the Press. For 26 years that institution had its censors for each newspaper, each journal, each magazine, each TV or radio program, for each play or film, for each book, for each exhibition or concert.

In 1974, Ceaușescu's regime abolished censorship. He knew how to win the home and foreign public opinion on his side and many other actions in the first decade of his rule proved it.

As a matter of fact the censorship was simply transferred to the directors and editors-in-chief. They bore the whole responsibility for the contents of the journals, magazines, books, radio and TV programs, shows, etc., etc. The great epoch of self-censorship had come.

As the confidence placed in the leaders of media was limited and restrictive, the party started its direct control through the press and propaganda sections, among which the Council of Socialist Culture and Education.

The control was very exigent and the limitations were higher than ever. The "Securitate" was always present to ensure the ideological, political, and artistic "accuracy" of the Romanian press and culture against any attack of the ... enemies inside and outside the country.

I remember that Wednesday evening in the summer of 1982 and the sinister classification we made while waiting for the *România literară* preprints to come. It was then that Ivașcu told me: "With all due respect, and taking into account my four-year' imprisonment, I have to tell you that Antonescu's censorship was, by far, the sweetest of all. When I think of what we have to invent today to edit our magazine, I can say that that was a piece of cake".

I was surprised by his words and I remembered that Mircea Grigorescu and George Macovescu had told me the same thing.

The incredibly high number of juggling acts he had to perform *week by week* seems incredible today. But I am sure that his closest collaborators at *România literară*, Nicolae Manolescu, Gabriel Dimisianu, Constantin Țoiu, Andriana Fianu, and the ubiquitous Roger Câmpeanu knew more, much more than I could learn in the evenings spent with George Ivașcu.

In spite of the fact that he was more and more timorous and confused, Ivașcu had remained a rebel. He often hinted at his peasant-worker extraction that had directed him to the political left, and was very proud that he had taught many "factors of power" their place. (He used to call the central institutions *Forums* and their leaders *Factors*.) It is hard to understand today that the energy he used for each issue could have been enough for a whole year.

He dearly loved the Romanian literature, the culture and history of the Romanians, the writers, journalists, and especially the students of this country. It is an error to consider that George Ivașcu wasted his time and energy in vain and that he had better resigned; he never wanted anything for himself. If he had resigned, Ana Blandiana's and Geo Bogza's columns would have disappeared a long time ago. The Museum in Focșani carefully preserves the only things dear to Ivașcu: his famous desk and his books.

When the present book was in print I found a resignation letter of April 21, 1980 that Ivașcu had addressed to Ceaușescu. Although it bore the mark of the "epoch of light", the letter showed sheer inner torture. Ivașcu referred to his poor health and also to the difficulties he had in his position. However, it was obvious that his patience had given way since in that time resignations were not accepted.

I do not know what happened to that letter.

Ivașcu remained the director of *România literară* till the last day of his life. (It was better so because, owing to him, pale pieces of information about the cultural world outside could reach us). As I read that resignation letter I remembered his pale face full of disgust for the life he had to live. In fact, when he died, Ivașcu had already resigned for a long time from his life.

Not long ago, after having finalized the volume, I read some words of appreciation made by two people having quite opposed biographies and political options. The former, Gabriel Țepelea, a member of the Romanian Academy and one of the leaders of the National Peasants' Party, mentioned Ivașcu several times in his memories inspired by the imprisonment years. The latter, Paul Niculescu-Mizil, an ex-communist leader and chief of press for many years, wrote in his *Lived History* only laudatory words about Ivașcu. Although the two approaches were different, both of them show the same respect for George Ivașcu, appreciation of his value, and high regard of his suffering. After all, he was a distinguished intellectual, ostracized in an impossible alliance with the communist power.

For a better understanding of the last years of Ivașcu's life I will quote here, with the kind permission of his daughter, Voichța Tessa Ivașcu, some lines from his last letters.

"Bucharest, Oct. 1, 1987

Dear Voichița,

I hope you have received my postcard from Bratislava. I attended there a congress of the literary critics.

I was very touched by your notes on the four postcards.

Aneta is quite well and… so am I. However we would highly appreciate if you could send us some *Gelusil*. It is the only medicine we need from you. We would like also – try not to "disturb" Andriana – some *spaghetti*, *coffee* (about half a kilo or so, some *instant coffee* included), *chocolate*, some lemon drops, and… that's all. You can add one or two magazines for me (*Le Monde*) and… nothing else. (See on the back).

We hug you and hope to hear you on the phone soon. Our best wishes to Jérôme.

G and Aneta."

Now the New Year letter of 1988

"Dear Voichița,

I am sending you the DECA records although I'm afraid they look rather worn. One is broken.

I enclose my latest book as well. (I think I have not given it to you when I was in Paris, in Oct.-Nov. 1986). I dedicate it to you and to Jérôme.

Likewise, I am sending the 1988 *România literară* Almanac and the latest issue.

Please pay 35 Fr. to the International Association of Literary Critics, my subscription for 1987. They should give you a vignette with 1987. But as you'll probably send the money by mail, Mr. Jean Dubacq will send it to Bucharest. However, it is important that the subscription for the last year is be paid.

I hug you. I am looking forward to hearing about your plans. I hug Jérôme and I wish you A Happy New Year.

G. and Aneta"

How many comments one can make on the lines sent to his daughter. I leave that to the reader.

I feel like telling about Ivașcu's last voyage abroad, as there were a lot of rumors. In April-May 1988, Ivașcu asked me: "What do you think? Shall I go to Warsaw to a Congress of the International Association of Literary Critics?" I advised him to consider it. I knew he was not quite well. After a few days he told me: "I've made up my mind. I'm leaving. What do I have to do?" I told him about the procedures he had to follow (Ivașcu hated all the red tape he had to go through for getting the required permissions and visas). He finally left. At the Congress he caught a cold and made a serious pneumonia. He was quite alone in a hotel room in Warsaw.

From Poland he wrote to Voichița a letter that arrived in Paris after his death. I learned later that one of the reasons he made that voyage for was that he wanted to write to her a *freer* letter. One cannot realize from that letter how close his end was.

"Torun, June 11, 1988

Dear Voichița,

I am in Torun, an old Polish town, where I attend an I.A.L.C. Congress about *Literary Critique and the Reception of the Foreign Literatures*.

On Monday morning I'll fly home by a Polish plane. Aneta is waiting there for me as usual. She is not very well (rheumatism, liver) and is even frailer than she used to be (less than 50 kilos). Her age and all the housework she has to do are beginning to tell on her.

We are thinking of your situation all the time and I am sorry I cannot help you.

Mrs. *Madeleine Gobeil* has attended this congress. She is *Responsible-Promotion des arts* and represents UNESCO.

I am writing this letter from Poland because it is easier and I'm under the impression of my meeting with this special lady.

I hug you with all my love.

I send my *très amicalement* greetings to Jérôme.

You'll probably have to pay the I.A.L.C. subscription for 1988.

In autumn, if you have the opportunity, please send me after-shave, a Rexona antiperspirant, and, perhaps some of the medicine you have already sent. That's all!

P.S. And lemon drops.

George and Aneta"

On Monday, June 13, 1988, Ivașcu collapsed in the arms of his sister, Aneta Ivașcu, his guardian angel for almost all his life. Dr. Voiculescu, our friend, came in a hurry and he diagnosed double pneumonia and all the signs of a severe heart effort. He insisted for immediate hospitalization. Ivașcu's rebuff made the doctor prescribe home medication. Ivașcu had already suffered two heart attacks and I had been with him in both occasions. Professor Victor Nicolaescu, a man of exceptional discretion and kindness, treated the first one, in 1984. It was Sunday afternoon and Victor Nicolaescu went to hospital to see Ivașcu and to ensure the best conditions for him. When Ivașcu left the hospital he was smiling and confident in the powers of medicine. The second time, it was New Year's Eve, 1987. He was admitted in the Elias Hospital and he was lucky again. Now, the third time, the situation was extremely critical, and Professor Voiculescu, a man of rare clinical intuition, expected fatal heart complications. That was why, the following days he insisted for a new hospitalization. But something seemed to have happened to Ivașcu. He refused again. He seemed to have been fed up with suffering. Although the conditions had been quite good, the previous stays in hospital had humiliated him. He did not like people to visit him. He listened to the doctor's advice; he also listened to what his sister told him to do. Until the evening of June 20, 1988 when, after the football match Great Britain-Argentina, that he had watched with much interest, he entered the last bend of the track of his life.

In the night of June 20-21, 1988, a great lord of the Romanian press, one of the fewest who had known how *to make* a journal, passed away.

(Several years before, after having read the manuscript of my first edition of *A Trip down Memory Lane*, Ivașcu made me certain recommendations and told me, with a unique mixture of cynicism, misanthropy, care, and tenderness: "What's the matter with you?

Why do you want to come up against them? Can't you see what's happening?" His words vexed me and I replied instantly: "You know why". After a few weeks he told me that he did not want me to draw the attention on him in my chapter about Mircea Grigorescu. I understood him but I published the book as it was.

In the morning of June 21, 1988 I made a promise to myself: Mircea Grigorescu will not remain the only journalist in *A Trip down Memory Lane*. I owe these pages to him for *all* he meant to me and for the confidence with which he encouraged me and taught me *how* to make a journal. Therefore I have written them "with all due respect" as he used to mock the grave notes of our conversations. Nicolae Iorga's words are as true as ever: "He who forgets does not deserve".

THE OLD MAN, THE SEA, AND THE MOUNTAINS

"On November 20, 1895, Fate filled Alexandru Rosetti's crib with a lot of gifts, but Goodness was the dearest one to him. The member of the Academy, Professor, and literate who left our world on February 27, 1990 took, with a huge inner power, the chance of being good: in all periods and under all dictatorships he offered as much help as he could. Goodness accompanied Alexandru Rosetti all along his life: from the peasants to whom he used to give food in his childhood, to his students who became famous later on. All his life he administered Goodness. His severe and accurate value judgements were always balanced by his Goodness. At the meeting organized at the Academy with the occasion of his 90th birthday, some of the instances were reminded when he saved people and institutions. But they are more, much more.

I give evidence – and everybody who knew him can do that – that Alexandru Rosetti used the telephone only when he could not move. Otherwise he used to go personally to all kind of authorities, sometimes frightening ones, to plead the cases of the other people.

He endured outrages (he was expelled from the University – once by legionaries, in 1940, then by Stalinists, in 1952) and injustice, but he could always find support in the endless power of his Goodness.

When he passed away, Alexandru Rosetti left us not only his *History of the Romanian Language*, all his philological studies and his literary writings, not only his vast correspondence, but also (according to Zoe Dumitrescu-Bușulenga) 'an entire epoch of Romanian culture'.

He left us the example of a life always guided by Goodness in a century and in a world tortured by wickedness. His wise smile seemed to encourage us: 'be good, be kind, and help your fellow people'."

I wrote these words under the overwhelming sadness caused by the tragic death of Professor Alexandru Rosetti. I published them in *Adevărul* of February 28, 1990 and now, more than eight years later, I think they can open the chapter about this man-locomotive of the Romanian culture in the 20th century.

I add now the following pages written when Professor would have been one hundred years old and his ex-student, Mrs. Andriana Fianu had the excellent idea of publishing, together with some friends and disciples, an evocative volume.

Here they are:

"What are you doing Professor?"

"Well, I write, I read! I read, I write!"

The above dialogue repeated day by day (excepting of course the periods when he or I were not in town) became a kind of rite. It was followed by the evening visits, usually after 10 p.m. At about 11 p.m. he used to prepare his coffee – a big cup – he would drink at about midnight.

It is said that young people are a comfort for older ones. With Rosetti, about 40 years older than me, it was exactly the opposite. He was a comfort for me. Always young, always wise, always lively. He, the eternal naïve, the eternal confident, the eternal enthusiast.

Some of the people of my generation kept telling me: "Why do you go to Rosetti? You are not a philologist, you are not a linguist, he can help you in no way". I did not go there to be helped or to help him. I went for the simple pleasure of a chat, more and more difficult to find anywhere else, and for the delight of listening to his words.

However, I most admired his nonchalance and his lack of awareness in taking the risk of being good.

It was in 1954–1955, after he had experienced the difficult recluse imposed on him by legionaries and then by communists (although he had been rather close to them). The department of foreign policy at the Radio, where I worked then, sent me to invite him to a program about peace. He received me, following a lot of telephone calls, in a winter evening in the old house at 56 Dionisie Lupu St. He looked at me rather severely, listened to me and said "no". I realized that he had no confidence in…fight for peace.

After 15 years, at the beginning of the 1970s, our relation suddenly started to develop and went on like that until the end of his life.

The hundreds and hundreds of evenings we spent together were as many stories about people who had lived long ago, about his family, his books, tragedies of life, and funny things. But as he never wrote about them I have no right to do it.

The most I can do is to disclose here and there some fragments of what he told me.

I shall give below some "samples" of letters I received from Rosetti.

Buc., Nov. 9, '73

Cristian Popișteanu
Buc.

Dear Mr. Cristian,

I highly recommend to you a distinguished young man who wants to work for *Magazin istoric*:

Mihai Hotea, a graduate from the Faculty of History, Latin and Greek (the son of Mrs. Hotea, a well-known professor of Latin and Greek).

He is a man of high quality and *very honest*!

He works for *Flacăra* now but he prefers your Sorbonne!

My best wishes

Al. Rosetti

Cristian Popișteanu – *Magazin istoric*

Bucharest, April 9 '84

Cristian,

– *Zevedei Barbu*. A smart boy. I met him several times when I worked for underground. After August 23 he left for England where he became a teacher (economist). Does he still live?

His address (if possible!)

Al. Rosetti

Marie Lamenciu!

Fr. Rainer's notes!

Al. R.

Jan.2 '86

Christian,

Thanks for *Le nouvel observateur*, a magazine full of life, written finely! Nice and instructive reading. (The sexy section well represented.)

P.S. *L'Express*, p. 55. Cioran's new book. *Maybe you have it!*

Rosetti

However, the "export" of his students had become the leitmotif of our evenings. Permanently he intervened on somebody's behalf to try and get a visa for them. Rosetti told me that in 1948 he wanted to get a passport for George Brătianu. He almost begged Brătianu to leave, on several occasions, but the latter's final reply was: "Dear Sandu, you know quite well that a Brătianu never leaves his country willingly. No, I am not leaving".

From then on, Rosetti kept persevering in using his influence to obtain passports and visas. I was there on several occasions and I can tell what he did to achieve his aim. First of all he called the President of the Romanian Academy, then the minister of Education or of Culture, as the case was. Then, if the situation was more difficult, he approached the "higher structures" – Ministry of the Interior, Central Committee of the Communist Party.

He had the direct phone numbers of all the bosses at the "passports" and, in the last years, when Elena Ceaușescu started keeping a tight rein on all the institutions, he called them. "Rosetti speaking". "X has to travel to that country". "He has to go by all means. He has to get a visa". "Good bye. Thank you."

He pretended he could not hear very well (that was partly true) and ended the conversation with no other words. If he did not succeed, he used to call again in a day, in a week…

I think that dozens of intellectuals left forever or for a while following such a tempestuous phone call from Rosetti.

Therefore, besides all Rosetti's qualities one more could be added: the risk he took of helping really talented people, mainly young ones, to create in a free world. Nothing seemed to be more important to him than the freedom he was expecting and nothing

helped him more in his expectations than his goodness.

To the end of 1989 he kept asking: "When? When?" I used to answer: "Soon", but he always replied: "Yes. But I have no more time".

The freedom finally came, but he was in the hospital then. Although he suffered a lot, when death came he was serene, reconciled, and confident.

I often think of Professor Rosetti and I should like to reveal some more things about this lord of the Romanian culture. As I cannot venture into judging his scientific work, I should like to write something about this man whose death, in spite of his 95 years, was extremely tragic.

Old Mr. Rosetti burnt in his own old house following a logical succession of unhappy and happy circumstances. In the last years of his life Professor Rosetti felt very cold. As a matter of fact he shivered with cold, similarly to almost all the inhabitants of Bucharest, subject to a chronic lack of heat, light, and food in the 1980s. The old house of the Rosettis, at 56 Dionisie Lupu St., had very large and tall rooms, impossible to warm in those hard times. Professor suffered a lot. Brave, proud, and stoical, he was never obsessed with his own self as it so often happens with old people, almost entirely concerned with their own needs. He used to drink a lot of tea and warmed himself keeping the hot cup in his hands. All kind of attempts to make the room warmer! Nothing worked. Until when his friend engineer Horia Cosma found an electric radiator for him. In that very day, Rosetti simply came to life and he became as alert as usual: like a big and kind bear, forced to hibernate in cold, hunger, and dark, that suddenly felt warmer and started to relax.

In the last years of his life, Professor came out very seldom, and in winters – extremely seldom. The radiator meant genuine holiday and restored the spiritual equilibrium in the old house. However, Professor was afraid of cold. As a matter of fact his fear was part of the general fear that had been invading us all for long years, dominating our minds, actions, and gestures in a hide-and-seek game. But with Rosetti that fear was fatal. He was home again after a severe heart attack that forced him to spend Christmas 1989 and New Year 1990 in the hospital. He felt exhilarated with joy, made plans for the future, thought of his everyday work. In that euphoric state, one night he pulled the radiator closer to his bed, although that was no longer necessary; he fell down with the radiator over it and a large part of his body was severely burnt. A terrible accident and a tragic story.

Now, when he has passed away, the researchers have to turn to account an immense heritage made up of hundreds of studies and papers – many of which fundamentals of philology. On the other hand, our duty, of the people who accompanied him for longer or shorter times in his life, is to reveal something about *him and his life*. Rosetti is much more than *A History of the Romanian Language* and *A History of the Literary Language*. He is not only *Romanian Christmas Carols* (1920) and *The Philosophy of Truth* (1980), and not only *Travel Notes* or *The White Book*.

Alexandru Rosetti also means George Călinescu's *A History of the Romanian Literature from Its Origins up to the Present* since, in those miserable times, Rosetti edited the book at the risk of his life. One of his favorite students (Marius Sala) said, on March 2, 1990, at Professor's incineration ceremony, that Rosetti had told him once that if he had succeeded to edit just *A History of the Literature* and nothing else all his life, he would have considered himself a very lucky man.

Alexandru Rosetti also meant Tudor Arghezi, Ion Barbu, Camil Petrescu, Mircea Eliade, Geo Bogza, Emil Cioran, Nae Ionescu and many others whose works he had edited in the publishing houses *Cultura Națională* and *Fundațiile Regale*.

Here you are George Călinescu's words characterizing Rosetti: "A member of the large princely family of the Rosettis, Al. Rosetti (b. Oct. 1885, son of Petre Rosetti and of Zoe C. Cornescu, married to Maria I. Rallet) is one of the most interesting figures of our literary life. His influence is very deep and will be serenely recognized later".

Prophetic words written about 60 years ago in his peerless *A History of the Romanian Literature* by George Călinescu who used to tell Rosetti: "The editor, even the noblest one, such as you are, does not live by himself but by his devotion to the writers of his time".

About himself, Rosetti said that: "As an editor I have looked for the new and for the private formula of each author, and I have also tried to publish our classical writers in critical editions". He told that to Liviu Călin, a writer and a critic, one of Rosetti's favorite students, who, unfortunately passed away much too early. It was also to Liviu Călin that Professor left many of his memories and manuscripts. He showed us some revealing dedications.

On *The Last Night of Love, the First Night of War*: "To Mr. Al. Rosetti, editor of the Romanian literature, with whom even the controversies have got charm and delicacy, this first copy of the book I would have liked to dedicate if he had agreed", Camil Petrescu, November 7, 1930. On *Mould Flowers*: "To Mr. Al. Rosetti, the repetition of words repeats the sound of souls", T. Arghezi, April 9, 1931. On *A Paradise of Sighs*: "To Mr. Al. Rosetti this collection of sighs wished and cared for by the editor as plants in a greenhouse, with all their author's gratitude", Ion Vinea, January 12, 1931. On the essay *Ion Barbu*: "To Al. Rosetti, who wanted this book and made it possible, to my unique friend with all my love", Tudor Vianu, March 19. On *The Dark April*: To Professor Al. Rosetti, a remarkable scientist, to the unique nobleness of his soul, the respectful homage of the author who settles an account with ghosts in the present book", Emil Botta. On *A History of the Romanian Literature from Its Origins up to the Present*: "To Mr. Al. Rosetti – a beloved accomplice to this book", G. Călinescu, 10.IX.1941.

I purposely left Călinescu's dedication to the end because it was Rosetti who saw, for the very first time, the huge breadth of the critic. When *Mihai Eminescu's Life* was first published, Rosetti welcomed it with the following words published in *Mișcarea* (The Movement) on May 6, 1932: "Călinescu's flexibility, his intelligence and his deep understanding of deeds and people make him the most adequate man able to give us a history of the Romanian literature populated with people and not with shadows".

At the same time, Alexandru Rosetti focused the connections with important Romanists all over the world. They all valued him, respected him, and loved him. At the beginning of the 1980s I made a voyage to Scandinavia. He called me and gave me an important message to the "patriarch" of the Swedish Romanics, Alf Lombard, and to his disciple Eugen Lozovan in Denmark. He asked for support for the Romanian philological sciences that were in great difficulty as the dictatorship in Romania was harder than ever. Likewise, Rosetti highly appreciated Eugeniu Coșeriu with whom he had been in touch all the time.

Rosetti crossed the Earth at a steady pace, like a mountain man, initiated in the long race of life. First of all through his scientific work as a famous linguist. Then by wandering through the fields and forests, along the banks of the rivers and in the mountains, all over Romania. And last but not least through his presence in different places on Earth: in Europe, Asia, Africa, North and South Americas. Al. Rosetti integrated people and places – Romanian and foreign alike – into his affective universe. His texts bear the mark of classicism, a characteristic of the inspired and hard-working editor of so many styles who brought to the modern time the tradition of some famous old publishers like Coresi or Șerban Cantacuzino.

He met so many heroes of the Romanian culture of the 20th century (from Sadoveanu to Arghezi, from Mateiu Caragiale to Mihail Sebastian, from Camil Petrescu to Ion Barbu, from Gheorghe Călinescu to Constantin C. Giurescu, from Miron Nicolescu to Gh. I Brătianu, from Tudor Vianu to Mihai Ralea and so many others); he was related to the great spirits of mankind (Michelangelo and Tolstoy, Rabelais and Wilde, Voltaire and Gide, Kafka and Hemingway, Camus and Rimbaud, Hugo and Michelet and with so many others; he meditated near the monuments of Greece, Italy, India, Israel, Brazil, Romania, Russia, Germany, Africa, Albania, the United Stated, or Great Britain. On all those occasions he used to send to the readers the signals of his deepest respect and of his great love for the genius of the human creation, the only witness of the time passing by.

His attitude was that of a classic.

A page written by Rosetti remains in one's memory even after a long time. Why? Owing to its perfect equilibrium – the main characteristic of his whole personality, the unaltered source of his unusual vitality in permanent search of new horizons and able to fight incessantly for the needs of people and of science.

It was the same equilibrium that always led him directly to the point when he spoke about people, situations, and places as the associations populating his imagination spread around an evoking fragrance that seemed familiar and proper to us.

Al. Rosetti used any opportunity he had to pay homage to life and always expressed his full emotion in contact with the new, faithful to his own words published in an interview about thirty years ago: "If I were to live again I should follow the same way".

Alexandru Rosetti deserves praise for his *daily* strive to help someone, to save something, or to repair some injustice. He never had any other power than that of his value, his intelligence, his perseverance, and his optimism. His authority as a head of a publishing house or of an institute, as a dean or as a rector at the University had intellectual fundamentals only, not administrative ones. Through his deeds and his work alike, Al. Rosetti helped Romania and its people in the hardest times.

A younger colleague of mine, Ioan Lăcustă from the State Archives in Bucharest, found a document on the visit of a Romanian delegation in USSR. I will quote below what Rosetti told me, on several occasions, about that visit. He broached the subject on February 20, 1974. I will write my notes below.

In December '45, I first heard from Pătrășcanu that I was a member of a delegation that would go to Russia. He told me that we had to prove to the Russians that we were their friends. After the New Year 1946, they called us to the Foreign Affairs and to the Academy and explained to us what was all about. It was an "information visit" and they told us again that we had to prove to the Russians that we were their friends and that we respected them. Before leaving we were called to the Soviet Embassy on Kiseleff Blvd. Great joy there: we were a delegation of the Society of friendship with USSR, after all.

Most of us knew one another. There was a beautiful woman with us, Dora, the wife of Egizzio Massini, director of the Opera. We were curious to see what would happen.

We traveled by train for about two or three days. It was like a voyage in the unknown. Large areas covered with snow.

Iordan was at the Embassy and he met us in Moscow. He had

arranged everything. It was a very important visit, Iordan explained. To persuade Russians that we wanted to go by their side.

The hubbub started. They took us everywhere. Excellent receptions. Excellent pictures. Excellent meals. But I also saw great disasters caused by war. I met there a lot of distinguished Russians and some superb women.

About two days before our departure we were told that Stalin would receive us. None of us knew what we were supposed to do. Iordan advised us to be sincere and respectful. The way from our hotel to Kremlin was quite unusual. Dozens of checks. Young and elegant officers. Stalin's secretaries were extremely polite.

When I saw Stalin I couldn't take my eyes away from him. He was short, very short. He was in sharp contrast to his photo; he seemed quite old and ill to me. However, our blood ran cold. He was courteous to Romania, was drawing something on a drawing block in front of him, and when he looked at one of us I could see how concentrated he was. We shook hands with him when we came and when we left; he did not smile at all and was very attentive. All of us had the same feeling: our blood ran cold."

Each time Rosetti remembered that first meeting with Stalin he mentioned that feeling.

I will give below some of Rosetti's deeds meant to support the Romanian culture and its people.

The diaries of King Charles II, of Queen Mary, and of Princess Martha Bibescu, of Constantin Argetoianu, and, more recently of Mihail Sebastian mention, as far as the 1930s, Rosetti's tenacity in launching young writers, many of whom later glories of the Romanian literature.

When General Antonescu ascended the power, a series of literati and scientists underwent great suffering. When Rosetti heard that his colleague Alexandru Graur had been arrested, he went to General Antonescu himself and he insisted until Graur was set free. Graur confessed in the meeting at the Academy dedicated to Rosetti's 90th birth anniversary that his release from prison had been "like a resurrection" for him. Some more quotations from Alexandru Graur: "Professor Al. Rosetti was very well connected and everything he suggested was listened at. He used to intercede for anybody was in trouble and he got what he wanted. On several occasions I asked him to help party members and he did it. He helped me as well. One morning I was arrested and taken to the police. They wanted to send me to a concentration camp and I would have been in Vapniarka from where I would not have come out alive. Comrade Rosetti went to the highest official there and he ordered his men to set me free; by noon I was at home."

Alexandru Rosetti invited me quite often to accompany him to lunch at The University House or at Capșa, at "Doi Cocoși, or at C.O.S. On those occasions he used to show his undisguised pleasure. Rosetti was the man who mixed a speck of sacerdotalism and a lot of joy in everything.

Once he told me what I already knew from Professor N.Gh. Lupu.

When the communist regime wrested the power, Rosetti learned that the future "party administration wanted to take over the park and the house in Dionisie Lupu St.". He started then campaigning for getting them for the professors and the staff of the Universities in Bucharest. When he finally succeeded, Rosetti inaugurated there The University House and became its first president. But the troubles and difficult years were to come.

Another case of Rosetti's solidarity and dedication.

At the beginning of the 1980s, the dreadful Office 2 (Elena Ceaușescu's) interdicted the publication of the scientific journals of the Academy in a cynical and stupid attempt to isolate and destroy the Romanian science and culture. Al. Rosetti had then the guts to start a crusade for saving those journals – the only journals where the scientists could publish the results of their research, but also the only exchange base with similar journals abroad. He even sent a card to Office 1 (Nicolae Ceaușescu's) with the words *SOS, Romanian culture* on it. That action of the old Rosetti (alongside the unthinkable efforts made by lots of other intellectuals to stop the disaster) proved to be salutary. In the same meeting at the Academy organized for Rosetti's 90th birth anniversary, the "miraculous effect" of that intervention was reminded as well. Professor Radu Voinea said then: "Just a few of us know that the words *SOS – Rosetti* saved not only the philological journals, but all the other ones for which we had not been able to do anything in spite of long-week discussions."

In fact, *SOS – Romanian* culture was the banner under which Alexandru Rosetti fought under all the dictatorships, but mainly under Ceaușescu's regime that attempted to annul our history by annihilating our culture in the first place. It is incredible how much energy the old man in his eighties used to send specialists abroad, to get the approvals for the Romanian delegations to participate to Congresses abroad, and to edit important books.

For a long time, for several decades, Al. Rosetti had no longer been just a member of the Academy, a professor, or a writer. *His name had become an institution.* I saw him many times pick up the receiver and speak for people, for books, or for ideas in a loud voice as trilling his r's: "Rosetti speaking". Of course his interventions could only cover the field of philology and they could not stop the cavalcade of the evil. Such was the case of the Center of Phonetic and Dialectal Research the director and founder of which was Rosetti. The Center had been dissolved by the Ceaușescu regime in 1970 and Rosetti had made over 200 interventions in 20 years to re-establish it again. He was happy to write the last one (the below document) as he knew he would succeed that time:

"To

Romanian Academy

Bucharest

I am addressing myself to the Academy, of which full member I am, with the request of taking into account the two notes sent by the staff of the former *Center of Phonetic and Dialectal* Research improperly dissolved by the Ceaușescu regime.

I have already sent a memo to the Academy, with the request of establishing an *Institute of Phonetics and Dialectology* instead of the former Center.

The re-establishment of this scientific institution will allow the resumption of the research work and publication of the papers in the journal that has been appearing for 38 years!

Acad. Al. Rosetti
36 Dionisie Lupu St.
Bucharest;tel. 11.34.78

Bucharest, Jan. 31, 1990".

The note was written just a few days before his accident.

Following the decision of the Romanian Academy of February 24, 1990, the *Institute of the Phonetic and Dialectal Research* was established (now Al. Rosetti Institute).

You have won Professor!

The revolution of December 1989 gave him his peace and his confidence back. In the last two months of his life he was very ill indeed but he was in a state of high spiritual loftiness. In the last years he used to ask me a question meant to have no answer: Why? *Why do we have to suffer so much?* In August 1989 he simply said to me: *I do no longer have time. It's a pure rhetorical question. I'm 94. My heart is weak and the by-pass is no longer enough. That's why I ask you, because I wonder 'When'. When will he fell down? I do not want to die before that.*

He overlived – in hospital, it is true – the dictatorship and he was lucky to see Romania's revival.

There are so many things I could write about Rosetti, about his love for his wife Maria, for his son Gheorghe, who had remained an eternal *boy*, and for Maria, his daughter-in-law, about his exuberant friendship with Gheorghe Brătianu and with Petru Dimitriu, with Alexandru Balaci and Valentin Lipatti, with Eugen Barbu and Sanda Golopenția, and with many others.

That is why, at the end of these pages a question keeps pushing me: Who will be the literary historian or the writer able to offer to the public the book about Al. Rosetti's life? In any case, the author should understand this man, a genuine democrat, that gave his wealth (similarly to his father) to the people and lived then the deception of the communist dictatorship, a leftist who helped a lot of people opposing the left, a friend of all the great Romanian writers, a guest of all the Romanian kings and dictators, devoted to Florence and in love with Paris, a traveler through the Romanian mountains and forests, an inveterate townsman overwhelmed by the nostalgia of the Black Sea, a famous Epicurean and a rigorous scientist, the man who discovered Mircea Eliade and Camil Petrescu, and a total adept of universality of history. A great lover of Good, Beautiful, and Equilibrium. A European with one country only: the Romanian language and culture. A noble subject and a difficult task indeed.

THE HUMAN ADVENTURE IN THE 20TH CENTURY

Each morning, for long, long years André Malraux has been looking at me from the cover of a book in my bookcase. It a mature Malraux, looking straight in your eyes, smiling casually, and pointing his forefinger at you. A half-joking, half-severe gesture: attention, another day has started! Take care not to waste it, not to let it pass without doing something good, something you have to do. It is a somewhat filtered smile, deeply engraved in the physiognomy of his face. It is an accomplice's smile at the same time. Malraux, his face propped against one of his hands, looks at you as if wanting to warn you smilingly. Nevertheless, that is a less severe Malraux than the one I met, with incandescent eyes and a waxen face, his brown eyes darkened by the force of his spirit.

"*A life is worthless, but nothing is worth a life*", his eyes, his forefinger, and his whole face seem to say from the photo. His words are worth being known by everybody as hundreds of thousands of possible deaths are on the watch in one's lifetime.

During my teens, shared between building sites and hospitals, André Malraux was the only writer whom I considered tangible and human in spite of his genius, grandeur, and distance. I first read La *Condition humaine* with a dictionary, in a sanatorium, in a very hot summer syncopated by haemoptises, when I was 16; I re-read it about ten years later, in the same hospital room no. 18 in which I am writing now. It was only in February 7, 1967 that I met Malraux in the flesh and from then on he has remained very close to me through all his books, be they older or newer. However, he has remained alive in my memory owing to the first, second, third, fourth, and fifth audience-talk we had. They were audiences, but the way he received me and the way we talked were not punctilious at all; they were rather visits to a friend. So…

THE FIRST MEETING

I was in Paris for the first time and I obviously wanted to meet Malraux. I had just come from a very interesting voyage in the Saharan oases, in beautiful islands, and in the places where Caesar had first stepped when he had gone to Africa, or wherefrom Hannibal had started with his army to frighten the Romans. In the very first day I succeeded to arrange a *rendezvous* with his private secretary, Marcel Brandin. It was neither easy nor simple to reach Malraux, then a minister. That was why I approached him from two different directions: through Jacques Fauvet, the then editor-in-chief and later on the director of *Le Monde*, and through Geneviève Tabouis, the famous Cassandra of the inter-war period. Thus, I succeeded to do it very quickly.

Suddenly, Paris had become for me just the background of my meeting with Malraux that had to take place at 3 p.m. on February 7, 1967.

It was a rainy and gray February. It had been raining for days. I remember someone asking me once what was the smell of Paris in the day of my first meeting with André Malraux. I instantly remembered my feelings then. Paris smelled of wet winter, of waste gases, of roast chestnuts, of coffee, of the perfumes of the Parisian women, and of cigarette smoke. In the first five days I was very busy: an interview, another one, appointments, long distances. Later on I realized that the distances were shorter than in London, Moscow, New York, or Peking. However, the fort I had to conquer was André Malraux. The building of the Ministry of Cultural Affairs added to my emotions.

Later on, Malraux told me that de Gaulle "had created" for him, in July 1959, the Ministry of Cultural Affairs and "had offered" Palais Royal to him, as a token of respect for the great writer and for the French culture as well.

The building of the Ministry of Cultural Affairs was a side of the quadrilateral made up from Palais Royal in front of the Louvre. It was its east wing. In the same palace, in other wings and sides of the quadrilateral there were the Council of the State and the General Direction of Beaux-Arts. The huge gallery with mythological statues on the ground floor of the Ministry of Cultural Affairs was the only reminder of the original royal palace it once had been. In fact, the palace had been built in about 1630 for Richelieu and the Cardinal left it to... Louis XIII. Then it belonged to Louis XIV – the Sun King. Then Napoleon took it, but he offered it too, in his turn. In 1967, the palace sheltered Malraux's history.

3 Rue de Valois. Doormen wearing empire uniforms, imposing by their posture and age accompanied me from one room to another, till they left me alone in a small drawing room in the most genuine Louis XV style. A few moments' later, Marcel Brandin, a short and thin man with a sad face asked me in. I realized that Brandin's role was to "filter" the guests, to select those he would introduce to his minister.

However, after a while our roles were inverted. I was the one who asked one question after another and put down the answers hurriedly. I found an excellent starting point for our discussion in Brandin's words: "When we were colleagues in the sixth form of the high school, Malraux used to dream of a huge theatre outdoors similar to the amphitheaters in the old Greece". Dozens of details followed about the years when Malraux and Brandin were pupils in the same grade. Long months Malraux used to be taciturn and after that, one day, he started speaking incessantly, from morning till night. One could realize then that everything he said was the fruit that had ripen in those months of silence. "He does not remember much about the school years, but he has never forgotten me." Marcel Brandin went on telling me episodes of his life as a humble clerk until Malraux called him and made him his principal private secretary. That man spoke about his minister with great affection. In 1971, when Marcel Brandin passed away, André Malraux felt – as he told me – that he had lost not only a devoted friend, but also the only witness of his teens and of his late maturity.

Brandin and I talked from 3 p.m. till 5.35 p.m., interrupted by tens of telephones, papers brought in to be signed, etc. He finally told me with a smile: "I hope to get the five minutes for you". He came back at 5.45 and told me to go to the minister's waiting room where Malraux would receive me. At 6.02, André Malraux entered: tall, wearing a classical navy blue coat, with a large leather case in one hand and his gloves in the other one. We shook hands and he invited me to sit down on a coach. He then asked me the question that he would resume each time I saw him: "What's new in Romania?" I told him some words about the political and cultural lives in Romania and then I confessed how much his books had helped me when I had been ill, *La Condition humaine* most of all. He listened to me without interrupting me, with the modesty characteristic of all the great people. When I came to an end he looked warmly at me and told me: "I haven't known that *La Condition humaine* would help somebody in Romania to live or that it could ever reach Romania, so I'm very happy about what you've told me. See? You have succeeded to live! Life is unique and it is a great mystery." (In our last meeting, in 1974 he would resume those words.)

He started asking me about my life and I realized that beyond that formal visit and the topic of our discussion, a human contact had been made. Was he moved? Maybe. Anyhow, the communication was much easier and I understood in that very moment that Malraux would not refuse to meet me again. From then on he accepted to talk to me, not just to speak for interviews, but to tell me what he was thinking *at a given moment*, about one issue or another, about one idea or another, or about people. As a matter of fact it was almost impossible for me to interview him in the usual meaning of the word. That was why I chose to look at him as he asked himself questions and searched for answers. I chose to watch him and "to learn" him; to learn him by heart. He agreed with that game from the very beginning. From time to time he told me what was not meant for publication and I respected his recommendations.

When I broached the subject of the Houses of Culture he started talking with great animation about that mission of his ministry.

In 1959 he became the minister of Cultural Affairs in de Gaulle's government. The Houses of Culture were created with the purpose of "making accessible the masterpieces of mankind, and mainly of France, to as many French as possible, of ensuring the vastest audience for the cultural inheritance of France, and of favoring the creation of new works of art able to enrich the human soul." For the first time, Malraux told me, France had a coherent policy in the fields under the umbrella of the Ministry of Cultural Affairs, that is: museums, archives, architecture, theatre, music, films, and last but not least the Houses of Culture initiated by Malraux. He told me that Houses of Culture would open in all the departments. France had to have a popular culture, and the Houses of Culture would become, Malraux considered, what cathedrals were for religion, or, better to say, places where people would meet what they have the best and the most beautiful inside themselves. Besides Paris, Houses of Culture would open in Lyon, Dijon, Grenoble, Bordeaux, Marseille, Strasbourg, Toulouse, and Avignon.

Malraux could not stay out of the current events. No matter the sophisticated arguments he put in his historical and art criticism books, he was quite straightforward and energetic when he approached the political problems of culture. He reminded me with respect and love of the Popular National Theatre and of its pillars, Jean Vilar and Gérard Philipe. In Malraux's opinion, Houses of Culture were to be established in each department and in each city as institutions joining together theatres, cinemas, artistic workshops, concert halls, and places where the audience could meet people of culture.

Another topic was the cleaning, that is the washing of the Paris monuments. When I told him: "Minister, I can see that some of the monuments in Paris have a new look" he replied shortly: "They do not have a new look – they have the look they should have".

Malraux's initiative of bleaching all the monuments in Paris caused great strife. Jets of compressed air and water were used to remove all dust and dirt that had covered the monuments during centuries. Malraux's idea to make the city more beautiful was gradually accepted.

Starting from the new look of the monuments, Malraux told me then about Georges Eugène Haussman, the prefect of the Seine, responsible for the transformation of Paris into a modern town. Between 1853 and 1869 the latter embarked on an enormous program of public work and cut wide, straight, tree-lined avenues through the chaotic small streets of which Paris was then composed. He opened up parks both in the center of Paris and at Bois de

Boulogne and Vincennes. Likewise, he built the Opera and the central market place known as Les Halles. Many of the ideas came from Napoleon II, but it was owing to Haussmann's exceptional capacity for work that those schemes were carried out so expeditiously.

Seven years later, Malraux would tell me about the years when he had been the head of the Ministry of Cultural Affairs. "I lived that decade 1959–1969, between the return to power of General de Gaulle and his final retirement, like in a whole epoch. After General's retirement in 1946 – that is after about 12-year interruption that I called 'the passing of the desert' – we were in action again. There were long days when we worked more than 12 hours; sometimes, even 16 hours a day. It was not an easy task to work with the General. I lived that experience with the same ardor I used to live all the other stages of action in my life. Action in itself has always been a priority to me – I mean an important action of course – because people are involved. Writing, on the other hand, involves ghosts only. For me, everything that implied governmental action was connected with General de Gaulle. When I was Minister of Cultural Affairs I had a lot of interesting things done: the cleaning of the Paris monuments, or the new ceiling of the Opera painted by Chagall, or the Odèon restored by André Masson. However, my greatest success is the new look of the Paris monuments. Now they look like a new spring. I was also enthusiastic about the idea of organizing education through television; that would have been equal to instituting compulsory education. I knew that I had to start by giving deputies full explanation. It was important to act then. I saw what the Japanese had done, although there had not been a national program with them; they had private foundations only. If that project had been implemented in the whole country, with the State support, France would have had an extraordinary cultural experience. But such an action is connected with people as well. I would have liked to achieve it together with General de Gaulle. We could communicate very well together. As you know, that is the only thing that gives 'color to an action'."

Malraux did a lot for making French culture known abroad. I mean mainly the exhibitions he organized all over the world. He was also the author of the first retrospective of Picasso's works at the Grand and Petit Palais, and at the Bibliothèque Nationale as well. Malraux seems to have been one of those who succeeded in persuading Picasso to leave a huge part of his works to the French State. They are sheltered today in Marais, in Hôtel Salé that has been turned into a permanent Picasso Museum.

He told me then about Jean Moulin, one of the heads of the French resistance. Ironically, I wrote these lines about Moulin in the very year when, four decades later, his assassin, Captain Klaus Barbie, was captured. Barbie is the man who tortured Jean Moulin, the then de Gaulle's delegate general for the unoccupied France, the chairman of the National Council of the French Resistance. Three years before my first visit to Paris, national funerals had been organized for bringing Jean Moulin's mortal remains in the Pantheon. It had been de Gaulle's decision. Malraux delivered then a speech of a highly emotional force. I asked Malraux if he wanted to speak about Jean Moulin and he answered "We have honored him, but we will have to offer him our eternal gratitude". It was his belief that the people who had fought in the Resistance and who had died would be martyrs forever. "Antifascism" he told me "was the latest Romantic movement in the history of Europe."

He rose to his feet and smiled. "Mr. Brandin will give you the record of the speech I delivered for Jean Moulin at the Pantheon. I am glad to offer it to you". Before leaving, he added "Please focus my answers to your questions on the actions I am most concerned with now: restoration of the Paris monuments; spreading of culture through the Houses of Culture and through theatres; TV role in education; art contribution to the international political détente.

He wanted to leave and I asked my last question: "When will you come to Romania?" "I want to come by all means. It is a country I am interested in although I don't know it. I know that some of my books have been translated; I met Ion Mihăileanu who translated *La Condition humaine* and *L'Espoir*[*]. It is not very important if I come to Romania or not. What really matters is that

---

*1 Some other names have added to the list of Malraux's translators: I. Igiroşianu and Modest Morariu, Constantin Ţoiu and Valeriu Râpeanu, Ştefan Augustin Doinaş and O. Cotruş, Cristina Isbăşescu Hăulică and A Erimicioiu, etc.

Romania is an independent country today." He started speaking animatedly about independence and I could see that he knew some things about Romania.

I left Rue de Valois with the feeling that I had conquered Paris that day. The rain, the unpleasant hotel, my tiredness, and the other interviews waiting for me had no importance! The meeting lasted about forty-five minutes. When the multitude of impressions started to calm down I realized that during our conversation Malraux's face was perfectly relaxed although he was generally known to have a lot of tics.

The following afternoon I went again to Hotel Prince in Avenue Bosquet where a large envelope from the Ministry of Cultural Affairs was waiting for me. I found inside the record of the speech made by Malraux at the Pantheon when Jean Moulin's remains had been brought to rest there.

I thanked Malraux through Brandin. A short discussion with the latter and a warning that shocked me: when I meet Malraux again I must not ask him about his sons! Those things were buried deep in his soul and any memory threw him in unbearable suffering. He cannot speak more. Silence.

I am thinking of Malraux who was 66 when I met him. Death had always been on the watch around him. At the beginning there were those who died during World War I – relatives, older acquaintances, and friends. The revolutionary moments in Indochina and China followed. Victims again. In 1930 his father committed suicide. A hard to bear shock! And then the deaths during the Civil War in Spain, those in World War II, his two brothers, and Josette Clotis, the mother of his two sons, Gauthier and Vincent, who both died in a car accident on May 23 1961, one at 21, the other one at 18 … "Almost all the people I loved died in accidents" Malraux wrote later. In the meantime, de Gaulle and Louise de Vilmorin had died as well.

In those days in Paris I browsed André Gide's journal: "I am reading again *La Condition humaine*. When it was published in a magazine, the book seemed to me extremely dense and hard to understand because of its complexity… now, as I am reading it again I find it perfectly clear, with order in its confusion, of a wonderful intelligence, and despite itself … deeply rooted in life, throbbing with unbearable unrest sometimes.” The *Journal* goes on: “Just like Valéry, Malraux is careless. His great force lies in being careless, in not giving a damn about the left behind listener who gasps and is only concerned (when I am the listener) to seem that he/she listens to him than to really follow him… Anywhere a right cause needs a defender, where a noble fight is going to start he is the first on the barricade. He offers himself, without a second thought, with a kind of bravery mixed up with a certain desperation behind which one can guess that he does not care much about his life. Life itself is less important than what consumes him, it is only sacrifice that adds meaning to it, and life is worth living only if you risk it in a valid adventure. At the same time, the word ‘adventure’ gets with him the most beautiful, the richest, and the most human meaning.”

Again Gide: “His work offers us wonderful reasons to love life […] and to make life noble through self-denial and sacrifice”. It was not only Malraux’s work, but also his life – I daresay – the life of a man who lived so many experiences (many unexplainable, many contradictory, and not all of them linear) that increased the forces of the contemporary people, their ability to be brave and to trust life.

Malraux explained why his first meeting in 1945 with the Gaulle had been a decisive one: “I preferred General de Gaulle to art because I was sure that by following him I could serve people the best”.

THE SECOND MEETING

May 1968 that has remained in history and literature like a rapid spring rain, despite the media of the time that saw in it a long storm in France’s life, brought us face to face again. He had invited me to the Cannes Film Festival but I could not reach the south of France because of the events in Paris. To better describe what happened in May 1968 in a Paris stirred up by the winds of spring and of revolt I shall quote the ex-Prime Minister Pierre Mendès-France who eloquently synthesized the events. “Behind the great grievance, small revolts took place. All the determined values and all the established organizations were being questioned. Physicians rose against medicine, architects against architecture, Christians questioned the Catholic hierarchy, workers and clerks denied the power of their bosses, teachers, at least part of them, were against their own trade unions, artists occupied the music-halls that paid them, writers invaded the offices of the Society of the men of letters, technocrats attacked technocracy, professional football players wanted to occupy the headquarters of the Football Federation, cinema people had interrupted the Cannes Festival, men of theatre tried in vain to shatter the structures that directed them. Of course, there was much talk, incoherence and utopia in the numerous meetings that took place almost everywhere. As they later used to tell: 'In May, the word was conquered the same way the Bastille had been taken in 1789'."

Without being complete or analytical, the above definition reflects rather correctly the state of spirit. Of course, with the exception of the general strike.

Nevertheless, I met Malraux under those circumstances.

Brandin had told me that whenever I came to Paris Malraux would be glad to meet me. The Minister of Culture himself had invited me. The meeting was a short one – a quarter of an hour or so, in an office close to the cabinet of the president of the Deputies' Assembly, his friend Jacques Chaban-Delmas. It was May 21, 1968, during the crucial session of the Parliament that decided not only the fate of the Pompidou government, but also that of the institutions of the Fifth Republic.

Malraux – the man who had understood a lot – felt that he could understand nothing. Malraux – the man who had always looked at the youth and at the future – stayed in front of the young people and the young people mocked at him. The students mainly. Of course, the minister was aware that the system of education had its flaws. But what did the young people on the barricade want? Part of them might have been confused, or irresponsible, or lacking interest, but the problem could not be solved with all that labeling. However, what was the problem?

I looked at him and that time his tics were more rapid – a face tortured by spasmodic movements. In 1968, lightening crossed

Malraux's face. I met him in the day when he had had a fight with the great man of theatre Jean-Louis Barrault. Malraux, the minister of Culture and not the writer, had ordered Barrault, the director of the Odéon Theatre and not the actor, to cut off electricity in the building occupied by the young people. André Malraux was almost exhausted

"What is your opinion about the events in France?" he asked me and, without waiting for my answer he went on: "I can't understand these young people. Or I can't understand them yet. I can't understand the artists." (The slogans covering the Odéon Theatre, where Malraux had been personally attacked, stigmatized and bantered the minister of Culture.) "I can't understand the writers. What I know about revolutions has nothing to do with whatever happens here. If it were a revolution I could feel it. A civil war caused by superficiality seems the gravest thing. However I hope that is not the case."

He was speaking gravely, in a febrile way. His eyes were gleaming and permanently looking for something around. When he said he could not understand his face showed it. Smiling shortly he asked me: "What's new in Romania?" and added then "In fact I know it better than you do, because the General told us about his excellent impressions."

He told me that de Gaulle's visit to Romania on May 13 was a historic fact. Malraux and the Prime Minister Georges Pompidou insisted that the visit should not be postponed or made shorter despite the dramatic events in Paris. Malraux had seen the President in the very evening of his return to Paris, when the situation was extremely serious, and de Gaulle had told him: "I am glad I have been". Malraux appreciated that the dialogue in Bucharest was a crucial moment in the evolution of the relationships between France and Romania.

We stood during our talk. Malraux kept walking across the room with his cat-like steps as I waited for him to calm down. Suddenly, in an unexpected gesture, he stretched his hand to me and said: "Sorry. Although I do not know exactly what to do I am very busy. See you soon."

THE THIRD MEETING

After two other attempts that had failed (André Malraux and André Holleaux, the director general of the National Center of the French Cinematography, kept on inviting me) I took part in the 21st edition of the Cannes Festival. I wrote to Malraux from Cannes to thank him and to ask him to receive me again. He answered me immediately and called me to Palais Royal on May 27, 1969 at 4 p.m. I was permanently astonished by the readiness and precision of Malraux's answering letters and also by his concern to send me the 13 volumes of his old and new books that I arranged on a shelf of my bookcase. (From where his photo looks at me every morning.) Malraux's habit seemed a sign of self-respect, of his respect towards the others and towards the very idea of letter as a form of communication. At that level and among those people, not to answer a letter or not to honor an invitation (without a solid reason announced in advance) meant total disqualification. (In total contradiction with the communist impoliteness that introduced the so-called "correspondence of silence" – the fashion of letters that were to remain unanswered for ever.)

I was at Palais Royal again. That time, Malraux was no longer a minister. Exactly one month before President de Gaulle had resigned following his defeat in the referendum calling for the acceptance of regional reorganization of France. Therefore, on April 1968 "Le charme est rompu et il a donné sa demission" (The spell is broken and he has resigned – Jean Lacouture). Malraux was to resign as well but he remained for a while to endorse France's cultural affairs. He met me at the door of his office and took my right hand in his both hands. Brandin was no longer there and Malraux would leave Palais Royal for good. Malraux, who was the first to speak about the "national destiny" of the deputy of Cantal, Georges Pompidou, when the latter was Prime-Minister, explained later that "to remain a minister under Pompidou would have been similar to remaining a colonel in the Civil Guard had the republicans won the Spanish Civil War". About Valéry Giscard d'Estaing, the president of the Fifth French Republic following Pompidou, Malraux said: "I am not interested in working with Mr. Giscard d'Estaing. I can't say I have anything against him but, for me, he is just a gentleman I happened to meet sometimes in the Council of Ministers."

My third meeting with Malraux took place during the elections campaign. In May 1969, Malraux was quite different from Malraux I had met before. I sat in an armchair and followed him for an hour and a half as he crossed his office, sat down for a while, and rose again and again. He was both concerned and enthusiastic. Almost all the time he told me about the state of things in France and about its future. He was concerned about history, and about the lessons of history. He had not agreed with the referendum calling, but he had accepted General's decision. Although skeptical, he hoped that the Gaullists would win. Actually I think that he had intuited defeat. Before the referendum he remembered that Napoleon had written: "I make my plans based on the dreams of my sleeping soldiers". Gaulle might have made plans based on the dreams of the sleeping France but he forgot that the majority of the French people did not want to sleep any longer. Unlike May 1968, when he had been alarmed, astonished, and sad, Malraux realized then that the public opinion was on the point of following another way.

Malraux thought of France and talked about its future. However, that time he did not do it in his quality of a minister, but as a man who had resumed his profession: writing. He easily approached one topic or another: he revealed the huge importance of the German problem, underlined an older opinion of his that the lives of the nations resulted from their own experiences, he mentioned Alan Peyrefitte's book *Quand la Chine s'eveillera*. He said that the world had to take China into account, as its historical role would be greater and greater. "All my life" he told me "I have believed, based on my experience, that peoples could understand among them without borders. That is not true. A nation is the depository of its national sovereignty. It represents collectivity and individuality alike". The internationalist Malraux in China and Vietnam, in Spain and in France expressed then his confidence in the future of the idea of nation and underlined the importance of national independence and sovereignty.

From politics he passed to culture. Brancusi was for him a forerunner of the art of future and he was sorry he had not been able to visit the native places of the famous sculptor. He was also sorry he had not visited the monasteries in Bucovina. Like Camus, Malraux was "against all those who think they are absolutely right". Art offered him the great pleasure of the dialogue. His polemic vocation, his pleasure to see his interlocutor make fantastic somersaults of intelligence mixed in him with another vocation: that of silence. Malraux's famous silence. In front of universal masterpieces, before each explanation there exists a moment of silence lying at the basis of understanding... "Talking with Malraux" Indira Gandhi said "means to start an adventure". I could add: *to keep silence and contemplate* beside Malraux is an equally impressive adventure. "An hour's talk with him" Jean Gabin said " is a huge gift. Owing to his own presence, Malraux forces you to become a little more intelligent."

In 1969, Malraux told me a lot about Spain, about the genuine nature of the events in Spain. He reminded me that he had been one of the presidents of the International Committee of Fight Against Fascism. He spoke to me about that mysterious chapter of his enlisting in the Spanish Civil War from the very beginning and put me in touch with a famous researcher of his work, Professor Walter Langlois, from the United States, who gave me the details I would resume. During that visit when I last saw Malraux at Palais Royal, the writer told me about that special mission, about the adventures of the voyage and mainly about the outburst of the right against him. He also remembered that in that period, Titulescu, the Romanian Minister of Foreign Affairs had shown his sympathy for the cause of the Spanish people. "I was surprised and glad to learn (from Pierre Cot and from my Spanish friends) how trenchant Titulescu's attitude had been. After all, until 1936 he was Romania's Minister of Foreign Affairs." In his quality of Commander of the aviation of the international brigades affiliated with the army of the Spanish Republic, Malraux learned that in the summer of 1936 Nicolae Titulescu had agreed that an order of French airplanes meant to be delivered to Romania should be postponed so that the planes could be sent to the Spanish republicans.

When I met Malraux, his attitude was the same as in 1936, when he had been commanding his famous international air squadron as writing *L'Espoir* (Man's Hope), producing and directing a motion-picture version of the book. In 1970, when the ship he was cruising with stopped over at Cadix, Malraux refused to get down and stayed on the deck his back towards Franco's Spain. He was determined, similarly to his great friend Picasso, that as long as Franco ruled in Madrid he would not set foot in Spain again.

"On July 18, 1936 Civil War broke out in Spain. Two days later Malraux was in Spain." That was all Janet Flanner, Malraux's first biographer, could say in 1954 about the beginning of that crucial moment in the writer's life and work. For more than twenty years, many other researchers have tried to enlighten Malraux's activity during the Spanish civil war, but certain episodes – mainly at the beginning – are still unknown. Not even the exact time of his arrival there has been found out for sure and nothing has been discovered yet about his mysterious stay there at the end of July 1936. However, all his critics agree that that short period could be extremely interesting. His experience then was used in the first part of his novel *L'Espoir* and could probably reveal the reason why Malraux dedicated almost three years of his life to the cause of the Spanish Republic. Professor Walter Langlois studied literary and historical archives to bring to light the circumstances of the journey in 1936 that seems to have had a great importance for Malraux's life and literary career.

"Malraux was probably interested in Spain long before the rebellion in July 1936" Langlois wrote. Owing to his works on art history he first traveled to Spain in order to study the Spanish old masters. Later on, following the heroic revolt of Asturias in 1934 and the victory of the leftists in the elections of February 1936 he started being interested in the economic and social changes in that country. He was so much concerned with the political experience of the so-called *Frente popular* that, at the end of spring of 1936, he traveled again to Spain. Back in France he described with much enthusiasm what he had seen and showed what important and logical "the workers-peasants alliance under which the Spanish revolution develops" was. Malraux is known to have belonged to the left intelligentsia, sympathizers of communists. During his stay in Indochina in 1924–1925, he had known the huge and inhumane abuses of colonialism and had returned to France decided to fight with all his energy against the authoritarian spirit spreading over Europe. According to Malraux, the only ideology that could withstand fascism - and that suggested a program for improving workers' and peasants' lives – was Marxism. That was why, similarly to many other intellectuals of his epoch, Malraux joined communists. However he kept intact his independence and was never a member of that party. Malraux was either a president or a member of numerous antifascist organizations and took part in a lot of congresses, meetings, and conferences, both in France and abroad. He thus made a lot of friends in the intellectual and political circles in several countries, Spain included.

Walter Langlois speaks then about the tense situation in Spain before Franco's military rebellion and about the way the French public opinion received it. The news about the insurrection that started in the Spanish Morocco in the night of July 17–18 surprised the large majority of the French. All telephonic calls with the Peninsula were cut at 1.30 a.m., on Saturday 18, and the borders were closed in a short while after that. Even the important journals lost contact with Spain. The only way of getting a piece of information was T.S.F. The Spanish transmitter went on broadcasting and during the 18–20 weekend the French stuck around their radios to get news. Thus, a genuine 'battle of waves' started between the two forces fighting in Spain. The radio station at Ceuta, North Africa and, a little later, that in Seville were among the first to be taken by the rebels and their generals used them to spread confusion and pessimism among the loyal republicans. They boasted about their victories (sometimes phonies) in provinces. The republican radio stations, mainly those in Madrid and Barcelona, tried to fight back that entire propaganda showing that the situation was under control and there was peace almost everywhere in the country. The French people in Paris could pick up almost all these messages. They used to listen passionately as trying to find out the truth. After 24-hour doubt, the French listeners got the impression that the government's situation started to improve. On Sunday morning they heard about the new cabinet led by José Giral and about his decision to organize popular armed militias. Their success against the rebels in several cities – Madrid and Barcelona included – seemed to ensure republicans' victory. On Monday morning, as they went to their jobs, the French thought that it was not for the first time that a handful of Spanish generals had tried to stage a coup against their government. "Spain is the country of generals' *pronunciamientos* par excellence", an article in *L'Humanité* wrote that day.

On Tuesday, the news from Spain was comforting for the French supporters of the republicans. Radio-Seville, regained from the rebels' hands, after they had had it for 36 hours, announced that the whole city was again under the control of the Madrid government and that the food shops would open soon. At the same time, Radio-Madrid confirmed that an important column of Asturian miners had come to Madrid to ensure the protection of the legal government against the rebels. Several groups in France started to take action for supporting the cause of the Spanish Republic. One of the firsts was the World Committee of the Intellectuals against war and fascism, the co-president of which was Malraux.

The leaders of the group met on Tuesday evening to decide what they would do for Spain. At that meeting somebody who was very close to the Blum cabinet showed them the ins and outs of the affair. Despite the news broadcast by Radio-Madrid, the government of José Giral took the revolt very seriously; he had already requested France to help Spain with war materials. Several members of the French cabinet convened in an unofficial meeting decided to accept the request and the preparations started secretly. The World Committee agreed that it was useless to challenge the conservative French in that moment so they did not try anything more important in Spain. However, in the long cable sent by Malraux and his friends to "the Spanish people, who fight heroically for the cause of the whole mankind", they promised them prompt humanitarian aid.

Likewise, the Committee decided to send immediately a delegation to Spain "to express the international solidarity" with the Spanish people against the fascist attack. The delegation led by Malraux was made up of Jean-Richard Bloch and Jean Cassou among others. They had to contact Madrid and the Blum government first so they could not fix the date of departure. However, they hoped that that would be soon. As the reports of the Spaniards arrived in Paris were both contradictory and fragmentary, the French government had no reliable information about what was going on in Spain. Nobody knew exactly how, but at a certain moment a high official – perhaps Pierre Cot, Minister of Air who knew and admired Malraux – suggested that the best solution to learn about the real state of things in Spain might be to get an authorized report. Obviously they could not send an official delegation as the World Committee had suggested. The risk would have been less if somebody had left for 48 hours only. Helped by the Spanish government, that delegate would have been able to come back with reliable information that would have allowed the French government to act. The right person was Malraux. He enjoyed the friendship and confidence of the Spanish and French authorities; he was courageous, intelligent, honest, clear-minded, and his international reputation would have given added weight to his report.

Malraux was delighted. He and his wife – who also wanted to go to Spain in her quality of representative of the Women's World Committee against War and Fascism – were very moved by the proposition and announced president Azana in Madrid about their plans.

Malraux and his wife were to leave on Friday morning, but there was one more issue to be fixed. The planes on the Paris-Madrid route had to stop for supply before reaching the French-Spanish border and, at the request of the Spanish government, the French Minister of the Interior had closed all the airports in the Lower Pyrenees region. The right press, already on the watch, would have made a fuss over the clandestine voyage of the "red" Malraux to Spain. The writer decided to issue a bulletin announcing his departure for Wednesday 22, before the official closing down of the airports. The bulletin published by several French newspapers mentioned that Malraux (in his quality of a delegate of the World Committee) had the mission to convey to president Azana "the proof of the solidarity of all the men and women who followed with great emotion the fight of the Spanish people" and also to see what happened "on the spot, so that he could inform world public opinion (and some members of the French government as well) about the events taking place in Spain."

Professor Langlois makes then clear the technical details of Malraux's flight by a Lockheed Orion plane belonging to the Training Center of the Ministry of Air. The plane was piloted by Edouard Corniglion-Molinier, one of the best pilots of France. Malraux knew him. Two years ago they had embarked together on a dangerous flight to Yemen to look for the Queen of Sheba's legendary city. Corniglion-Molinier was enthusiastic about the new project; they were to fly by a Farman plane. The departure to Spain was arranged for the morning of Friday 24, but in the last minute – out of unknown reasons – the Farman was no longer available. Corniglion-Molinier got the permission from the Ministry of the Air to use an American Lockheed Orion, a special plane belonging to the Training Center of the Ministry of the Air. The plane was in the hangar of the military airport Villacoublay, not far from Versailles. As the weather was rather bad till early afternoon, they had to delay the departure hour.

A usual Paris-Madrid flight lasted then five hours and a half, including the thirty-minute supply. The Lockheed plane with Malraux, Clara, Corniglion-Molinier and Lenormand, the mechanic, landed safely at Forgas, a military airport not far from Biarritz, on Friday, in the late afternoon. Some other difficulties appeared there. The ministerial order issued the previous day had closed down all the airfields in the Pyrenees and the commander at Forgas seemed to have asked a delay in order to get from the Minister a confirmation concerning Malraux's mission. However, the travelers had to spend the night there.

On Saturday morning, July 25, the weather was fine in the south of France. The plane took off with no other difficulty. When they had crossed the Pyrenees, Malraux asked Corniglion-Molinier to fly lower. As soon as they were above the Spanish land they could see the somnolence of the region; everything seemed to be in a deep slumber. There was almost no move. There were no cars on the roads, except for some military trucks, and everything seemed frozen in the railway stations. The outskirts of the industrial towns and the building sites look deserted as the funnels of the factories were dozing. There was life in barracks only: trucks, cars, vans, and ammunition wagons around which groups of people moved to and fro. When they heard the noise of the flying plane all of them ran away to hide in the nearby buildings. Almost all the squares were empty. The only exception, Malraux told later, was a small village in Navarra. "Seven-eight persons, their backs against a wall, were guarded by armed people. I asked later and I learned that they were communists. The soldiers were to shoot them. In about two hours, the plane was not far from Madrid. The town looked calm in the dawn. The plane landed on Barajas, the international airport lying northwest of Madrid. Five other planes were shining in the morning light. They were planes of the Spanish National League commandeered by the government at the beginning of the insurrection. [...]

The officer in Biarritz had told them about the fall of Madrid so Malraux and his companions did not know what they could expect there. Clara Malraux told that "once they were above Barajas' military base" they all had their faces "pressed against the plane windows" and wondered "if they were going to meet friends or enemies down there". When they saw the red flags their hopes revived.

After landing, the plane was took to a hangar where about forty militiamen were on guard.

Two days before, Madrid had been announced about Malraux's voyage and *Politica*, the pro-Azana newspaper, had written very enthusiastically about the visit. The journal wrote that Malraux, president of the World Committee against War and Fascism was "one of the most distinguished international personalities engaged in the fight against fascism" and that "he came to Madrid to support the brave Spanish combatants". His visit to Madrid was authorized and supported by the highest officials of the republic. However when Malraux and his friends opened the plane door, there were only armed militiamen that surrounded them. Suddenly a car came and the representatives of the Spanish government got down to meet them. Malraux did not know the first one of them, Carlos Montilla, but the second, José Bergamin – one of the greatest Catholic writers of the country – was a friend of his. Malraux had met him at several international congresses. At the congress in London in the spring of 1936, during some long philosophical discussions he had come to know better Bergamin's ideas; some of them are to be found in Guernico's opinions in *L'Espoir*.

Bergamin greeted Malraux warmly and introduced him to the third man: the famous Spanish aviator Navarro, the head of the Barajas airport, ex-pilot on the French route Toulouse-Casablanca. Navarro – who later became a friend of Malraux (when he commanded the Espana squadron, at Barajas) and the model for Sembrano in his novel – was a great lover of France.

Accompanied by his friends, Malraux left to Madrid in the official car. On their way, Bergamin tried to brief him on what had happened in the country lately.

During their first day in Spain, Saturday, July 25, Malraux and his wife were accommodated at the Florida Hotel but they did not stay there long. In the short time he could afford he wanted to see as much as possible. He discussed first with the leaders of the government and, of course with president Azana whom he had met a few months before. Then he visited the places where important fights had taken place in the first hours of the rebellion in Madrid. Among them, the telephone station built by Americans; it still worked and was often the only communication means through which the government was announced about the situation in the country. Among all the things he saw in Madrid, Malraux was most impressed by Montana. The barrack, reconquered five days before, had turned into a sacred place for the inhabitants of the city. The fight had been fierce. In the inner yard, militiamen from all over the country were being recruited; most of them where very young, about 16–18 years old. Malraux was extremely interested by the story of a soldier, Modesto Romero, who was in Montana when the rebellion started. He was stuck there in the first day of the encirclement, but then he succeeded to escape. He went to the republican headquarters and he told them that the colonel of the regiment had misled his soldiers. Everybody in Madrid spoke about the soldier's clear-sightedness and Azana himself was told to have received him. Malraux did not forget the story of the young soldier and retold it as such in his novel. Montana impressed him because it symbolized the saga the people in Madrid lived.

Malraux spoke for Radio-Madrid then he got the permission to make an aerial reconnaissance. [...] Back in Madrid, Malraux sent a cable to his friends in Paris and assured them that the military situation was in favor of the republic.

For more detailed information Malraux wanted to learn the opinions of his friends, the journalists. On Saturday evening he visited several editorial offices in Madrid: Politica, president Azana's newspaper, and *Mundo obrero*, the most important communist newspaper.

The next morning, on Sunday, July 26, he left together with Corniglion-Molinier to Barcelona, but unfortunately there are very few data about what happened there. He might have discussed with several political leaders, visited probably the battlefields and discussed with the officers about the military situation in the province. It is supposed that Malraux wanted to fly directly to Paris, on Monday, July 27, but in the evening Corniglion-Molinier was called from Madrid and asked to fly to the Capital, as he had to take an important person to Paris. It was the new Spanish ambassador to France, Alvaro de Albornoz.

Unfortunately, when the rebellion started, Spain had no ambassador to Paris. Juan de Cardenas had taken that position in the spring of 1934, but he was a conservative and disliked the left governments. Following the victory of the Popular Front in France he had to be replaced. Personal reasons delayed Albornoz' departure to Paris and Cardenas agreed to keep the job until his successor came. It was then that the rebellion started and any communication between Paris and Madrid was interrupted. On July 20, when José Giral ordered the planes and arms from France he had all the reasons to be afraid that the negotiations could be compromised by Cardenas and the following day he called urgently a socialist friend, ex-minister Fernando de los Rios, who was in Switzerland, and asked him to go to Paris and take care of the arms acquisition himself.

De los Rios arrived in Paris and learned that despite

difficulties and hesitations Blum government had accepted to send war material to Spain. Unfortunately, three days later, a fierce campaign of the right press started and several conservative members of the Spanish Embassy in Paris resigned. That event and multiple diplomatic pressure led to a hesitation of the French government concerning the validity of that act. De los Rios sent then a long and pessimistic letter to Giral and asked for the absolute necessity of the presence in Paris of the new ambassador. The letter reached Madrid on Sunday at noon and all the afternoon Giral discussed with the members of his government. Albornoz took part in some of those meetings. It was probably then that somebody remembered that Malraux was in Spain. They called to Barcelona and that very evening Corniglion-Molinier returned to Madrid. Very early the following day, Corniglion-Molinier took the ambassador and at about 10 o'clock the plane was back in Barcelona, where Malraux and his wife were waiting for them. [...]

Malraux had met Albornoz at the Paris Congress in 1935 and took advantage of the voyage they made together to strengthen their friendship. Malraux promised to help him as much as he could, but he could not guess then the important role he would play in the evolution of the situation in Spain. That is, in short, Langlois' story.

***

I find it proper now to answer the questions of a young Romanian writer, a great admirer of Malraux: what is the place of history in Malraux's life and work and what is the place of Malraux in the history of the 20th century? Two difficult questions that could by answered by writing a book. However...

History holds the first place in Malraux's life. "History has crossed my life like a tank" he used to say. If Malraux had lived in another century that extraordinary impact between the man and his age would not have been possible. Without the history of the 20th century Malraux would not have been Malraux. Like other important representatives of our times Malraux knew how "to catch" the opportunities offered by history, knew how to get involved. Malraux was dominated by history. Sometimes he dominated it. Or, more exactly, as he said "I went on through history together with my books".

Malraux's relation with de Gaulle lasted a lifetime – twenty years of shared ideals in the service of France, of that France they both wanted independent, sovereign, and brilliant. Let's remember what the first president of the Fifth French Republic thought about Malraux: "His mind has no borders and travels even during the meetings of the Council of Ministers. And now, the final judgment. "The Council of Ministers used to meet once a week and it was always presided by me. André Malraux was always on my right. The presence by my side of this genial friend, an admirer of the great destinies, gave me the impression that I was covered in that direction. His opinion about me made me feel stronger. I knew that during the debates, when the topic grew graver, his quick judgement would help me to make things clear."

De Gaulle resigned, rose to power again, resigned again, and Malraux was all the time by his side. Malraux told me more than once that he did not think that he was a "rightist" by simply going into politics. He insisted: "Capitalism has always hated de Gaulle". He used to say the following about General's policy: "He wanted the unconditional obedience of capitalism to the State". Malraux wanted to revive the French cultural institutions similarly to de Gaulle who tried to revive the political institutions and the economic structures of the traditional French society.

However, let's remember that after the war Malraux was one of the firsts European intellectuals to show his attitude against communism. His discourse in 1948 at the Winter Stadium in Paris is eloquent. The fact that he was a leftist and was close to the Soviet Union in the 1930s gave added weight to his words.

One of the greatest shocks of his life was the moment of the 1968 events. He, the writer who could turn any experience of history into a literary page, used to say that he was not able to write a line about that period. I think that Malraux's life is best defined by the title of the biography Pierre Galante dedicated to him: *Quel roman Malraux que sa vie!* His life was a genuine adventure in the 20th century. "If I were to choose another life," he said, "I should chose mine." Malraux was a great historical writer! I could prove my words by simply mentioning what he wrote about the saga of the 20th century in his novels and in *Antimémoires*. (He said that memoirs were the only genuine literary genre, because they were lived.)

Pierre Galante said: "A novelist, since his novels reflect his life. An art historian, since his writings reveal his basic concern: to explain the work through the man who created it. He wrote less than Aragon, Sartre, Giono, or Montherlant. When Gide asked him ' Why don't you write more?', Malraux answered: 'Because I live. And life takes all my time."

Drieu de la Rochelle, one of the important writers between the two wars, who committed suicide to the end of the war after having been a collaborationist, wrote: "Malraux, the new man". In his will Drieu asked for Malraux's presence at his funerals. When a relative of André Malraux visited Drieu in 1943 to ask him to save Roland Malraux who was a prisoner in a German concentration camp, Drieu answered: "I have got but little influence. I prefer to keep what have remained of it to help André in case of need".

A legend of our century, Malraux expressed by his gift, originality, and his complex work both the overwhelming vigor of the human condition and the *historical and revolutionary activity* that is more tragic and greater than ever.

THE FOURTH MEETING

That time I met Malraux at the Vilmorin residence in the little village Verrières-le-Buisson, not far from Paris. Verrières-le-Buisson, the old residence of the Vilmorins, became the castle of Malraux, the pilgrim, when he left Palais Royal. On my way to Verrières I remembered the circumstances of Malraux's moving to that castle. The writer was extremely discreet about his private life and he very seldom disclosed his feelings. When I met him on May 27, 1967 he showed me the windows of a flat in rue Montperisier. "It is there that I have lived happily for twenty eight months". He digressed then and told me that he had written the following dedication for a lady: "Courage and hope". He said that one needed as *much courage* in love as in war. Sometimes more… And *hope*, because audacity had its roots in hope. "Love cannot be understood by those who do not share it." Although he had to leave power he felt strong because he was living together with the novelist Louise de Vilmorin. She was for him the total woman, the woman with whom he had never been bored. Louise de Vilmorin told that she once had asked Malraux: "What kind of a woman do you need?" He answered "I don't need a fatal woman, but a total one". They met in 1933–1934, when the young and victorious Malraux had been awarded the Prix Goncourt for *La Condition humaine*. He asked her in a small restaurant near *Rive gauche*: "Do you know with whom am I going to end up my life? With you." There followed his marriage with Clara, his love affair with Josette Clotis, the second marriage with Madeleine, his brother's Roland ex-wife. When Madeleine Malraux had left for the United States for good, André Malraux and Louise de Vilmorin met again, in 1965–1966 and they started living together there, not far from Palais Royal. Louise died unexpectedly on December 26, 1969. The separation was painful and it shocked him. "The death of the woman you love is like thunder." After that he lived in that castle, at about 30–40-minute distance from Paris.

With all those thoughts I entered the park of the small castle and Malraux met me.

Malraux was still interested in Romania. That time he asked me about the folk songs, about the folk art, about the Danube Delta – the birds' paradise. He told me again that he was sorry he could not visit our country. "I need any minute I have to write my *Antimémoires*." (That autumn Malraux was present in the bookshops in Paris with three new books: *La Tête d'obsidienne*, *Lazare*, and *L'Irèel*). He then expressed his admiration about Romania's independent policy. "You are the owners of a fabulous spiritual and historical heritage that offers to the present Romanian artists the creative force of a universe having a strong inventiveness and a rare vitality. You can built on that ground genuine caryatids that would raise the Romanian culture to a world vision."

I have put down in a notebook some of Malraux's thoughts when I met him for the fourth time. "All my life I've been historically *committed* in everything I've done: in my writings, in my deeds, in my thoughts. A historian's mission is to make clear the human adventure and the adventure of mankind. It is due to Marx and his historical interpretation that that adventure has become intelligible. It is not an extravagance to assert that Marxism has revolutionized history as a science. Similarly to Darwin who revolutionized biology with his theory of species. Likewise, I think Hegel is very important too. I doubt that Marx would have been able to produce his conceptions without Hegel. Hegel has to be admired because he found the essence of the historical phenomena. Let's not forget Freud, the pathfinder in psychohistory and phychosociology."

The dialogue with Malraux is confusing. His old ideas expressed in almost the same words alternate with new observations, with extraordinary shades of meanings. "We live in an unprecedented age, in which the old historical structures have dissolved, and the new ones, much more complex, are budding. The ideas of civilizations are much alike living bodies: they develop according to their own laws and each of them has its structure. That is why I think that the genuine historian has to be appreciated following certain laws. History is, by all means, the most authentic judge. Sometimes history defeats death itself. I had time to think about that a short while before, when I was very ill, almost dying. The result was the novel *Lazare* in which I describe the thoughts and fights of a man before his death."

He was concerned about the future. "We live at the end of a history and at the beginning of a new one, of some extraordinary changes. The age of the electronic devices will change completely the face of civilization on Earth. I have the courage to say that I am the last writer of our civilization who lived in the epoch of the British Empire; I mean in an epoch that has gone forever. The fact that history is unrepeatable is more valid than ever. Humanity is looking for a planetary conscience, the only one able to take it close to the discoveries of the technical-scientific revolution as a whole. It is no doubt that Napoleon and Ramses could have understood each other, but it is obvious that Napoleon could not have understood John F. Kennedy. Voltaire would not have understood anything from Albert Einstein, but despite their total disagreement he would have found a way of understanding with Saint Augustine. For long centuries and even millennia communication kept its continuity; now, in our age, the communication has been placed in the light of a new semantics, an expression of a new revolutionary technique. Everything depends on the way people will become aware of the level reached by science. Science is able to do everything for people, except people themselves. The demiurgic element has remained the man, and it is to them that we entrust our hopes. I am confident that what is indivisible in man and what brings humanity together will be eternal. Now we have to learn to warn history."

There, in the Vilmorin castle, Malraux had several cats. He introduced two of them to me "Lustré" and "Fourrure". The other cats were called "Touffu", "Foutras", etc.

He told me that his cats helped him, due to their sphinx-like silence and their attentive, tense eyes, but they inspired him as well. Smilingly, he told me a joke. An English home. In front of the fireplace, the husband, wife, and their black cat were seated. The cat looked at them and said, "Your wife has cheated on you". The choleric Englishman stood up, took down his gun and shot his wife. The cat looked at him, its green eyes half open and told him as it went away: "I've lied to you. I've been bored."

In that kind atmosphere I told him about my project of writing a book about him. I even showed my plan to him. "I want to go back from today to yesterday," I said. "It will be a five-part structure – The Wise Man, The Minister, The Combatant, The Writer, and The Adventurer." He answered: "I'll be at your disposal with advice and documents." And he gave me plenty of them…

THE FIFTH MEETING

On November 24, 1974, in the early afternoon, I was again at Verrières-le-Buisson. Between two cups of tea and two sips of whiskey (for the guest, of course, because Malraux gave up tobacco and alcohol and drank ice-tea only) he showed me tens of small and large sculptures of cats, masks from the Pacific islands, naïve pictures, a crown from Tibet, paintings by Braque, Picasso, Chagall...

On his desk a lot of written pages, letters, a magnifying glass, a lamp, and some small art objects from Latin America… "I still have a lot to do" was the key-sentence of the last afternoon we spent together. There was no agenda prepared beforehand for our discussion.

"I still have a lot to do! The book I am writing now is *Hôtes de passage*, the title of which has been inspired by my friend Max Torres."

He told me, as he had done previously as well, about some people he had met, loved, or understood. He also told me about his book of comments and discussions with de Gaulle *Les Chênes qu'on abat*, a part of the volume II of *Antimémoires*. (Malraux had put down some of the General's word and then transcribed everything they had discussed for several hours while waiting for the train to Paris.)

When *Hôtes de passage* was published, Léopold Sédar Senghor, the first black member of the French Academy, a friend of Malraux, said. "If Malraux's style turns the grammar rules upside down by brilliant periphrases, he does it so to let himself plunge into the depths of the popular language and to find again the dynamism of the Celtic genius: to express what cannot be expressed. When *Hôtes de passage* was published a lot of people thought that it was a kind of genial swindle, but I can say how surprised I was when I read the 32 pages dedicated to our talks. I recognized my sentences as written in his book; I uttered them often and I used different words, but Malraux took them and recreated them in a new context, gathered and imagined by him. After all, that was Malraux's genius that explored our existence to the farthest possible limits and created a dictionary of images and of analogies. Malraux has the power to express the essential as recreating the world according to his vision about the future. A true revolutionary vision by his defying of destiny, like a creator reshaping lives and the civilizations on Earth in accordance with his heroic and human dream."

"I still have a lot to do!"

"I fought without loving war"– he told me or he told himself. "I fought but I thought of creation, at man's creation, the absolute divinity; the only valid answer given to death is art." Malraux's thoughts. "In order to learn to die one must get accustomed to live with death." "You suffer alone and you die alone. Suffering and death cannot be shared. [...] I am not afraid of death: that I'll die or that I'll be killed. What annoys me is the irreducible fact. Death is one of the most powerful representations one can have about the meaning of life. To talk about death is one of the most reasonable ways of talking about the meaning of life."

"I still have a lot to do!"

"Hydrogen bomb is the Apocalypse. Nothing is equal to it. If Napoleon could say to his soldiers 'Forty centuries of history are looking at you', the generals and politicians of today do no longer have that privilege, as the H bomb is deaf. And blind. An if there is no fatality of history then we have to trust the human faculty of reasoning. That means that the H bomb can disappear only if people oppose to it everywhere; I repeat, that must be everywhere."

Our meeting took place exactly twenty years since the day Malraux had entered the first, ahead of his soldiers, the Cathedral in Strasbourg. "Then I lived history in a different way than in an adventure of mankind. I wondered if the succession of the millennia of humanity is simply a range of circumstances or if the succession of the human adventures gets a meaning in time. That is, in my opinion, the strong part of history. That is also the main reason that hinders us to throw it to the wastepaper basket: people's will to understand – not just to know their past. That is the strongest idea that justifies history. Otherwise it would be completely meaningless. History means the effort of human thinking to systematize and explain the past, to render its meaning. Man wants to understand. On the Earth and in the Universe as well. My opinion about history is that man tries to define the meaning of mankind's past, of the human adventure, similarly to the astronomer who wants to make order in the world of starts. I think that our present civilization is deeply preoccupied to invent something that is comparably important to what the 19th century brought to us. However we do not know yet the way that future will follow. We do not know yet what it would be like..."

"I still have a lot to do!"

Malraux speaks as quickly as ever. As usual, he seems driven by a tireless internal tumult.

Night stealthy comes in the park of Verriéres-le-Buisson. I walk to the gate of the small castle through the roses forgotten by the late autumn. In the doorway, André Malraux watches me. Farewell.

Two years later, on Tuesday, November 23, 1976, the great adventurer, writer, combatant, and minister, the wise André Malraux passed away. He was first buried in the park of the castle Verriéres-le-Buisson, beside Louise de Vilmorin, to whom he had promised forty years ago that they would spend their last days together. In 1996, on the 20th anniversary of his death, his body was enshrined in the Pantheon in Paris.

After a while, when I was again in Paris, I went to Malraux's burying place in the park of Verrières-le-Buisson. It was there, beside the two tombs, that I remembered what Malraux had once told me: "When fight starts there is no need to hurry because it takes sixty years to make a man and just one instant to destroy him".

FATHER OF THE DECLARATION OF THE RIGHTS OF MAN

When I left for Teheran, one April morning in 1968, I did not know who had conceived the International Pact of the Rights of Man. It was during my flight to Rome that I read a text issued by the United Nations and I came across Cassin's name there. In another two weeks I met him. For the time being I was extremely happy to travel alone (I've always preferred that). I stopped for three days in Rome, in the house of the Romanian ex-press correspondent Octavian Paler, a friend of mine. At that time Nicolae Puicea lived there, at 110 Viale Tizziano. I knew Puicea as well. In January 1967 we had visited Tunisia together, from Carthagina to Hammamet and the oases in the desert; we had traveled as far as Kairouan and Soussa. Puicea was very busy in Rome, so I was on my own: I could see the city the way I liked. I left Rome and after an eight-hour night flight and an unpleasant stop in Baghdad (because of the soldiers that checked on us ten times in an hour) we arrived in Teheran.

The first thing to happen there was a misunderstanding. I was met at the airport and a Mercedes took me to the Palace Hotel. As I was tired, I took a shower and went to bed. A quarter of an hour later a pestering thought woke me. I got up and I looked at the price list. My room cost USD 167 a night and I had been allotted $ 20 only. I had come to Teheran to take part in the International Conference of the United Nations dedicated to the anniversary of the Declaration of the rights of man. *Lumea* magazine that had sent me there could not afford all that money. I called the Romanian Embassy. The Romanian diplomats were very amused and they took me to another hotel that better suited my daily fee – Caravan Serai, where the Romanian delegation to that important event stayed. In several days I solved the mystery of my accommodation at Palace Hotel. The young lady who had met me at the airport had confused me with an Italian secretary of state (the plane had come from Rome and she had mistaken my Romanian accent for an Italian one).

In the opening day of the Congress I met Mr. René Cassin and he could not get rid of me how long the Congress lasted (three weeks). What does that mean?

Among the personalities attending an international Congress, the journalist has to carefully find his/her "prey" in advance. Numerous colleagues-rivals watch their future interlocutors during meetings, receptions, breaks, and places of entertainment. A journalist has to know how to exploit any opportunity to get an exclusive story or interview. Based on my 50-year experience as a journalist and on my over 5 000 interviews, discussions and press conferences (sometimes about 30 a week), I can say that the interview is a journalist's forte. It is very difficult to obtain an exclusive and the "technique" of luring the interlocutor and of removing obstacles makes a good journalist. I can say that of my 200 very important interviews (the rest of them were also important but easier to obtain) I had only to failures: the Italian tycoon Carlo Ponti and Joseph Aslop from the *New York Times*.

In Teheran, René Cassin was among my priorities. I did not know him more than I knew about the Pact of the Rights of Man. I looked for him and I found him in the very first day. A short old man, with extremely brisk gestures, with a short and white beard, and piercing, intelligent eyes. Professor Tudor Popescu of the Romanian delegation introduced me to him. I took advantage of my double quality – radio and press correspondent and asked from him a cycle of commentaries for Radio Bucharest. The magic word, a kind of "open sesame" was Titulescu. When I asked him: "Did you know Titulescu", the answer came immediately. "If I knew him, young man? I admired him, I loved him, I respected him." We arranged to see each other that very evening, after the opening meeting.

"I visited Romania to the end of the 1920s. Bucharest was wonderful. I had worked in Geneva with Titulescu, Elena Văcărescu, George Oprescu and with other famous Romanians. I have always appreciated and liked your co-nationals' intelligence and vivacity. We succeeded then in Geneva to accomplish some things in the field of intellectual cooperation. We wanted to give a new dimension to the solidarity of the intellectuals that had experienced the traumas of a war. We did not suspect then that another one, much worse would come! Genevieve Tabouis was right to call the two decades between them 'the strange interlude'. As a matter of fact, Mrs. Tabouis is a great friend of Romania.

It was then that I met Albert Einstein a couple of times. Titu, as his French friends used to call Titulescu, impressed Einstein as well. I admired him till his tragic end, when he died exiled, longing for his country. What I admired most was his inquiring mind. The fact that he was a bright jurist and knew the law systems *à fond* allowed him to imagine the best solutions for the entangled international relationships after the war.

Speaking about Bucharest: I met there some of the most beautiful women I have met in my all life."

I remember now my deep emotion when I listened to him then, in the broadcast booth in the Parliament building in Teheran. There were more meetings and adjacent talks out of which I have selected a few samples of Professor Réne Cassin's thoughts, number one in that Conference of the United Nations. Why? It is simple. Réne Cassin was the principal author of the UN Declaration of the Rights of Man drafted immediately after World War II and adopted by the UN General Assembly in 1948. The Conference in Teheran was organized to commemorate the 20th anniversary of its ratification. The atmosphere was relaxed and friendly, and the socialist countries were present beside the other ones, under fully equal conditions; the communist totalitarianism was almost not mentioned at all with that occasion.

It goes without saying that the delegates in different countries had their clear points of view concerning the human rights and liberties in the communist countries but diplomacy was also present there; however that topic was not on the agenda and there were instances of infringements of the human rights in a long range of other countries as well.

That was why there were not open confrontations between the representatives of the Western democratic countries and those of the socialist ones, as dialog and general consensus animated the whole conference. During the Teheran Conference I had the opportunity to learn some important data about the future Vietnamese-American contacts and peace negotiations and about the role played by the

Romanian diplomacy in preparing them, a beneficial aspect indeed. It was at the same time that the French Prime Minister George Pompidou visited Iran (whom I accompanied during all his stay there) and the French President Charles de Gaulle visited Romania – both events having a huge echo as concerns the East-West dialogue and détente.

However, René Cassin explained to me in detail the topic of the rights of man.

Who was René Cassin after all? He told me a few words about his life, there in Teheran and later on, in summer, in Paris.

His family originated in the south of France, but he was born at Bayonne, not far from the Spanish border. When he was four the family moved to his father's native city, in Nice. He was educated first at home, together with his brother and sister, in the good French tradition and when he reached the proper age he went to a public high school. He would have liked to study law, but his father, a merchant, wanted his son to be a merchant too. It was the Dreyfus Affair that tipped the balance scale in the favor of law. Before graduating he was enlisted as a soldier, a fact that enabled him to know the sons of France. He decided then that nothing could be achieved without the support of the "deep" France – its people. "The army" he wrote later "enabled me to know the people".

In 1910 he went to Paris and joined the leftists gathered around *L'Humanité*, Jean Jaure's newspaper that was to become a communist journal later. Young Cassin left politics soon. He was called up at the beginning of August 1914, but for him the Big War was to end on March 22, 1915. He sustained then a severe abdominal wound, the effects of which troubled him for the rest of his life. He told me that it was to his mother that he owed his life: she insisted on immediate surgery as the gangrene had already set in. In 1918, in Lyon he became the deputy secretary of the Federal Union of the combatants, maimed persons, and war widows for whose rights he would be fighting his whole life.

The little man in front of me rose not only for the rights of widows, mutilated men or orphans, but also for the French-German reconciliation. From 1924 to 1938 he served as a French delegate to the League of Nations assemblies and disarmament conferences in

Geneva together with Edouard Herriot, Léon Bourgeois, Aristide Briand, Louis Loucheur, George Bonnet, Maurice Sarraut, Joseph Paul Boncour (Maria Ventura's friend, the grandfather of Mrs. Dominique Paul Bouncour-Lafaurie who helped me so much with the present chapter), Henry de Jouvenel (Martha Bibescu's lover), Leon Jouhaux. It was there that René Cassin asserted for the first time that the League of Nations was not a superstate, but "a league of independent nations, freely and equally associated, ready to ensure a superior moral rule among them: Law."

The belief that war had to be eliminated and to be declared against law was put to the test when muses became silent and the guns of war began to shoot. After the fall of France in June 1940, Cassin joined General Charles de Gaulle in London and served as a key member of the Free French government in exile.

I found among the documents I studied – with the help of the French League of the Human Rights – numerous letters written by the leader of the free France, which attest the great role played by René Cassin for legally justifying General de Gaulle's work in exile. Despite all his work, Cassin could not join De Gaulle during his triumphant parade along Champs-Elisée. He stayed for a while in Algeria to soothe away his pain caused by the deaths of the 27 members of his family, deported together with many other Jews from France.

The fundamentals of his activity and theory lie in his belief that *the absolute* exists in each individual. "The massacre of the civil, noncombatant populations on racial grounds, the inability of the norms of humanitarian law to prevent that catastrophe, and the indifference of the great powers that made war a priority played the role of an explosive for a theory of the human rights that was no longer satisfied with the humanitarian benevolence. Something new had to come."

General de Gaulle wrote in his war memoirs: "René Cassin who was, during times of war and of peace alike, a champion of democracy and an apostle of the human rights presides now over the debates of the Council of State. He told me directly so that I can judge, and sincerely so that I can understand what we have to give up". Words meant to certify France's will to propose *something new* to the whole world. Since November 1944 until 1960 Cassin was the vice-president of the Council of State, France's highest administrative court and held also other high legal and administrative offices in France.

Following World War II, René Cassin lived the supreme adventure of his life – he tried to establish the conception of the human rights within the new international context. Each evening, for ten days, Cassin told me in Teheran about the huge effort the Council of State had made to install the legality of the French administration in the whole country, to update it, and to ensure the observance of the human rights as well. "I accepted that position in the Council of State" Cassin told me "because that body, the highest administrative court in the country was the guarantor of the citizen's rights against power." That was René Cassin's basic idea of the contemporary democratic state – the state of law.

He was thus the advocate of the individual's protection against the collective power of administration; of the reestablishment of the republican institutions alongside an absolute observance of the citizen's individual rights according to the republican tradition. That was just a part of his mission.

His dearest wish was to find a legal formula for the peaceful organization of the world.

"Well, the moment had come" he told me "to try to achieve that project. I welcomed the foundation of the UNO and saw in it some miraculous news. Although I had not been in San Francisco I was glad to find out that an auxiliary body had been created – Commission of the Rights of Man, with the aim of preparing a Charter of the Rights of Man. I embarked with all my forces on that ship and I had to face many tempests and lots of deceptions."

In May 1946 a small group of personalities gathered to establish the directions of the future UN Commission of the Rights of Man. Mrs. Eleanor Roosevelt, the ex-first lady of the United States was elected to lead that small group to which René Cassin belonged as well. Unfortunately, the second meeting was so disappointing that he called UNO "a Penelope that weaves international pacts". His main disappointment was generated by USSR that imposed the idea that the members of the Commission should be appointed by the respective states instead of being elected by UN according to their competence. Likewise, René Cassin regretted that no European had been elected in the staff of his Commission. More than that, his proposal that the Commission should be authorized to receive individual complaints and to study them before being forwarded was rejected as well.

However he never gave up. After having tried to get a revision of the Charter of the United Nations so that it might include the extensive chapter on the human rights, he took over the British idea of preparing an international pact having a compulsory character where the interested states could adhere.

Cassin made clear several points in the British proposal so that it could become an essential document. As the UN General Assembly was due to open in Paris in autumn, the Commission decided to prepare a Declaration-Manifesto susceptible of being adopted.

Long months of hard work were dedicated to the preparation of the Declaration-Manifesto. Cassin wanted the document to be a quintessence of the historical evolution of the human rights as proclaimed by the French Revolution, enriched with whatever mankind had experienced since then, mainly the dramatic events of the two world wars. He and the other members of the group debated the theses of the philosophy of the human rights, opposed sometimes to the Soviet ideas and to Mrs. Eleanor Roosevelt who was expressing the idea of the freemasons' lodge she belonged to. Cassin's starting point was the 1789 Declaration, but he did not forget the 1776 Declaration of Independence of the United States.

The hard work of drafting the Universal Declaration of the Rights of Man was an endless confrontation of varied points of view, harmonized by concessions and mutual compromises among the representatives of the respective states. The final text has got perfect equilibrium. René Cassin saw that fundamental document of our age as a monument supported by four pillars. "The first one is the pillar of personal rights, among which the rights to life, to liberty, and to the inviolability of the person. The second is the pillar of the relationship between man and people, family, the groups surrounding them, things, and places. People get married. They have families, build houses, live in towns, in countries, and owe all kind of possessions. The third is the pillar of public liberty and of the fundamental political rights from the liberty of thinking, of expression, of gathering, of association to the quintessence of all the political rights, that is the will of people – the fundamental of each government's authority." René Cassin showed then that "this monument cannot be supported by three pillars only. It needs the fourth one, that of the economic, social, and cultural rights. This pillar embodies everything that concerns people's material lives, the right to work, to social protection, to education, and to rest."

The Man of the Rights of Man that was how Cassin was called. In his speech on December 7, 1948, at the UN General Assembly he said: "These four columns would be of no use if they did not support the structure of the social and international order that permits the guarantee of rights and establishes their limits as each individual has rights but also duties towards society.

The debate in the UN General Assembly was very animated and plenty of viewpoints were advanced. The atmosphere did not calm down until Mrs. Eleanor Roosevelt succeeded to assure the delegates of the 58 states that it was not a treaty that entailed legal obligations, but a Declaration of the fundamental principles of the rights and liberties of the man meant to be a model for all the peoples and nations.

The Declaration was passed by 50 votes to 8 abstentions (the then socialist member states of the UNO – USSR, Ukraine, Belarus, Poland, Czechoslovakia, Yugoslavia, and also South Africa and Saudi Arabia). There was no vote against. René Cassin called that moment "the first document of ethical value adopted by the assembly of the mankind organized at the end on an unprecedented war".

The Declaration was finally ratified. Cassin's expectations were fulfilled as the Declaration was included in the documents of the International Israelite Alliance, to which he belonged due to his origin, in the Pope's encyclical, *Pacem in Terris*, in the European Convention of Human Rights (France ratified it much later, to Cassin's great disappointment), and mainly in the international pacts of the human rights adopted in 1966 by the UN General Assembly.

His last success was the inclusion of the ideas of the rights of man in the Helsinki Final Act. On December 20, 1968 Cassin was awarded the Nobel Prize for Peace and he used the money he received to found the International Institute of the Human Rights in Strasbourg so that the youth could continue his striving.

All the events concentrated within the period December 1948 and April 1968, when I met Professor Cassin in Teheran, proved that his fight had been right. The United Nations Conference for the Human Rights in Teheran was an incentive that the fight must go on and the resolution adopted there reasserted the value of the 1948 document.

That was the end of the series of talks I had with Professor René Cassin at Teheran first, and then at his place in Paris where he received me in June, the same year.

The award in 1968 of the Nobel Prize crowned René Cassin's lifetime career.

Ten years after his death his mortal remains were moved to Pantheon. "Let's imagine" François Mitterand, the then President of the Fifth French Republic said, "the courage and lucidity required to oppose that moral and legal principle to the nationalist mystic in the Europe between the two world wars. His tenacity, intransigence, modesty, and virtues were characteristic of a free man, dedicated to France and to brotherhood among people. As this man belongs to nobody he is entitled to receive the homage of us all."

The Father of the Rights of Man who sleeps in Pantheon beside so many glories of France and of the whole world still inspires new generations of defenders of the great cause to which he dedicated his entire life.

ISBN 0-88033-542-4

9 780880 335423 90000